Mountain Heritage

Fourth Edition

Edited by

B. B. Maurer

McClain Printing Company
212 Main Street
Parsons, WV 26287
http://McClainPrinting.com

Standard Book Number 87012-279-7
Library of Congress Catalog Card Number 75-299047
Printed in the United States of America
Copyright © 1980
McClain Printing Company
Parsons, West Virginia

FIRST PRINTING 1974
REVISED EDITION 1975
REVISED EDITION 1977
REVISED EDITION 1980
FIFTH PRINTING 1984
SIXTH PRINTING 1989
SEVENTH PRINTING 1991
EIGHTH PRINTING 1996
NINTH PRINTING 1999

MONTANI SEMPER LIBERI

Arts and Crafts Chapter illustrative Art Sketches by John Randolph

Biographical resumes by Betsy McCreight

FOREWORD

In one of his minor tales written in 1845, Edgar Allen Poe described the wild mountains of Western Virginia as "tenanted by fierce and uncouth races of men."

In his book, *Our Southern Highlands,* Horace Kephart wrote in 1922 -- the year I was born:

> "Time and retouching have done little to soften our Highlander portrait. Among reading people generally, south as well as north, to name him is to conjure up a tall, slouching figure in homespun, who carries a rifle as habitually as he does his hat, and who may tilt its muzzle toward a stranger before addressing him....

> "Let us admit that there is just enough truth in this caricature to give it a point that will stick. Our typical mountaineer... is a man of mystery. The great world outside his mountains knows almost as little about him as he does of it; and that is little indeed."

If these perceptions of Appalachia were ever valid, they are changing rapidly as the world comes to know us better. Modern means of communication and transportation have opened the isolated areas of Appalachia to the outside world. At the same time, we have come to know and appreciate our own heritage.

West Virginia is our home -- by birth or adoption. Sometimes it has been neglected, but one of which we are still proud. This state and its people have not had many advantages afforded to other states. West Virginia was conceived in the most difficult of times, situated in the most rugged of places, and constructed of the hardest of materials.

Its founders were not always refined or elegant, but neither was their task. The hills, with all their majestic beauty, were difficult places to carve a home. The roads were steep and muddy, hardly more than cow paths; the creeks flodded frequently; the land was uneven, filled with rocks, and not always the best quality for tilling; travel and communications were difficult; work was hard. Yet, out of this inauspicious setting, the builders of this state made a home.

What we are today as a people, we have made ourselves. We need look no further than our own conscience for the cause of whatever problems plague us. At the same time, we need look no further than our own pride to take satisfaction in our great achievements.

v

With better luck or with a different combination of historical circumstances, we might have created other conditions. Fate and fortune might have obviated whatever deficits exist in state character or purpose. However, we are not judged by what we might have been but by what we are. Whatever our lot, we are judged in reaction to it - to good times as well as to bad.

The same premise which describes the past explains the future; what we will become, we will make ourselves. In the making, we must understand, appreciate and respect our heritage. We must share mutual faith, trust and cooperation with today's people. With these attributes of character, we can face the future with a faith and courage as solid as the foundations of our state and our heritage.

Cecil H. Underwood
President, Bethany College
Twenty-fifth Governor of West Virginia
(1957—61)

PREFACE

If you were born in the hills of West Virginia, you are fortunate to have this book in your hands. For from its pages, you may learn of the background of us folk from the hills and hollers who proudly call it our heritage.

If you are from anywhere outside the bounds of our Mountain State, you can learn why its sons and daughters are such individual, independent and friendly people.

Actually, there are ten books inside this cover. Each by a separate author who has lived, loved and taught in the confines of our hills. Over the years, and in many cases a lifetime, they have been drawn to and fascinated by the segment of our heritage of which they write. They have spent years searching every nook and cranny where they might find information on their subject and have written it down so all may see.

They have been kind enough to turn over this priceless treasure to us of the Mountain State Art & Craft Fair to publish in book form.

It is with humble pride that we present these works to you so that you may know and understand these wonderful, unforgettable things that are a part of our everyday life.

You will find why some of the words and phrases we use, and some of our ways of doing things are at times not understood by those around us.

These have come naturally from the combination of salmagundi of cultures from our forefathers.

There is one outstanding characteristic which may not be spelled out specifically in these pages, but is understood by everyone who comes to our borders -- this is friendliness.

You will learn of our music, our songs, and our dances. And you will learn of our faith, the faith that came into the Appalachian Wilderness with those hardy sons and daughters, and which prevails today.

All these things you will find in the following pages, and from these has come the pride we have for our Mountain State, which we call ''Almost Heaven.''

> O. L. (Tubby) FitzRandolph
> President
> Mountain State Art and Craft Fair

INTRODUCTION

The Mountain Heritage program of the Mountain State Art and Craft Fair has developed as a part of the Fair's growing emphasis on cultural education. From the beginning, the Fair has attempted to assemble a select group of West Virginia's finest craftsmen and their handiwork. This it has achieved to a remarkable degree over the initial years of its existence.

With the growing maturity of experience came the realization of a deeper dimension of the Fair. As the craftsman gives of himself in the act of creativity, so his handiwork carries the indelible stamp of his personality. The fair-goer purchasing his handiwork is thus investing in the way of life exemplified by the craftsman. Fuller understanding of the importance of this in the world today led to the development of the cultural education dimension through the Mountain Heritage program.

The Mountain Heritage cultural education program was developed by the West Virginia University Extension Service, one of the six sponsoring agencies of the Fair (other sponsoring agencies are: West Virginia's Departments of Agriculture, Commerce, Education, and Natural Resources, and the West Virginia Artists and Craftsmen Guild.) Originally designed for West Virginia youth through the 4-H Program, it quickly spread to homemakers, senior citizens, and West Virginians of all ages. The primary purpose of the Mountain Heritage program is to develop understanding and renew appreciation of West Virginia's rich cultural endowment and pride in its achievements. Its intent is not veneration of the past, but understanding of the cultural heritage for the light it has to shed on the present and the future.

To achieve this goal, West Virginia University sought to develop a balanced cultural education program covering the natural environment, culture, language, vocal and instrumental music, dance, religion, folklore and literature, Black culture, family and home, and arts and crafts. The Mountain Heritage program was a natural for the Fair.

Housed in a special tent, the Mountain Heritage program goes on daily from 9:00 a.m. to 9:00 p.m. during the Fair. Music, dance, crafts demonstrations and special cultural features, augmented by the instrumental music of native mountain musicians and special exhibits, provide an experience for fairgoers which enchances cultural understanding and appreciation.

Responding to increasing requests for Mountain Heritage resource materials by individuals, groups, communities, schools, and other organizations, the Mountain State Art and Craft Fair Board decided to launch publication of a collection of cultural heritage resource materials for the first time under one cover, hitherto available only to a limited group of educators as the Mountain Heritage resource series. Scheduled date for the publication's release was set for the July 3-7, 1974 Art and Craft Fair. Reception of the first edition prompted revision and enlargement from seven to twelve chapters for further use as a textbook. The Fair Board, with the approval of the West Virginia Bicentennial Commission offers the publication as a part of the American Revolution Bicentennial celebration.

The Mountain Heritage resource book is in the best tradition of the Fair. It is written by the finest group of West Virginia scholars available on the State's cultural heritage. Beginning with man's entry into the mountain wilderness, the contents progressively moves through his cultural development, arts and crafts, use of language, folklore and literature, folk music, family and home, religious faith, Black culture, and a cultural overview of the Mountain State on the eve of the Bicentennial. These are followed by sections on folk and religious songs and folk and square dances of the region. It is a resource book designed to produce understanding and appreciation of the cultural heritage and aid development of cultural educational programs. West Virginians and others sharing experiencially in the programs thus become recipients of the heritage as it is preserved and passed along from generation to generation.

Lois Hammer, of Charleston, a member of the Fair Board, provided the art work for the Chapter Title pages, and John Randolph sketched the illustrations for his Chapter on Arts and Crafts. Betsy McCreight of Huntington, prepared the biographical sketches. Rush Butcher of Nicholas county gave oversight to the section on dances, and son Keith Butcher fit the guitar chords to the songs.

The number of West Virginians who have shared in the development of the Mountain Heritage program are legion. Those who assumed major responsibility for its development at the Fair are Fair Board President, Tubby FitzRandolph, former President, Don Page, Fair Board members Betty Crickard, Virginia McTeer and Ancil Cutlip, the authors of this publication, Rush and Ruby Butcher and the Nicholas County Dancers, Judy, Crystal, Jerri, Kim, Sherri, Janet, Kaye, Pam, Kay, John, Randy, Steve, Rodney, Larry, Donnie, Harold and Dot Brown and the Putnam Highland Dancers.

The support of the West Virginia Arts and Humanities Council through Norman Fagan, Ewell Cornet, and Jim Andrews made the development of the Mountain Heritage Program a reality.

At West Virginia University, across the board support has been received from President James G. Harlow, Provost Ralph Nelson, WVU Foundation Director Donovan Bond, Dean Ronald L. Stump and the Cooperative Extension Service, Mildred Fizer, Harley Cutlip, Larry

Cavendish, 4-H Agents, Home Demonstration Agents, 4-H county camp instructors, 4-H dance and singing groups, Homemaker clubs, volunteer leaders and secretaries Edith Dean, Dawn Poole, and Julie Wood.

Likewise the response of resource persons across the state has been tremendous. The hills and hollows seem to rejoice in yielding their hidden treasures of native cultural lore and wisdom to the searching soul. Again the names are legion. To mention a few: Russ Fluharty, Franklin George, Aunt Jenny Wilson, Jim Comstock, Ruth Ann Musick, Maurice Brooks, Louise McNeill Pease, Muriel Dressler, Matt Hanna and Harv Webb, Wally Dean, Rose Chiazza, Eleanor Maillaux, the Helevtia dancers, Bill Hairston, Karen McKay, Rhonda Wallace, Mike and Lora Meador, the Morris Brothers, Dave and John, Ann Williams, the members of the West Virginia Artists and Craftsmen Guild, and Louise Gerrard of the Commission on Aging.

The experience of sharing in our cultural heritage is a richly rewarding one. If you're from the mountains, this book is for you!

To all readers of these pages, we invite you to share that wonderful experience which prompted the spirited exclamation (in somewhat less than theological terms) of a native son, swelling up and bursting with pride, "West (*by* the Grace of *God*) Virginia!"

B. B. Maurer
1st Vice President
Mountain State Art and Craft Fair
August, 1975

CONTENTS

Man and the Appalachian Wilderness

Mountain Men

Lois Hammer

N. BAYARD GREEN, professor emeritus of Zoology of Marshall University, is one of West Virginia's most distinguished academicians, in addition to being an active contributor to varied aspects of state and community life.

Dr. Green has been a West Virginian since the age of one year, and is of the Scotch-Irish ancestry so often found among Appalachian people. He was raised in Elkins and received his BS degree *cum laude* from Davis and Elkins College. He earned his MS degree at West Virginia University, and his PhD degree at Ohio State University. He has taught at Elkins High School and been a member of the faculties of Davis and Elkins College, Ohio University, Ohio State University, West Virginia University and Marshall University, where he taught from 1938 until his retirement in 1971.

Dr. Green's field is herpetology, the study of amphibians and reptiles, and he has published widely on the subject. He is now working on a Herpetology of West Virginia. He has held major office in national professional societies and has been president of the West Virginia Academy of Science.

In addition to his specialized interests, Dr. Green has had a continuing interest in the entire world of nature. He has been active in the Audubon Society, the Izaak Walton League, the Soil Conservation program and the West Virginia Conservation Education Council.

Dr. Green is an avid black powder marksman who delights in making the world of the early American woodsman come to life for today's young people.

2

CONTENTS

THE FORMATION OF THE APPALACHIANS

In order to fully understand the unique manner in which the mountains of Appalachia have influenced its peoples, their culture, their arts and crafts and their life style, including their occupations as well as their leisure, it will be necessary to go back many millions of years to that point in the earth's history which led up to the formulation of the Appalachians.

The Appalachian Mountains were formed from vast sediments which were deposited at the bottom of a sea which covered most of what is now our United States. At that time there was no North American continent as we know it today. Instead, there was a large land mass lying along what is now our Atlantic coast and out into the ocean for some distance. This land with its high mountains provided the sediments which were washed off the western slope of this mountain mass into the sea which covered the land to the west. This land mass was called "Old Appalachia", the name being taken from a tribe of Indians which inhabited Florida many millions of years later. The erosion of Old Appalachia with the subsequent deposition of its sediments started approximately six hundred million years ago, or, roughly, more than half a billion years.

This vast sea which extended from the western foothills of Old Appalachia to what is the approximate position of the Rocky Mountains today varied in depth, the deepest part being along the easternmost side. In fact, this deep area extended as a trough along what is roughly today the Appalachian Mountains from southeastern Canada down into Alabama, Georgia and Mississippi. This trough served as a vast depository for the materials which were washed down the western slope of the eastern land mass. To these materials were added the remains of the various forms of animal life which were living in the sea at that time and which today appear in these rock layers as fossils; animals such as corals, sponges, trilobites, straight and coiled shells of the nautiloids and many others.

As the sediments were deposited, their weight caused the deposits to sink. The sea would then become deeper and thus additional deposits would build up. This went on for millions and millions of years. These deposits which accumulated at the bottom of the sea in layers eventually became compacted to form the sandstones, limestones and shales which today are present near the surface throughout the state.

After millions of years the accumulated weight of these sediments brought about massive pressure changes in the earth underlying this mass. This resulted in the buckling and thrusting upward of these sediments above the surface of the sea to a height of what has been estimated as high as 30,000 feet in some areas. These uplifted sediments formed the Appalachian

4

Mountains and the phenomenon of buckling and upheaval has been termed the Appalachian Revolution.

This uplift occurred westward into what is now central United States with the highest portions in the Appalachian region. The seas drained off toward the West leaving what is now West Virginia elevated above the sea. This all took place from about 220 to 250 million years ago leaving the Appalachian Mountains as the oldest mountains on the North American continent. During their upheaval large amounts of salt, gypsum and potash were deposited which have played an important role in the economy of the region.

For more than a million years after the Appalachians were uplifted they were eroded. Many rivers which originated in these mountains carried the gravel and silt down their slopes until there was very little left of the mountains as they had first appeared. Most of the Appalachians were worn down to a level plain.

The levelling of the mountains to a vast plain was followed by a gentle uplifting which resulted in the formation of an immense plateau which then occupied what is now our Appalachians. This occurred in the East at the same time the Rocky Mountains were being formed in the West. This was about 70 million years ago. Since that time the rivers, which were carried to the tops of the mountains by the last uplift, have been cutting deep gorges and gentle valleys in the plateau so that today our land is dissected into a rugged terrain with which we are to deal in the rest of this story.

If you stand on any of our tall mountain ranges today and look across the hills to the mountain ranges in the distance the skyline will look fairly level. This represents the original plain after it had been uplifted. The valleys are not very distinct in the distance but you know from the land around you that they are present.

MINERAL WEALTH OF THE APPALACHIANS

During the formation of the Appalachians numerous minerals were formed: some came from the plant and animal life of the sea or the emergent land mass while others were present as various elements combined with other elements. The extraction of these minerals from the earth has provided a basis for much of the economy of our state.

Coal, Oil and Gas

Coal is our principal natural resource. Most of our coal was formed during a period of about fifty-five million years just before the formation of the Appalachians. By this time the accumulation of the sediments nearly filled the trough in the Appalachian region and much of the area was covered with vast swamps. In these swamps grew giant tree ferns, seed ferns, horsetails and other closely related plants. In the course of time the fallen trunks, branches and fronds of these plants formed layers of compacted organic material under the accumulated sediments which collected on top of them. These layers formed a rich organic sediment called peat. As the layers became thicker and thicker most of the moisture was squeezed from the peat and the layers became compacted into bituminous coal. Under somewhat similar conditions and usually found associated with the coal are the other two fossil fuels found in our state. These are oil and gas. West Virginia lies in the heart of the Appalachian Coal Field and more than half of the state is underlain with this resource.

Limestone

Limestone is a sedimentary rock which is composed of minute particles of lime fused with a variable amount of clay. Some limestone may contain the fossils of plant and animal life embedded in its matrix. Limestone is an important building material but its most important use throughout the state is as a source of lime. When roasted in a kiln, the stone breaks down into a fine powder which, because of its alkaline reaction, is used on the soil to counteract acidity.

Much of the southern part of West Virginia is underlain with limestone where numerous caverns have been carved through the action of the underground water. These caverns have served as temporary shelter for people, as well as many kinds of animals. They are homes for many species of animals, particularly bats. Down through the ages, the accumulated excrement of these bats formed a rich organic substance called guano. In the days of the early settlers, these wastes served for the extraction of nitrates which could be manufactured into gunpowder.

Iron Ore

The mountains of Appalachia are rich in iron ore. The early settlers badly needed iron for many household implements and utensils such as hinges, rifles, kettles, axes, farm tools and many other uses. It was far more convenient to mine the ore, melt it down and separate it from foreign particles than to try to transport it from coastal sources. The mountain stone furnace was utilized for this purpose. Many of the tall stone columns which were used for the smelting of the ore are still to be seen over the state.

Most of the iron furnaces were heated by charcoal. The obtaining of charcoal in itself was an important mountain industry. The melted ore was run off into sand molds to form "pig iron". The bar iron was then taken to a nearby forge for shaping. Some early mountain forges were built along fast-running streams so that the triphammer forge could be powered by the water.

The first iron furnace west of the Alleghenies was built near what is now Weirton in the Northern Panhandle. It is said that cannonballs were cast here for Commodore Perry's fleet which engaged the British in the Battle of Lake Erie.

Salt

Salt was a very important commodity on the early frontier. As the early settlers moved farther and farther away from the coast, its transportation from coastal areas became too difficult. The center of the Appalachian salt manufacture was the many salt springs and licks. These attracted large herds of elk, buffalo, deer and other animals. As the settlers moved into these regions they frequently located their settlements close by. Many communities throughout the Appalachians still bear such names as Salt Springs, Salt Lick and Saltville. One outstanding salt area was located near Malden in the Kanawha River valley. Daniel Boone frequented this area during some of his hunting trips.

Other Minerals

Other minerals which occur in West Virginia of economic importance are potash, zinc, gypsum, dolomite, saltpeter and mica. Lead was a metal of major importance to the early settlers because of its need in the making of bullets. Lead ore was discovered in the New River Valley in western Virginia in 1756. A number of lead mines, furnaces and forges operated along New River throughout the late eighteenth century. Large quantities of lead were supplied to Washington's army from the New River furnaces.

RENEWABLE RESOURCES: THE APPALACHIAN PLANT WORLD

The renewable resources include water, soil and the living plants and animals. All of these are dependent, to some degree, upon each other, as well as upon the physical environment. Thus the plants depend upon the soil for minerals and for support. The water depends upon the soil for retention and upon the plants and animals for recycling. The soil depends upon the animals and plants for its formation and maintenance, and the animals depend upon the plants and the water, as well as the soil, for sustenance.

The Great Deciduous Forest

The Appalachian Forest is one of nature's greatest miracles. Nowhere else in the world is there to be found such a variety of broad-leafed trees as is to be found on the slopes of these mountains. The great variety of woods with their multitude of uses, coupled with the fruits and products of these trees, is one of the wonders of nature. Each season of the year reveals the glories of this great forest. In the spring the multitude of trees bearing their strikingly beautiful blossoms attract viewers from throughout the East. In the summer the changing shades of green add variety to the hillsides. The beauty of the reds and yellows of the autumn slopes present an almost unbelievable picture of loveliness. Even in winter, the stark shadows of the naked branches are enhanced by the scattered evergreens of the pines, hemlock and rhododendron.

More than fifty species of deciduous trees are indigenous to this region; almost twice as many as occur throughout the entire continent of Europe. Most of the types such as maple, oak, beech, birch, elm, chestnut and others are also found in Europe although the variety of species do not exist there. Hickory is the only well known genus present in Appalachia that does not occur in Europe. This was a new wood for the early settlers. There are about twenty species in Eastern North America and one in China. Deciduous forests also occur in central China and in other areas scattered throughout the world, but nowhere is there the diversity, nor the splendor of the broad-leafed trees, as we find in Appalachia.

Here is a good place to comment upon some of the reasons for this diversity, as well as some of the results which it has had on the culture of Appalachia. Foresters refer to the forest type in mid-Appalachia as "cove hardwoods". Where soils are good and moisture is abundant, these trees grow rapidly and attain their optimum size. There is probably no other region in North America which is so favorable to the development of a deciduous forest.

Although the number of species of broad-level trees in the Appalachians will exceed fifty or sixty different kinds they are not uniformly distributed. In every stand there will be certain species which outnumber the others. These are called the dominants and their number is determined by the rainfall, temperature, soil type, light and other environmental factors. In other words, the environment is ideal for their development while the other species in the stand may have some difficulty in competing because they are not so ideally adapted to the environment. In the northern part of the Appalachians the dominant trees are more resistant to frost and cold weather. In fact, the limiting factor in their distribution is their ability to withstand late spring freezes which would interfere with their ability to produce seed. This gives rise to what is termed the "Northern hardwood forest". Such species as the maples, birches and beech belong to this forest. Southeast of the Northern Forest grew a forest which was dominated by the oaks and the American chestnut. To the west there developed another forest type, which, in this instance, was limited by the amount of water available. In this forest, which is

8

referred to as the "central hardwoods", flourish such species as the oaks, hickories, elms and sycamore.

Man and the Forest

When the white man first settled along the Atlantic Coast, his progress inland was blocked by an almost impenetrable wall of trees that extended to the Mississippi River. Except for the coastal forest which was coniferous, being composed of various species of pines, this forest, or, I should say, these forests because there were several different types, were all deciduous. There was one exception; at higher elevations, along the crest of the Alleghenies and other mountain ranges, there grew conifers such as spruce, fir, white pine and hemlock.

The first settlers who came to West Virginia found the entire state covered with forests. The forest was an integral part of their existence. It was the central factor in their mountain life. It provided a product for building their homes, and fuel for heating and cooking. It provided wood for many necessities, as well as luxuries; furniture, implements, toys and recreation. It provided the game upon which their life depended. And when the land was cleared, the rich forest soil provided the space for growing corn, squash, tobacco and other crops.

The Appalachian forest provided three woods, unequalled in their beauty of finish, for the making of fine furniture. These were black walnut, black cherry and sugar maple. The early settlers used these woods in the making of their cabinets, tables and other furniture which is so eagerly sought after today.

The early rifles which were brought to this country by the settlers from Europe had stocks made of walnut. Soon an industry began to thrive in the area around Lancaster, Pennsylvania for the making of these "Pennsylvania rifles". But the stocks of these rifles were made of maple. The early riflemakers liked the honey colored wood of the maple. Today, one of the distinctive characteristics of a genuine "Pennsylvania" or "Kentucky" rifle is its maple stock, usually striped to form what is referred to as "tiger maple" stock. Modern manufacturers use black walnut for stocking their rifles but the early settlers preferred maple.

One of the most versatile woods of the early settlers was the white pine. At one time it was the dominant tree of the central Appalachians. It flourished from Pennsylvania to the southern end of the Blue Ridge. It was used for building cabins, making the flooring and furniture to mention just a few. During the Colonial period many of these trees attained a height of 150 feet. Trees of this size were desired for ship masts for the King's Navy. The British sent timber cruisers through the Appalachians to locate trees of this size and, when found, to mark them with a broad arrow mark designated as the King's arrow. This meant that these trees were to be reserved for the Royal Navy, a practice which the early Colonists resented as an intrusion upon their rights. It is said that there still may be found some of these trees in the southern Appalachians with the mark of the King's arrow.

The mountaineer's life depended upon the forest from the day of his birth to his death. As a child he was rocked in a cradle of walnut or cherry, fed homemade remedies from the bark and fruits of the forest trees for his colic, and played with a doll carved from a basswood trunk. He lived in a home made of wood, warmed by a wood fire, washed with soap made with wood ashes. As he grew older he hunted with a mountain rifle with a maple stock, cut wood for fence rails and when he was finally laid to rest it was in a wooden coffin. Oftentimes the only marker which the family could afford was a slab of hard wood with a crudely lettered inscription.

In these days of plastics, metals and other chemical substitutes we may look back on the Appalachian highlander as the last breed of man who could truly say the Great Forest was his way of life.

Space does not permit a lengthy discussion of the many uses to which such a variety of woods has been put. Many woods such as walnut, beech, maple, birch and cherry are used for panelling. Maple, oak and beech are used for flooring. Hickory is a versatile wood of many uses even to the chips which provide the smoke in curing ham. Oak casks, charred on the inside, are used for curing liquor. Basswood, tulip poplar and holly are widely used in wood carving. Cedar used to be much in demand for fences but is now used for lining chests and closets. Hemlock bark provided a rich source of tannin used in treating furs and pelts. Ash used to be made into church pews, furniture and wheel spokes. It is now used for baseball bats, tennis and badminton racquets.

Fruits of Deciduous Trees

The fruits of the deciduous trees, as well as such by-products as the sap, provide an important group of commodities which have become an integral segment of our Appalachian heritage. The ravages of the chestnut blight which destroyed the entire stand of American chestnut was one of the greatest catastrophies to befall the game population of these mountains. Introduced from Asia in 1904 the fungus, spread by wind and probably insects, travelled the length of the Appalachians like a forest fire. In just a decade or two the hillsides were covered with the dead relics of their former grandeur. To this day there are occasional stories of a tree here or there which has withstood the blight. But even these trees die after bearing a few fruits for a year or so. The native chestnut was probably the most important plant food for turkeys, grouse, squirrels and many other animals. The loss of this species brought about many changes in the plant communities in the mountains.

The passing of the American chestnut brought about important changes in the food habits of many of our game species, as well as other wildlife.

Fortunately the deciduous forest provided a variety of trees whose fruits could be used as food. Among these fruits were the many varieties of nuts. Their kernels contained highly concentrated foods rich in protein. Some served as a source of fat or starch. Among the most common nuts to be found in the Appalachian forest were the black walnut, the white walnut, better known as the butternut, several species of hickory nuts, beechnuts, hazel nuts, and many kinds of acorns.

The various species of squirrels devour a variety of these nuts including both black and white walnuts, hickory nuts, beechnuts and hazel nuts. The black bear, gray fox and cottontail rabbit feed on hickory nuts. Many species of birds include nuts in their diet. Wild turkey, ruffed grouse, pheasants, blue jays, grosbeaks and nuthatches feed on hickory nuts, hazel nuts, beechnuts. Acorns are the staff of life for many wild animals. They furnish up to 50% of the diet of wood ducks, black bear, raccoons and the white tailed deer. Some species of oaks such as the white oak, the post oak and the chestnut oak mature their acorns in one season while a group which includes the black oak, the red oak, and the scarlet oak and others take two years to mature their acorns. Some have interpreted this as God's way of assuring food for wildlife every fall; if the weather was too bad one spring, the acorns which started the previous year were there to fall back on.

The early settlers, as well as the present day mountaineers, were keenly aware of the food value of many of these fruits and seeds. Black walnuts, as well as the butternut, are much in demand and provide a supplement to the income of many mountain families. Many of the soft fruits and berries are eaten by both man and beast. Mulberries, paw paws, service berries, persimmons, the fruit of the mountain ash have all been eaten, at one time or another, by the mountain folk. Many fancy recipies have been made available for the utilization of these fruits.

The Colorful Spring Pageant

One of the earliest signs of the coming of spring in Appalachia is the appearance of the multitude of spring flowers which carpet the hillsides before the leafing of the trees. This is another unique Appalachian phenomenon. In the coniferous forest the understory is devoid of the blanket of flowers because of the exclusion of sunlight by the dense canopy of foilage. In a deciduous forest, many flowers actually push their blossoms through the snow to bask in the warming rays of the feeble spring sun. Among the early ones to appear are the jack-in-the-pulpit, hepaticas, spring beauty, trout lily, bloodroot, wild ginger and the trilliums. Overhead the trees begin to display their expanding buds. Among the first of these is the red maple, soon to be followed by the red bud, the wild cherries and the wild plum.

As we move into April, the ground cover changes to the reds of the wild columbine, the Indian paintbrush, wild bleeding heart, fire pink and wild phlox. Overhead the dogwood forms the most spectacular decoration for the Appalachian hillsides. Later the service trees, the magnolias, which include our tulip tree with its pale green and orange tinted blossoms, the buckeye, silver bell, black locust and fringe tree appear to decorate the landscape.

The Heaths

One of the most characteristic sectors of the Appalachian flora are the representatives of a family of plants known to botanists as the Ericaceae. The word is derived from the Latin, Erica, meaning heath. Although representatives of the family are found throughout the world, they form a characteristic part of the plant life of our eastern mountains. They have been referred to as our true mountaineers. It was a wise choice when the rosebay rhododendron was selected as West Virginia's state flower back in January 23, 1903 by a joint resolution of both houses of the legislature. It is one of the glories of the state when it attains its greatest splendor in late June when its flowers, ranging from white through deep rose, open in handsome waxy racemes.

Our Appalachian heaths range in size from the early flowering, sweet scented, prostrate trailing arbutus to the one member of the family which attains tree size in Appalachia, the sourwood. Between these two extremes range an assemblage of some of our most strikingly colorful shrubs.

The catawba rhododendron or purple laurel is confined to some of the southeastern counties where it has invaded this region through the New River valley from the southern mountains. The mountain laurel is another strikingly colorful heath. The burl of its roots is fashioned into tobacco pipes. In the mountains of West Virginia the evergreen heaths are called "laurels" while the deciduous members are called "honeysuckles". The correct name for these deciduous members is azalea.

Among the azaleas, the flame azalea has been described as one of the most beautiful flowering shrubs in the world. Other heaths whose fruits are edible are the teaberry or wintergreen and the blueberries and the huckleberries.

There are areas in the state where the rhododendrons form such an interlacing network with their trunks and branches that the jungle is almost impenetrable. Such jungles are referred to as "laurel slicks" or sometimes just plain "hells" to mountainfolk. Since these are usually located on slopes that are deeply shaded with a cool mountain stream flowing along the floor of the valley, they provide an ideal location for hiding a moonshine still.

Plant Dyes

The early settlers spun or wove many of their own fabrics. These were basically linen or wool. The Scotch-Irish that settled in the Appalachians were a rural people. They kept flocks of sheep. They grew flax. They spun

12

and wove their basic fabric which was called linsey-woolseys. From the plants in their surroundings they developed bright dyes to color these clothes. Dyeing is one of the oldest Appalachian home industries.

The mountain people relied upon two basic colors: blue and red. The blues were obtained from indigo and the red from madder. Both of these plants grew wild but were often cultivated in patches behind the house for convenience. By skillful handling, mountain women could produce many shades of red from the dye.

Other colors were also obtained from the hillside plants. Butternut, also walnut, bloodroot, hickory, poke berries, sumac, oak bark and goldenrod. These plants gave various shades of yellow, browns and even green when mixed with alum or other substances. The dress-up jacket of the early mountaineer was the hunting coat or rifle jacket. These were fringed cloth jackets such as the mountaineer is seen wearing on the obverse side of the West Virginia Seal. These jackets were brightly colored. They wore them to dress occasions, dances, and even in the fields and the woods. It was indeed a poor mountaineer who could not afford at least one of these colorful jackets.

Sweetnin'

One commodity in short supply in the early settler's household was sugar or some form of sweetning. Salt was a necessity but sugar was a luxury. Even so the frontiersman had a sweet tooth and such dainties as pies and cakes and candies were part of the holiday fare at times of celebrating. Since transportation of sugar for any distance was about as costly and prohibitive as salt, it behooved the settler to fall back upon his natural environment for this condiment. The two principal sources were maple sugar and honey.

The Indians taught the early settlers how to tap the maple trees, secure the sap and boil it down into a syrup for use on their pancakes and in cooking. In many sections of Appalachia today the maple syrup industry is a thriving business. Vermont is noted for its maple sugar industry. West Virginia has many localities where the processing of the syrup is a thriving trade.

The mountaineer searched the forest for a "bee tree". This would provide him with a source of honey and, if skillful, he could capture the swarm of bees and take them back to his cabin to set up housekeeping in a "bee gum" which he would provide. The one who found a bee tree automatically became the owner of the honey. When the time came to cut the tree to harvest the honey, it was his right to do this regardless of whose land the tree was on. This tradition is still followed in many parts of Appalachia. The "bee gum" was a primitive type of hive made from a trunk of a black gum. Because black gum rots from the center outward, an old trunk would provide the necessary shelter with very little effort in remodeling it for the bees.

Backwoods Remedies

Many plants, in one part or another, provided the basic ingredients that were used in the preparation of medicines and remedies by the backwoodsman. There seemed to be a belief among the early settlers that the more distasteful or obnoxious a concoction was, the more effective it would be. Some of their remedies are still used today in patent medicines. Wild cherry bark for cough medicine is one example. The principal ailments of the early settler included a variety of stomach troubles. Inasmuch as the diet of the mountain men left much to be desired, a diet which included fatback and sowbelly along with many other greasy items, there is little wonder that they had any stomach at all.

Sassafrass, catnip, horehound and pennyroyal were all brewed into teas. The leaves and twigs of red cedar were boiled and inhaled for bronchitis. White and black willow leaves and bark were made into a tea to break up a fever. Bloodroot, golden seal, wild ginger and the corm of the jack-in-the pulpit were used in a variety of concoctions. The pitch from the white pine healed wounds and sores. Powdered bark of the hemlock was used to staunch the flow of blood from a cut. Tannin in the bark of the hemlock was good for burns. Cooked pine needles were used for toothache. Rhododendron oil was used for rheumatism. Whether these remedies were effective or not, is not recorded. Who dared to get sick, with all that facing them?

RENEWABLE RESOURCES: APPALACHIAN WILDLIFE

The term "wildlife" here is used in the broad sense to include all forms of animal life which are native to the Appalachian Region. This does not necessarily mean that all forms of animal life were of direct interest to the frontiersman. In fact, those animals which were of interest to the mountain men could be placed into one of three groups. The first of these was the fur bearers. Another group would be those used for food, while a third group was also of interest in that they were either feared or avoided by the frontiersman.

The Fur Bearers

It was the early trappers, in their quest for furs, who penetrated the wilderness, who crossed the Alleghenies, who migrated through Cumberland Gap to open routes of communication between the eastern coast and the Ohio Valley, and later the Mississippi Valley. As the supply of furs decreased they pushed further westward, trapping, hunting and fighting Indians. Although many species of furbearers were trapped, the one in greatest demand was the beaver.

The Beaver

The beaver is the largest rodent in North America. It ranges from thirty to fifty pounds. Before the white man arrived to what is now West Virginia,

14

beavers probably occupied every stream that offered suitable habitat. Their principal foods are the bark and twigs of the service berry, willow, black cherry, yellow birch and alder although they will feed on any deciduous tree and even on evergreens.

Beaver pelts are prepared by stretching the skin across a circular hoop made from a slender willow branch. The diameter of the hoop is determined by the size of the pelt. The largest grade for the pelts ranges from 65 inches or over. After the pelts are dried, they are removed from the hoops and stacked. The trappers usually transported their stacks of furs on horseback or canoe to the trading station or the market.

The Indians trapped only those beaver for their immediate needs. The arrival of the white man increased the importance of the beaver to the Indians, for pelts could be traded for practically anything the white man had. This stimulated the Indians to trap more beaver. By 1660 Virginia traders were buying furs from the Indians as far west as the Blue Ridge Mountains. In 1748 the Ohio Company of Virginia was formed with a large storehouse containing 4,000 English pounds worth of trading goods located at Will's Creek where Cumberland, Maryland now stands. By 1753 explorations had penetrated West Virginia and western Pennsylvania. The French and Indian War was the outcome of a struggle between the French and the British for trading posts along the Ohio River.

During the Revolution the fur trade declined temporarily, but after 1785 it again became big business. By 1825 the beaver had declined in West Virginia until it was no longer commercially practical to trap. By the early 1900's the beaver was declared extinct in West Virginia. During 1933-34 the West Virginia Conservation Commission secured 14 beaver from Michigan and Wisconsin and released them in Randolph, Webster and Pocahontas Counties. Within the next five years, fifty additional beaver were released in several other counties. By 1947 a total of 340 beaver colonies were accounted for throughout the state. The first trapping season, inaugurated in 1948, resulted in the trapping of 135 beavers.

Other Furbearers

Although the beaver was the most sought after of the furbearers, there were other species of wildlife trapped for their furs. The forests of Appalachia were rich in many of these animals. Among the more desirable furbearers were the muskrat, mink, gray fox, raccoon, otter, opossum and the fisher. It is thought that the wolverine may also have occurred in West Virginia. Even the black bear, hunted for its meat and fat, provided a fur that was much in demand for the shakos worn by King George's Palace Guards.

Muskrats were probably more plentiful than beavers. They are still to be found along many mountain streams and in swamps where they build their dome-shaped houses. Many a youngster has bought his first rifle with the money he made trapping the muskrat.

Today in Appalachia there are two different kinds of foxes, the gray and the red. Both of these are native to North America but at the time the white man came to the eastern shores of the new continent the red fox was found in the Rocky Mountain region and did not reach that part of the country east of the Mississippi. The English gentlemen brought with them the tradition of fox hunting and with it the red fox for their hunts. The red fox of eastern North American today are the descendants of those which were introduced by the early colonists.

The woodland buffalo, hunted for its flesh as well as its hide, was a different species from that of the plains bison. It was larger, darker and lacked the hump of the bison. They roamed the eastern mountains in large herds moving northward and southward as the seasons changed. They followed well defined trails which later served for the location of highways. U.S. Highway 50 which runs through West Virginia from Parkersburg to the Maryland border at Redhouse, was supposed to have been stamped out by thousands of these animals enroute to salt licks. The last buffalo to be killed in West Virginia was shot at Valley Head, Randolph County in 1825.

The fisher, a member of the weasel family, was last recorded in West Virginia in 1863. It was restocked in 1969 through the introduction of 25 animals secured from New Hampshire and released in Tucker and Pocahontas Counties. At one time the fur of the fisher commanded prices as high as $125 for a pelt. It is hoped that the reintroduction may eventually provide additional income for the trappers in the state.

Meat For The Table

The early frontiersman frequently lived on meat for extended periods of time. He was able to vary his diet, or supplement it, with plant foods such as fruits, berries, nuts, roots, etc. His provisions usually included a supply of parched corn but when this was exhausted, he was on the land. Now it was his trusty rifle which he depended upon for his supply of food. Many accounts by the early settlers emphasize the abundance of game in the Appalachian wilderness. Many of the animals, adapted to a woodland habitat, undoubtedly flourished. Wild turkey must have been one of the most abundant. As the pioneers cleared the land for settlement and for growing crops, the woodland animals suffered, but others, better adapted for an agrarian culture began to increase.

Early accounts pertaining to West Virginia leave no doubt that the turkey, as well as the grouse, exhibited little fear of man in those days. When John James Audubon visited the Ohio Valley around 1810, he found the area abundantly supplied with game. A wild turkey could be procured in a few minutes. The American Indian made much use of the turkey for food, tools such as awls, weapons such as arrow points from the spurs, feathers arranged and tied together to form cloaks and blankets.

16

A fruitful source of information about the food habits of the Indians, as well as the early settlers, are frequently obtained from shellheaps or "kitchen middens". These are huge piles of shells, bones and other remnants from feasts. One of these would usually be associated with an Indian village. The Globe Hill Shellheap in Hancock County, dated some 3,000 to 7,000 years ago, was found to contain many fragments of turkey bones, along with remains of deer, soft-shelled turtle and box turtle.

Among the larger game favored by the frontiersman were the elk or wapiti, the woodland caribou and the white tailed deer. The elk must have ranged throughout much of Appalachia if the number of localities such as Elk Mountains, Elk Rivers, Elk Licks and Elk Garden are any indication of its abundance. As late as the 1820's elk were abundant in western Pennsylvania. The last one recorded in West Virginia was killed in Pocahontas County in 1867. The white tailed deer was abundant throughout the state until the early 1900's. It reached its lowest numbers about 1910 when, under more rigid protection and management, it began to stage a comeback.

Mountain hunters, to whom venison once may have meant life or death, knew that deer were far from abundant in heavy woodlands. In this instance, a knowledge of the deer's habits paid off. The hunter knew that sooner or later the deer would have to visit a salt lick for salt is a necessity in the diet of a cud-chewing animal. The location of a salt lick was a carefully treasured secret. In many of the valleys of the tributaries of the Ohio River salt licks were common. If the salt licks were absent, the settler had to provide one by boring large holes in logs and filling them with salt.

It is easy to understand why the hunter preferred the deer or elk, and even the turkey, to the smaller game which must have been present in the woodlands. One deer could provide food for a family for some time. The meat could be cut into strips and smoked and dried to form a "jerky" which was palatable. Meat could also be salted for preservation since ice and refrigeration was a luxury far removed from the early log cabins. However, there were times when the smaller animals of the forest were shot for food. The ruffed grouse and the gray squirrel were considered delicacies by the early hunter much as they are today. The muskrat and the beaver, particularly the tail, were eaten. Rabbits, as well as the varying hare or snowshoe rabbit, provided the protein supplement during the long, cold winters. Aquatic life such as fish, mussels and turtles were also eaten. Many other forms of animal life were eaten, especially when the more desirable ones were scarce. Ducks, geese, doves and other birds were hunted.

Surrounded by this abundance and variety of game, it would seem difficult, if not impossible, for a pioneer family to suffer for lack of food. But many of them did, time and time again. During severe winters, famine could stalk the settlements and death and disease was a constant threat. A resourceful hunter could usually provide his family with game but many of the early settlers were unfamiliar with the habits of the wild creatures, or they were poor shots. The wilderness life was truly a survival of the strong, the cunning and the resourceful.

Tygers and Other Fearsom Beasties

There were many times when the life of the early settler was anything but pleasant. Many problems plagued him and even the strongest of heart became discouraged at times. Lonesomeness, sickness, fire, famine and Indians were a constant threat to the Appalachian pioneer. There were also several animals which were native to the mountains that brought a constant threat to one's safety. Among those were the cougar or panther, the eastern timber wolf, the black bear and the snakes.

The mountain lion is the largest member of the cat family in Eastern North America. When William Bartram, a famous American naturalist, explored the southeastern states in the late 1700's, he wrote of "tygers" that roamed the mountains. This big cat was referred to locally as puma, cougar or panther. But the hill folk in the mountains of West Virginia know them only as "painters". It is a tawny, unspotted cat with a long tail. They may attain a total length of close to eight feet. It is a predator which originally fed on deer, elk and bison. As the white man began to settle the Appalachians, the panther preyed upon his livestock.

Mountain people feared the animal for many reasons. It was capable of making tremendous leaps and it had great power in its paws and jaws. It was elusive and swift. Many stories relate to panthers following a solitary hunter to his home in the dusk while the terrified hunter expected to be attacked at any moment. Its scream has terrified many frontiersmen and its voice has been variously described as that of the whimpering of a child and the cry of a woman in distress. Although the stories of panthers attacking humans are greatly exaggerated there are a few authentic accounts of people being killed by panthers.

The most puzzling stories associated with the panther are the frequent accounts of sightings of these secretive creatures in Appalachia today. The last recorded kill of a panther in West Virginia was one on Tea Creek in Pocahontas County in 1887. Yet one can be sure that as soon as he mentions the last recorded kill in the State, someone in the audience will come up with a recent sighting. As late as 1936 panther tracks were spotted on Kennison Mountain in Pocahontas County by two mammalogists from the United States National Museum.

Second only to the mountain lion, the eastern timber wolf was probably the most feared animal in the Appalachians. The timber wolf is a large, broadheaded wild dog. The males may attain a total length of almost six feet and weigh as much as 150 pounds. Under certain conditions the wolf could instill greater fear in the hunter than the panther. Their habit of travelling in packs and their fearlessness in attacking when hungry made them very dangerous. The wolf population began to decline in Appalachia in the late 1800's. Such measures as bounties, hunting, poisoning and traps proved ineffective. The most important factor in their decline was the settlement of the country with its attendant harassment. The last recorded kill of a wolf in West Virginia was in Randolph County in 1905. Today, reports of the appearance of wolves in the east, prove, under investigation, to be coyotes or police dogs.

The Dr. Jekyll and Mr. Hyde of Appalachia is the black bear. Unlike the wolf and the mountain lion, the black bear has been able to "hold its own" throughout most of its range in the East. While it seems to prefer the remote forested wilderness for its habitat in the mountains, there are many instances, such as in the Great Smoky Mountain National Park, where they seem to be adapted to civilization. While hunting seasons on the black bear are established in most of the Eastern States with bear range, there are occasions when the black marauder intrudes upon a flock of sheep and the local farmers demand its demise.

Full-grown specimens may attain a weight of 500 to 600 pounds, although the average lies between 200-300 pounds. They may stand over five feet high. Although they are classed as carnivores, their diet is almost omnivorous. They eat a variety of animal food including small game, snakes and fish while their plant food covers blackberries, acorns, roots and fruits of many forest plants.

The black bear is considered awkward, clumsy and comical by many but there are times when they can be dangerous. He is an extremely fast and agile animal and extremely adept at a lunge. When they emerge from hibernation in the spring, they are lean and hungry and ill-tempered. When a sow bear is with cubs, she is to be avoided. Many hikers and campers, as well as tourists have been mauled or clawed by the black bear when it was cornered or tempted with food which was withheld.

The early settlers hunted the bear for its meat, as well as its oil or fat, which not only was supposed to have a therapeutic value but was used in greasing patches to be used in the rifle. Furthermore the fur or hide was made into coats or rugs. Many hides were shipped to England where they were made into shakos: the tall black fur hats worn by the palace guards in London.

Woven into the folk lore of the early Appalachian settlers were the numerous stories about snakes. Migrating mostly from Ireland where snakes were nonexistent, or from the mother country of England where they were uncommon, it was a traumatic experience to encounter a deadly viper with a buzzer on its tail. Rattlesnakes are a New World creation and the tales the early colonists carried back to the Old Country or wrote to their friends or relatives were wonderous indeed. Man has always held the serpent in fear and awe ever since it was selected to be the symbol of man's first temptation.

The early colonists selected the rattlesnake as their emblem and incorporated it in several of their flags with the motto, "Don't tread on me". Bradford's Journal of December 27, 1775 defends this selection in the following passage: "I recollected that her eye exceeded in brilliance that of any other animal and that she has no eyelids. She may therefore be esteemed an emblem of vigilance. She never begins an attack, nor, when once engaged, ever surrenders. She is therefore an emblem of magnanimity and true courage. As if anxious to prevent all pretensions of quarreling with the weapons with which nature favored, she conceals them in the roof of her mouth, so that to those who are unacquainted with her, she appears most defenseless; and even when those weapons are shown, and extended for defense, they appear weak and contemptible; but their wounds, however small, are decisive and fatal. Conscious of this she never wounds until she has generously given notice even to her enemy, and cautioned her against the danger of treading on her. Was I wrong, sirs, in thinking this a strong picture of the temper and conduct of America?"

Snake stories make up an important chapter in Appalachian folklore. Some of these stories may be traced back to the fatherland such as the story of the mother snake swallowing her young in time of danger. Others, because of the diversity of types, originated among the settlers of the early frontier. Stories about "hoop snakes", snakes milking cows and vipers that blew their poisonous breath in the face of the attacker to cause blindness, convulsions and even death, originated in the Southern Appalachians where the counterparts of these fictional serpents may be found. Much of the folklore centered around the snakes had to do with the treatment of their poisonous bite. Unfortunately many of these treatments were not only useless, but many were downright dangerous. As one competent authority stated: "More people had died from using the wrong treatment for a snakebite than doing nothing at all". The Appalachian teller of snake stories is very sensitive about the veracity of his tales and takes offense when one doubts the truth of his account. As one old-timer stated, "I believe all snake stories until they are proven false". How do you go about proving a snake story false?

Three species of poisonous snakes are found in Appalachia. Two of these are rattlesnakes -- the eastern timber rattlesnake and the ground rattler. Rattlesnakes are found in every state east of the Mississippi River except Maine and Delaware. The other poisonous snake is the copperhead which is more widely distributed. Water moccasins are found only in the swamps of the coastal plain and the southern diamondback rattlesnake is also confined to the southern coastal plain and some areas in the piedmont.

Snakes held an important place in the life of the American Indian. They were used in ceremonial dances. Their fangs, rattles and skins were used to adorn necklaces and other ornaments. The oil had a distinct therapeutic value

20

and they also served as food. Many early remedies of the frontiersman contained rattlesnake oil. The powdered rattles were mixed in medicines.

MAN'S INTRUSION INTO THE WILDERNESS

The story of Appalachia is, more than that of most lands, the story of man confronted by nature. What spirit or quality of the early pioneer guided him away from home and his loved ones into an unknown land of trees, wild and sometimes dangerous animals, and savages? These early trappers and explorers were not searching for gold. Some were searching for living room where they could rear their families surrounded by the intoxicating profusion of natural resources. Others were looking for the only treasure their horses or canoes could carry: some of the finest furs in the world.

The Mountain Men

The early settlers were preceded into the wilderness by a group of men of unique characteristics who differed from their fellowmen in quantity, if not quality, of manly vigor. They were a brave, tough, resolute group. Many were obsessed with the spirit of adventure. Many belonged to that breed of man who felt the security of a rifle nestled in the crook of his arm.

From these explorers have emerged such names as Daniel Boone, Simon Kenton and Lewis Wetzel whose contributions to the opening of Appalachia have been well documented. All three of them have played an important role in the early history of what is now West Virginia.

Daniel Boone

Of the early mountain men, Daniel Boone is probably the most famous. Whether this is because he was deserving of the fame, or because he had a better "press agent" in the person of John Filson who was a ghost writer for his autobiography could still be argued.

Daniel Boone was born in Berks County, Pennsylvania in 1734. His father took him to the Yadkin Valley of North Carolina and here he learned the frontier wisdom from friendly Cherokees from which he was to benefit for the rest of his life. He served in Braddock's campaign against the French and Indians. When he returned he married and settled down on a farm of his own. But the plow was not for Daniel. There was the lure of adventure and the chance to test his backwoods skills. And in 1769 he left his wife and the farm and, along with several adventurous neighbors, plunged into the wilderness and thus became one of the founders of the State of Kentucky.

Daniel Boone made numerous trips into what is now West Virginia. He was a frequent visitor of Fort Lee along the Kanawha River at what is now Charleston. He frequented Point Pleasant and trapped extensively in that large triangle between Charleston, Point Pleasant and the Big Sandy River. In 1791 he was elected to the Virginia Assembly to represent the new county of "Kenhawa". The county then took in a great expanse from below Huntington north along the Ohio River to Parkersburg and east to Charleston. Boone lived in Charleston until 1795 when he again moved to Kentucky. He died in Missouri in 1830. His remains are now interred in Frankfort, Kentucky.

Simon Kenton

There are many who lean to the belief that Simon Kenton was Daniel Boone's peer. They were good friends, saved each other's lives on several occasions, and their careers show interesting parallels. He fought in border wars against the Indians and was captured numerous times. He also acquired large holdings of land in Kentucky and built himself a large brick home. He could neither read nor write and lacked any administrative experience. Eventually he lost his holdings and died in utter poverty on a farm in Ohio.

Simon Kenton was born in what is now Fauquier County, Virginia in April, 1755. When he was fifteen years old he fell in love with a maiden, whom he subsequently found was to be married within a week. In a fit of jealous rage he attacked the man and dealt him such a fearsome blow that he thought he had killed him. Because of this he ran away from his home and it was not until thirteen years later that he returned home to find the man alive. During these thirteen years he had trapped, explored and fought Indians in what is now West Virginia, as well as Ohio, then the Northwest Territory, and Kentucky.

An incident in Simon Kenton's life illustrates the hardiness of the early frontiersmen. On March 9, 1773, Simon Kenton was camped along the Kanawha River near what is now the city of Charleston. His companions were John Yeager and George Strader. Yeager, the older man, stayed in camp and did the cooking and the skinning of the animals. It was a cold, wet, rainy day and Kenton and Strader had returned to the camp with a disappointing catch of furs. They had killed a turkey and this meant fresh meat in the camp. While Yeager was preparing the turkey, Kenton and Strader cleaned and oiled their rifles and stacked them against a tree. Then they took off all their clothing and hung it over the fire to dry. Suddenly there was the crash of rifle fire from the darkness and Yeager fell to the ground. Kenton and Strader escaped into the forest. Six days later they reached the Ohio River, more dead than alive. They were half frozen and starved when they burst out of the forest and saw three canoes beached on the bank of the Ohio with several men around them. They recognized the men and while running toward them Strader fainted. It was ten days before Simon and George had recuperated from their ordeal.

Lewis Wetzel

Lewis Wetzel had been acclaimed by many as the greatest scout and Indian fighter that the United States ever produced. He was born in Lancaster County, Pennsylvania in August 1763. When about a year old Lewis' parents with their three sons and a daughter, along with four other families left their home and moved westward where the Wetzels settled along Big Wheeling Creek, Marshall County, West Virginia. When Lewis was 13, he and his younger brother were captured by Indians. Although they escaped, Lewis never forgot the ordeal and vowed vengeance on all male Indians, a vow which occupied most of his time the rest of his life. During his lifetime he journeyed to New Orleans and into Texas twice and spent four months with the Lewis and Clark expedition but left it because of boredom. He died of yellow fever while visiting a cousin in Natchez, Mississippi in 1808. His remains were transferred to the McCreary Cemetery near Moundsville on August 2, 1942.

The Mountain Men's Weapons

The Rifle

The rifle was the most important implement in the everyday life of the frontiersman. It provided him and his family with food and it was a protection against wild animals and savages. It gave him a sense of security at all times and it was not uncommon for him to attach pet names to it. Simon Kenton called his favorite rifle Jacob.

The rifle used by the frontiersmen was of an ignition type known as a flintlock. This type of rifle, or some variant of it, was the popular type for over three hundred years. It emerged in Europe sometime before 1550 and was widely used until it was replaced by the percussion rifle about 1840. The mechanism consisted of a hammer with a pair of jaws which held a flat chip of flint. An internal spring permitted the hammer to be brought back to a cock. When the trigger was pulled, the hammer moved forward and struck an upright plate called the frizzen. The frizzen covered a pan which contained a small amount of fine blackpowder. This pan was connected with the posterior end of the barrel, or breech, with a small hole. When the frizzen was struck by the flint it was pushed forward and sparks resulting from the striking flint ignited the powder in the pan which produced a flash which travelled through the opening and ignited the powder in the barrel. The resulting explosion forced the projectile out the muzzle.

This was a complicated mechanism and there were many ways in which it could go awry. The first aphorism the rifleman learned was to ''keep your powder dry''. Blackpowder would not burn nor explode if wet, so the powder had to be dry at all times. When the rifle was carried loaded in wet weather, the frizzen was down over the pan and the entire mechanism was covered with a piece of skin. Usually the oiled urinary bladder of an opossum was used. Oftentimes the flint striking the frizzen did not produce enough sparks to ignite the powder. The striking surface of the flint had to be "napped", that is, constantly sharpened in order to produce sparks. Even when the sparks did ignite the powder in the pan, there may have been an obstruction in the touchole and the flash would not ignite the powder in the barrel. This was called a "flash in the pan" and has given rise to the expression which is used today to denote a brief period of popularity in an individual. And last of all it may not have ignited the powder in the barrel, because in the heat of an encounter, or the excitement of a chase, the hunter may have forgotten to put any powder in the barrel.

The rifle used by the early mountain men was the Pennsylvania rifle. It was referred to as the Kentucky rifle in a ballad which was written in the decade following the battle of New Orleans in the War of 1812. In this battle the ballad refers to a company of men from Kentucky with their "Kentucky rifles". Some refer to it as the Pennsylvania-Kentucky rifle.

In the early part of the eighteenth century, German migrants began to settle around Lancaster, Pennsylvania. They brought with them a heavy, short-barreled hunting rifle called the "Jaeger". The word "Jaeger" means hunter. The rifle was accurate but it was adapted for hunting larger game in Europe than would be required in this country. It frequently had a bore of .58 —.68 of an inch. Furthermore the large bore required more powder and lead shot, two components which were in short supply in the colonies. The resulting rifle which was evolved from the Jaeger had a longer barrel to ensure the complete burning of the powder and a smaller bore: .36 to .45 caliber which was sufficient for their purposes and saved lead. The first rifles made by the German gunsmiths in Pennsylvania were exactly the same as those they had made at home. During the second quarter of the eighteenth century, however, the evolution became more and more noticeable. By 1750 the true American rifle had developed. The next sixty years saw the rifle reach its highest peak, both in performance and design. The stock became lighter and much more graceful as it developed a sweeping drop in the butt. Inlays began to appear of brass, pewter and silver and the patchbox became more elaborate.

With such an excellent rifle and such constant practice, fine marksmanship became commonplace. Shooting matches were held and prizes of turkeys and cuts of beef were offered. Although some of these fine rifles saw action in the French and Indian War, it was not until the outbreak of the Revolution that it was given an opportunity to prove itself. The principal weapon of the Revolution was the musket, a large calibered smoothbore which could be loaded faster than a rifle. Furthermore they could be fitted with bayonets. Although companies of riflemen scored victories at Saratoga, Cowpens and King's Mountain, the musket was the workhorse of the Revolution.

The accuracy of the Pennsylvania rifle was almost unbelievable. There are authentic reports of men being shot at range of 300 to 400 yards. These were instances where the one shot was the only one at the target so it was not just a case of chance. Accuracy was dependent upon many factors but it finally boiled down to a careful coordination between the rifle and the marksman. The rifle was loaded by carefully introducing into the muzzle of the rifle a previously measured amount of black powder. The amount required had been accurately determined by the marksman by shooting his rifle over the snow and checking the surface of the snow for unburned grains of powder. The idea was to use just enough powder to propel the bullet the necessary distance. Unburned powder meant waste and not enough meant loss of accuracy. Now, a greased cloth patch was placed over the muzzle and the round lead ball of the proper size for the bore placed on it and the ball driven into the muzzle. The excess cloth was trimmed from around the muzzle and the ball rammed down the barrel until it reached the powder. The greased patch served several functions. As it was rammed down the barrel with the ball it cleared the barrel of scattered grains of powder, as well as the residue of the previous shot. The principal function was to permit a closer fit between the riflings of the barrel and the ball. A small amount of fine, priming powder was placed in the pan and the frizzen closed down over the pan. The hammer was kept at half-cock as a safety measure. The weapon was now ready to fire when the hammer was brought back to full-cock.

The Flintlock Pistol

Loading the flintlock rifle took time and no matter how proficient the frontiersman was, the best he could do would be to get off three or four shots a minute. If he missed his first shot, he was in trouble. The savage, or the bear, could quickly close in on him and attack. For this reason, many hunters carried a pistol in their belt for such an emergency. The pistol was also the flintlock type, of a caliber somewhat larger than the rifle, usually .50 to .58, with a barrel length of ten to twelve inches. For close fighting this weapon could be deadly. Its accuracy was limited, however, partly because of the short sighting radius and partly because of the difficulty to steady the aim.

Many of these pistols were produced by local gunsmiths, as were the rifles. The Kentucky pistol became a tradition and collectors place a high value on an authentic Kentucky pistol.

The Knife and Tomaahaken

The knife was not only a weapon for close infighting, but it was an indispensable tool and implement of the mountain man. He used it for skinning his catch of furbearers, for cutting saplings and branches for his shelter, for scalping his Indian victims, for cleaning and cutting his game into smaller portions, to mention a few of its many uses.

The knife was usually carried in a fringed, buckskin sheath attached to his belt on the left side, out of the way of the bullet pouch and powder horn which were usually worn on the right side. The blade was heavy, about ten inches long and with a very fine edge. Mountain men practiced throwing their knives and many became very adept at this art. Throwing the knife was resorted to when the element of surprise was important and to fire the rifle would be to disclose one's presence. It was used in hand to hand combat after the rifle became useless.

The tomahawk was the white man's contribution to Indian weaponery. The Indian had his battle axe which was a heavy stone fastened at the split end of a stick and tied tightly with wet buckskin. When the buckskin dried the stone was held securely in the handle. The tomahawk of the white man was a small-handled axe. It was light in weight and thus provided no burden to the many other implements carried by the frontiersman. The Indian envisioned its potential and offered many skins in trade. A good tomahawk could bring several beaver skins. The Indians called it a tomaahaken, which literally means, "cutting edge". While the Indian used it to cut saplings for his weigeia (wig wam) he frequently put it to more deadly use in combat. Many a settler's head has been split from the blow of the tamaahaken in the hands of a savage. While throwing the tomahawk is mentioned frequently in stories of Indians, it is doubtful if the Indian threw it in defense or offense. In the heat of battle it may have slipped from the hand, as the owner swung it. Few frontiersmen wanted to part with the tomahawk or risk losing it when thrown; it was too valuable in close combat.

His Clothing and Accoutrements

The frontiersman on television or in the movies is usually pictured in fringed buckskin, moccasins, fur cap, as well as other articles of dress. This was the traditional garb of the trapper, scout, Indian fighter or hunter. Buckskin was the hide of the deer with the hair removed. It was soft, pliable and warm. Furthermore, it was easily obtainable when in the wilderness. It wore well and withstood the friction with the branches, briars and other obstacles. The shirt was usually slipped over the head with the chest partly open with laces to close it if necessary. It contained no pockets. Occasionally a vest was worn open or a coat style which could be closed with buttons. The shirt or coat was usually worn in a length almost to the knee. The fringe along the sleeve and across the back must have been adapted from the Indian style.

The Indian decorated his clothing with many ornaments such as shells, bear claws, tusks of animals, porcupine quills and later, after the coming of the white man, with brightly colored trade beads. The frontiersman also used these ornaments. Bracelets and necklaces were worn by men, as well as women. Plant dyes were used in intricate designs.

Cloth woven from linen and wool also served for shirts and breeches. These "linseys-woolseys" were usually worn around the home, to church and to social gatherings. One item of apparel was the traditional hunting shirt or rifle blouse. It was a cloth coat of knee length, fringed down the front, as well as along the sleeves and the yoke across the back. It was usually dyed a bright color such as yellow, blue or green. It was worn in the field, the woods, to church and to dances on Saturday night. It was a poor man, indeed, who did not have at least two of these hunting shirts. The obverse side of the State Seal of West Virginia contains, in the center, a rock covered with ivy. To the right of this rock is a farmer clothed in "traditional hunting shirt". Such was the popularity of this garment that it was included in our State Seal.

The hunter, trapper and scout wore moccasins with buckskin breeches and/or leggings. They were frequently decorated with beads. The breeches usually had pockets. The leggings and breeches were also fringed.

Headgear was somewhat more varied. The early settler brought with him the high crown, broad brim black hat. When this wore out, or he traded it or lost it to an Indian, he replaced it with a fur cap made from the skin of an animal such as a fox or wolf.

The term, "accoutrements" has several connotations. It was formerly used to include those side arms and necessary implements of the soldier. In its broader sense it was taken to include all those necessary articles which were worn by the frontiersman into the wilderness. His wide leather belt held his shirt closed if it were open in front. It also held his knife and his tomahawk. If he were so affluent to have a pistol, it was also stuck in his belt. Over his shoulder he carried a leather bag or pouch. It is sometimes referred to as a bullet pouch, but more often was called a grab bag because it held just about whatever the hunter carried as his coat had no pockets. The grab bag held his lead bullets, maybe a quid of tobacco, some parched corn and jerky, some salt, cloth patches for his bullets, and some extra flints.

Slung over the same shoulder and riding alongside the grab bag was his powder horn which contained his supply of blackpowder. Attached to the strap of the powder horn was a powder measure made from a piece of deer horn and hollowed out to hold the exact amount of powder for a charge for his own rifle. Occasionally a smaller horn which held the priming powder for the pan of his rifle was carried along with the larger powder horn.

If he planned to be away from home, or from his base of operations, for an extended time he had to carry an extra supply of lead with a bullet mold to form his bullets. Tools needed to keep his rifle in operating condition included a "worm", somewhat like a corkscrew which could be fastened to the end of his ramrod to extract a lead ball from the barrel if it stuck there. He also carried a priming wire and brush to keep the touch hole in the barrel clean.

BIBLIOGRAPHY

Brooks, Maurice
    1965   *The Appalachians.* Houghton Mifflin Co., Boston, Mass.

Connelly, Thomas L.
    1968   *Discovering the Appalachians.* Stackpole Books, Harrisburg, Pa.

Janssen, Raymond E.
    1964   *Earth Science:* A Handbook on the Geology of West Virginia. West Virginia Department of Education, State Capitol, Charleston, W. Va. Gene A. Maguran, Editor

Kauffman, Henry J.
    1960   *The Pennsylvania-Kentucky Rifle.* Stackpole Books, Harrisburg, Pa.

Kephart, Horace
    1913   *Our Southern Highlanders.* The Macmillan Co., New York, N. Y.

Peterson, Harold L.
    1962   *The Treasurery of the Gun.* Western Publishing Co.

Udall, Stewart L.
    1963   *The Quiet Crisis.* Holt, Rinehart and Winston, New York, N. Y.

Weatherford, W.D. and Earl D. C. Brewer
    1962   *Life and Religion in Southern Appalachia.* Friendship Press, New York, N.Y.

Culture

Rural Farms

O. NORMAN SIMPKINS, chairman of the Department of Sociology and Anthropology of Marshall University, has been a leader in bringing the distinctive culture of Appalachian America to the attention of the scholarly world, as well as a prime contributor to the development of pride in their heritage among Appalchians themselves.

One writer has said that his family is ''100-proof Appalachian, being Scotch-Irish who came to West Virginia by way of Kentucky.'' Dr. Simpkins was born and raised in Wayne County and began his higher education at Berea College in Kentucky. He served as a combat photographer in World War II, and returned home to earn his AB and MA degrees at Marshall University. While earning his PhD degree from the University of North Carolina, he taught at North Carolina Central University, and later at Bowling Green State University in Ohio.

From 1957 to 1960 Dr. Simpkins was a member of the faculty of the School of Public Health of the University of North Carolina, doing field research among the Pueblo Indians of New Mexico. He then returned to Marshall University as a member of the Department of Sociology and Anthropology which he has headed since 1966.

In addition to his work in establishing the academic importance of Appalachian culture, Dr. Simpkins has engaged in many research, community development and action programs aimed at his main goal: helping the people of Appalachia develop the pride in themselves, their background and their accomplishments, which he sees as essential to rebuilding the strength of the region. He is currently engaged in writing a formal statement of his theory of social change, a major development of his past decade of thought.

CONTENTS

AN INFORMAL INCOMPLETE INTRODUCTION
TO APPALACHIAN CULTURE

I'm going to try to give you some of the background of Appalachia from the cultural point of view rather than the historical point of view. I'm not going to be so much concerned with dates and names as I am with patterns of behavior.

Now there isn't a great deal published in this area available to you. The most accessible source is a paperback book available from the University of Kentucky called "Yesterday's People" by Jack Weller. Some of you probably have it. It's mostly about Boone County, West Virginia. However, it presents enough of the picture that you can understand something of the cultural characteristics of the people of rural Appalachia.

CULTURAL BASIS

There are four basic reasons why Appalachian people are the way they are.

Rural Farm

We've always been *rural farm oriented.* I'm talking about the people that came in and settled the area and not necessarily the people of today.

Isolation

We've always been *isolated - physically, socially* and *culturally* isolated from the rest of the country, and whenever a group of any kind is isolated it tends to change less rapidly than the rest of society.

Subsistence Economy

I used to say it's always been poor, but I don't do that any more since the war on poverty; what I'm saying now is that it's always been *under-capitalized.* I mean that in several senses. Unlike most of the rest of the country not as much capital has been invested in the region as in most sections of the country, so it is an underfinanced region of the country.

Celtic Roots

The fourth reason why we are the way we are is, to me, the most interesting. Though there is some controversy about it, I think I have the facts fairly straight. The *culture* of this region *is basically Celtic.* Now this doesn't mean that only Celts came into this area to settle because there were a number of Englishmen, a number of Dutchmen, many of them were really Germans. We know them as the Pennsylvania Dutch. Some French Huguenots—the French Protestants who got pushed out of France, even a few Portuguese, a few Indians, and some blacks. All these went to make up the early population. Later, whenever the coal mines began to open up in the

1880's and '90's, there were Italians, Greeks, Hungarians, Austrians, Polish, and even Russians who came into the coal mining regions of Appalachia. By the time they came, the culture had already been set in its pattern and that's what I want to talk about because the way we act and think today is determined in a large part by who we were, where we came from, and the conditions under which we originally came here.

Now in more technical terms, the Celts who came in here were known as the Scotch-Irish. They weren't exactly Scotsmen and they weren't exactly Irishmen; that's why they're known today as the Scotch-Irish. My tall tale consists of telling you (a) how they got over here, (b) why they got over here, (c) what happened to them before they came, and (d) some little something about their cultural patterns, so that you can probably look at your next door neighbor and recognize something in him as having been around for a long time. I could go back to about 900 B.C. but I'm going to start at the time the Romans conquered England.

The time the Romans invaded what is now England was something like 55 B.C. The people who lived there were of Celtic origin. There were the Britons in what's now England, there were the Irish in Ireland, and there were the Scots in Scotland.

The Celtic peoples were prone to hard fighting, hard drinking, feasting for days on end, and just plain enjoying life. They were incapable of concerted action and thus no match for the Roman Legions. They loved music and many forms of oral literary competition. They were great believers in magic and the occult. Their priests, the Druids, were believed to possess special powers.

The Romans did not conquer either Scotland or Ireland; they conquered only the English part of it, what later came to be known as the Anglo-Saxon area. Now the Britons were pushed back into the hills, into Wales, into southwest England and northern England. The Romans stayed in England for about 400 years. The Romans were a city-dwelling people; they didn't get out in the country much. They built a lot of magnificent towns and cities, and eventually even built a wall across the northern part of England known today as Hadrian's Wall to try to keep those wild Scots from coming down and raiding the towns and cities. Hadrian's Wall still stands today.

When Rome got into trouble around the fourth century A.D., they pulled all their troops out of England which very quickly reverted back to the countryside. The towns went back to the forests and so on, and the Britons had it all over again. That left a vacuum, which was filled promptly by the Angles, the Saxons and the Jutes. These were Teutonic or Germanic people who came in and conquered what is now England. They spoke what later came to be the English language. That's where we get the word English, from the Angles. Whereas the Celtic people spoke Gaelic.

Then along about the seventh and eighth century A.D. the Vikings started coming in and raiding the coasts. Ireland by this time had developed its own brand of Christianity, and Ireland missionized England and the larger part of Germany. I won't go into the story of Saint Patrick but you know there's a rumor going around that Saint Pat wasn't an Irishman but may have been an English Protestant.

The Vikings, after raiding the coastline, virtually destroyed Irish civilization and Christianity because it was built along the coast around the cathedral towns. After they raided all around the coasts of the British Isles, and after they had been raiding for twenty or thirty years, they began to settle down. So all along the sea coast you have people descended from the Vikings. They had their own language, but they gave it up and adopted Gaelic or Anglo-Saxon depending on the area they happened to settle in. So the population of the Scots, the Irish, and even the English today has a high percentage of Viking ancestry. These are the people who came from Denmark and Norway mostly. These same Vikings you know settled over in Normandy in France and became known as the Northmen or Normans. Later on they came over into England and we'll have another part of the story. The Anglo-Saxons finally conquered all of what is now England. They didn't conquer Ireland; they didn't conquer Scotland.

Then in 1066 came the famous Norman invasion. These were Vikings who had only lived about eighty or ninety years in France, but in that length of time they had already given up their original language and had adopted French and had become thoroughly Frenchified, if I can create a word.

They brought the feudal system with them. Now the Anglo-Saxons had always been a minority in England because you know when a conquering army comes in they are really very few though they control the area, and you speak their language if you're going to talk to them. The Normans came in and did the same thing to the Anglo-Saxons. These Anglo-Saxons had already converted much of England to speak English or what later came to be English--Old English, we call it. The Normans conquered England and required everybody to speak French. And they introduced the feudal system.

Things began to settle down, and in the twelfth century, actually 1155, something happened that started another whole chain of events (this is really probably where I should have started, but I had to set the stage). King Henry II was on the throne of England and was having trouble with those wild Irish over across the sea. They were trading and trafficking with the Spanish, and you know the English and the Spanish never got along. King Henry was afraid the Spanish might, with the help of the Irish, attack England from the back door. And he couldn't have that so he had to do something. He appealed to the Pope. Back in those days Popes were extremely powerful; they had a habit of giving land all over the world to whomever they wanted. Well the Pope had been trying to figure out what to do with those Irishmen because they were deviating from Roman Christianity. They had developed their own brand of Celtic Christianity. The ceremonies were not quite the same, and they didn't listen to Rome too well. So Hadrian IV, the reigning Pope in 1155 gave Ireland to the King of England. In effect he said "You go over there and civilize those uncivilized Irish and bring them back into the true church". At the same time the English government was trying to conquer the Scots who had been causing trouble up in the North of England ever since Roman times. By the twelfth century the English had managed to conquer Lowland Scotland but not Highland Scotland. So from about the thirteenth century on, Lowland Scotland had been speaking English. Of course, after the Normans came in, their French combined with the old Anglo-Saxon resulting eventually in our present day English language.

Now, the English tried to subdue the Irish with the feudal system. The King would give a big grant of land in Ireland to some lord or noble or somebody that had helped him in battle or something and in effect make him the duke of that area. He was required to go over there and build a castle, subdue the local people, and provide the king with so many knights in armor, so many foot soldiers, so many spears, so many bows, so many crossbows, and so many horses whenever the king had to go fight. These dutiful Englishmen, many of them were really Normans who had learned to speak English, would go over and as very loyal Englishmen, try to subdue the local Irishmen. In about two generations they would become Irish themselves and were fighting the English.

This is a characteristic of Celtic culture and it still holds today. They absorb strangers and make Celts out of them whatever their biological ancestry. Only you don't see this in the history books because so many people from Ireland and from Scotland have been labeled in the history books as English. You have to get beneath the surface to get at it. George Bernard Shaw was one of these Irishmen who was really an Englishman who was really a Norseman. His family was one of those who had been sent over to Ireland and given a grant of land. So too, the famous Irish family of Burke's were originally Normans.

Well this went on from the twelfth century up into the fifteenth century. The English King would give grants of land to these loyal Englishmen and in two generations they had become Irish.

Then in the fifteenth century some of the native Irish chieftains in Northern Ireland, known as Ulster, committed treason. Some of them were former Englishmen who had become Irishmen. They absconded: left their estates, and escaped to France. So suddenly now the king had a problem. He had a whole hunk of land in Ulster and he couldn't let the Irish take it back over. So the British government, this was in the time of Queen Elizabeth, conceived the idea of moving all the Irish out, advertising for good solid English yeomen to come over and settle in Northern Ireland or Ulster. They promised them the land, and after they had been there five years they'd get a title to their land. Well, the English farmers weren't too happy to do this; they weren't in any great trouble; they had plenty of land. The Lowland Scots, however, were being foreclosed off their land because of the Enclosure Acts. (England and especially Scotland was beginning to bring in sheep to raise, forbidding the peasants from raising their crops, and turning the land over to the lords to raise sheep). This was the merchantile period in which the theory was the way a country got rich was to sell something you've got to some other country and bring the gold in, and the more gold you had the healthier the country was thought to be. The English were selling wool to Holland because the best weavers were there. So instead of English yeomen coming in and taking advantage, it was the Lowland Scots farmers who seized this chance to get their own farm land. They already spoke English. Roughly a hundred thousand Lowland Scots farmers and twenty thousand English farmers took this new opportunity to get land and move over into Northern Ireland, into Ulster.

They were such good animal raisers they soon were running the market for horses and cattle and sheep in England. The English farmers began to protest. So the British government began to levy taxes on these Ulstermen to import their products into England. The Ulstermen simply planted their rows a little closer together and worked on the horses a little bit more and they still had the best horses and livestock.

So England finally adopted the practice of what's known as "rack renting". First the English reneged on their promise to give them the land after they had lived there five years, and required them to bid in their farm every year and they could make only one bid. If they didn't have the high bid, they didn't get any land to tend. And of course this broke them up since they often had to pay as high as 75 to 80 percent of what they raised to their landlord with all this rent money going to England.

So these Scotch-Irish got fed up with it. From about 1700 to 1776 over a half million of these northern Irishmen who were Protestants, who were Lowland Scots, (that's how they got to be known as Scotch-Irish) left the area and most of them came to the United States. They settled in the "out-back" country because they didn't have enough money to buy land along the seacoast where the colonies were. This was before the United States had declared its independence. The colonies were glad to get them because they wanted to use them as buffers between the colonies and the Indians. The Scotch-Irish moved into the "out-back" country of Vermont, New Hampshire, upstate New York, western Pennsylvania, (the Germans were already in eastern Pennsylvania) the Shenandoah Valley, and the Piedmont Area of Virginia and the Carolina's because that was the frontier then. They formed a buffer zone between the colonies and the Indians.

They came in with a horse, a cow, a sack of corn, an iron pot and a wife and several children, an ax and a long rifle. Now the highly accurate long rifle had been developed by the Pennsylvania Germans. It was a rifle rather than a smooth bore musket. To this day the governor of Kentucky and the governor of Pennsylvania quarrel over whether it's a Kentucky rifle or a Pennsylvania rifle.

These Scotch-Irish settled largely in the western part of Pennsylvania, the Piedmont area of Virginia, and the Carolina's. They filtered down the Shenandoah Valley along with some of the Germans that had settled in eastern Pennsylvania and into the mountains. Some came down the Ohio river and virtually eliminated the French who had earlier come down and settled a few places such as Marietta. The Scotch-Irish were English speaking when they came. Therefore you'll find very few evidences of the old Gaelic language. There's one or two places in West Virginia where it was spoken up until fairly recently. And they gradually moved over into the Yadkin, and through the Cumberland Gap into Kentucky and down the New River over into the Kanawha, into West Virginia; down the Ohio River into Ohio and Kentucky. This is how they got into Appalachia.

Daniel Boone is a prime example of the Scotch-Irish pattern of migration. Born in western Pennsylvania, he moved down the Shenandoah Valley into Western North Carolina, then over the Cumberland Gap into Kentucky and so on. Andrew Jackson was born in America six months after his parents came from Ulster. And the same kind of people incidentally later on moved out into the Ozarks. They have basically the same culture. They also moved out into the great plains area and are the people who started the cattle culture. I'm talkin about the real old cowboy West not the Hollywood kind. They were Celts, too. You look at the names of places out there and the names of families that started the early ranches and nearly all of them were Scotch-Irish. The history books call them English, but they were Scotch-Irish. For example, the Chisholm Trail is probably the most famous and Chisholm is about as Scotch as you can get.

CULTURAL CHARACTERISTICS

Livelihood

Live On The Land

The Anglo-Saxons, who are the English, were town dwellers. The Scotch-Irish were not. They were rural or country dwellers. And if you look at the settlement patterns in New England and the settlement patterns when you get into the Alleghenies, you'll see the difference. The Puritans, the English Pilgrims, were largely Anglo-Saxon in descent. They settled in towns and farmed the land roundabout. As a matter of fact for a long time up until after we became a nation, many of the towns in New England (and you know a town in New England is different from the towns in this area in terms of political structure) had laws requiring the people to build their houses within a half-mile or a mile (different towns had different distances) of the church. You couldn't live out on your farm, you had to live in town within a mile of the church. As the town got larger they had to expand the distances slightly.

We've got our history all twisted around; we give them all the honor when actually there were other people settled in Virginia long before the English settled. Harry Caudill in his *Night Comes to the Cumberlands* says the people in Appalachia were descended from the scum of London. Now that's a lot of hooey. If the scum of London had gotten over here in the mountains fighting the Indians, they'd all been killed off. Most of the names in the region that were originally here are of the Scotch-Irish name pattern rather than the cockney London pattern of naming. The Scotch-Irish lived on the land. The Celtic pattern is, if you have land you live on it.

So, they built their houses on their land; it's what technically in sociology is called "open settlements" or dispersed farmsteads. There are several names for it, and this established the pattern of settlement from here on through. Of course when they got over into Ohio the government came along and surveyed the land out in squares. But in this area they used the old "metes and bounds" system. And if you had land you put your house on it. You didn't live in town and drive out to it. And this means you're isolated and you had to be a jack-of-all-trades. And that's why they needed their neighbors to come and help whenever the rain was going to get the hay, or something, and when there's more work to be done than you possibly can get done, you swapped work. They didn't have much money so they swapped work.

Animal Raisers

The Scotch-Irish or Celts were animal raisers primarily, while the Anglo-Saxons were crop growers basically. This results in a different way of life. For 2,000 years the Celts had been pushed up into the hills where they don't like authority, where they're always tryin' to be taxed, and that's the reason why they're animal raisers. They could always take a flock of sheep or cattle or pigs and run them over across the valley behind the next ridge and hide them from the tax assessor. If you have a field of wheat or corn or potatoes you can't do that very easily. The pigs run wild in the mountains anyhow and out of this comes an interesting aspect of the Hatfield-McCoy feud. If you remember—it originally started over a pig and whether the notches on the ears meant it belonged to one family or the other.

Going back to the old country, stop and think, most of the standard breeds of horses, cattle, dogs and sheep have Scots names or Gaelic names or Irish. They were developed either in Scotland or Ireland. The biggest horse and the smallest horse, the Clydesdale and the Shetland pony, they're both Scots. Outside of the Brown Swiss cow and the Holstein cow most of the others--the Angus, the Hereford, the Jersey and the Guernsey--were developed by the Celts, and I don't know how many breeds of dogs except the English Bulldog, the Anglo-Saxons bred that one. The pattern persists even when the people have to go to Detroit where they can't keep cows and horses and so on. They'll have some kind of animals around the place. A good sign of a Celtic home is a bunch of cats and dogs and if they can't have anything else, a parakeet or canary.

Swapping

They did not have a money economy; they had a barter economy. Around here it's called "swapping". The pattern is still with us you know. This is one of the reasons why you see abandoned cars along the side of many houses in Appalachia. They originally swapped horses and cows and dogs. They transferred that pattern to automobiles and up until the 30's when the state passed a law requiring a use tax, they would sometimes swap cars two and three times a week. They'd just sign over the title to somebody else. I've seen a title back in the thirties that had eight or nine people who had signed the title and that was accepted. Finally one of them would turn it in and get license for it. Back then the license ran from January to December and so in the wintertime with no paved roads they'd just jack them up and not buy a license 'til after the first quarter had expired and that way they got them for three fourths price. The State changed the law, that's why the State changed it, to make it the first of July to the first of July so to make them pay twelve months for license tags. So every time they'd turn around, these people have been pushed around by government, by authority. They merely wanted to be left alone and live their life the way they wanted to live it.

"Toot" Work Pattern

There is a characteristic in Appalachia of working very hard for a time and then doing something else to relieve tensions or redevelop equilibrium. There are various terms you can use. So they tend to go on a "toot" every month or six weeks. The workers in Detroit do the same thing. Supervisors up there know the Appalachians as people who will suddenly, without any reason whatever, from their point of view, take off and go home to visit. They'd take the whole family. The cowboy did this when he got paid; he went to town and shot it up at the end of the month. You find this pattern somewhat in your religion. You don't find it as much today as you used to in the rural areas. It's kind of a backsliding pattern. They get religion at a revival meeting and hang on to it for awhile; the preacher doesn't come around very often; they try religiously to live a new life and they hold on for a month or six weeks and they backslide. And they go up next year when the revival comes around again. 'Course they had two revival seasons you know in the region, originally, in the Spring and in the Fall. So a guy could stay pretty religious most of the time if they had enough revivals. I'm being a little facetious here but I think this will make you remember this pattern a little bit more. You may have this pattern in schools. I've noticed it somewhat in some students at Marshall; they'll work very hard for a month or six weeks and then suddenly they'll just start cutting, start being absent for three, four or five days and then come back and work real hard again. The Army has encountered this with Appalachians; as a matter of fact, some areas of the Army, the infantry particularly, make allowances for this. If they're from the hills, eastern Kentucky or West Virginia or Tennessee, they expect them to go AWOL and they don't punish them too severely; they know they're going to come back.

Easy Going Pace

Appalachians get their easy going way of life from the Scotch-Irish influence. An Appalachian can sit on his porch and rock all day without getting an ulcer over it. Most Americans have to be up and about doing something all the time.

Personality

Open Faced Outlook

A personality characteristic of Appalachian people that tends to get them into trouble in the big cities and sometimes in our consolidated school systems, is their "open-faced" outlook on life and acceptance of strangers once they get over their initial suspicions. They're too ready to accept them as "home folks". They haven't learned to build up a "front" to protect their ego. The smaller a kid is, the more likely he is to do this. He'll tell things on himself, or he'll say things that will give you insight into his behavior that will damage his ego, and he's not aware of this because he hasn't built up, as urban people have, this front of protection.

Now the reason for this is they come from an area where they know practically everybody; they don't meet many strangers and everybody knows you. So you can't build up a front if everybody knows your inner most thoughts. After they go to the city it takes time for them to develop this. Some of the older ones never develop this. That's one reason why they're not satisfied in Detroit and Cleveland and so on. You might watch for this, they do not have this -- I don't have a good word for it, I never have found a good word for building up of a front to protect their ego with strangers. Some of you may have a better name for it than I have. I haven't been able to develop a good name for it or find one in the literature that is satisfactory. If you see this kind of thing, they tend to hurt themselves by what they say and what they do, because they're not aware that they can be used by other people.

Person Oriented

And if anything I say is of any value, this next statement is probably it. *They see other people as whole individuals.* Unlike the city person who tends

40

to see other people as objects. Now to see persons as wholes means that you do not see them in roles. A city person has to meet a lot of strangers in specific roles and tends to see them only in a narrow section of their life. He sees the clerk in the store, the official in the office, he sees the policeman in his role. The Appalachian does not; he sees the whole person. He does not see roles and this gives him difficulties in a bureaucratic situation. They go down to the Welfare office or the Employment office and they can't understand why the first person they meet can't solve their whole problem whatever it is. You know in a bureaucracy that person is only an intake clerk that merely sees that they fill out all the words properly on this form and then refers them to somebody else. And whenever the mountaineer is told to go over here to line number so and so, desk number so and so, they get hot under the collar about it because they think they're abused, or that she's got something personal against me, or she'd have taken care of it. I've stood at the complaint counter at some of the stores and I've seen this same thing happen. They can't understand why. Well, I get the same feeling. When something happens at school like no chalk available or something, I can't see why the person I approach can't solve that chalk problem even though they're not the ones that are supposed to provide chalk. I can't understand it myself. I get a little hot under the collar about it and I mutter about the bureaucracy at Marshall. Some of you probably had this kind of situation, or I come in and somebody's moved half my chairs out and put them in another room. Well I assume that the janitor has charge of this so I go to him. He hasn't any responsibility for this, he's supposed to sweep the floors. I can't understand why he couldn't have been there and kept those chairs from being moved out.

Lack Conversation Ritual

Living in an area that is hard to get to, where they want to be left alone, they interact at a high rate with each other whom they know very well, but they don't interact with outsiders because there's few outsiders. And this has developed certain character traits. They're somewhat suspicious of strangers: "foreigners" from the next county. "Foreigner" in this area doesn't mean from France or somewhere; it means in the next county or over the hill on the next ridge or something like that. Now their patterns of interaction are the kind that develop in rural situations anywhere in the world where you have people who don't meet strangers very often. They're not necessarily uniquely Celtic. If you know all about the people you meet and you know all the skeletons in their closets, you don't have to have the usual ritual for getting the interaction started and then cutting it off. So here's a characteristic you find true today among kids in school from this rural background. And if you have them from town, they're only one generation in most cases removed from a rural background, so we still have much of it. The Appalachian has no need of a ritual for getting interaction started and then cutting it off, so it takes him a long time to get started and it takes forever for him to cut it off and break away and get away from it. I've seen people when they go visiting and they're leaving, go out to the car, get the car started while the host comes out to say goodbye and the guest lets the clutch out on the car and moves down the road and the host is right along beside it and moves a quarter of a mile down the road trying to break away. They just don't know how to say good-bye and do it. They don't know how to start a conversation and they don't know how to end it. The more rural you get the more you're likely to see this.

Another thing, Appalachians have difficulty saying thank you and have difficulty accepting thanks. It hurts them; it's actually agonizing.

Staring Impolite

The urban-middle-class society and, of course, our school system teaches upper-middle-class values. Appalachian values are not upper-middle-class urban, they are rural. They're not necessarily lower-class, although if they get out of the mountains, they're classified as lower-class in many cases. But in the upper-middle-class urban society you have a belief that whenever you talk to somebody you look them in the eye, that shows you're honest and you've got nothing to hide. Not so in Appalachia; we have been taught that if you looked people in the eye that's staring, and staring is impolite. And so your hillbillys don't face each other and talk like this, they stand this way. And if you look them in the eye their eyes will shift off. And you get the suspicion that they're shifty or dishonest and that's not true. They're just trying to be polite in the only way they know how. It's impolite to stare. This stems from a time when strangers were suspect because they were likely to be a witch, and witches had the evil eye. And if somebody looked at you long, hard, and intensely, they'd give you the evil eye and make you get sick, or your cow's milk would dry up, or the milk get bloody, or somethin' like that. So Appalachians stand this way. Try this sometime. I have watched this at Marshall in the hallways where kids are talking to each other and the kids never stand this way, they stand this way. You walk up and start talking to one of them this way and you look him in the eye and he'll back off and turn this way and you come around this way. I've run them around in circles. They don't know they're doing it, but they do it never-the-less. This is simply because it's their value system, and just as it's impolite to point, it's impolite to stare. And they define staring as looking somebody in the eye. You watch a rural Appalachian, he will not look you in the eye. There is a time when he will; whenever he's lost his temper and he has become aggressive or hostile. He'll look you in the eye when he's coming at you, so watch yourself. So when you see a rural person in this region who looks you in the eye, it means they have already become anatagonistic and they're aggresive. You've already breached the bounds of common courtesy.

Word of Mouth

The primary means of passing news among Appalachians is by word of mouth. While they may read about an incident in the paper, they don't really believe it until they get it first hand from someone else. Gossip and rumor are rife - and often times quite effective - and fast - and embellished. The word gets around the community that so and so's been all cut to pieces in a fight and carted off to the hospital. You rush over to the hospital thinking you're going to get to say howdy to him at his dying breath and find there's a three-stitch cut on the back of his hand! I've seen it happen more than once. You hear somebody's just cut all to pieces and you go over and all that's wrong with him is he's just mad - that's hillbilly for angry.

Proud People

Another characteristic of the Appalachian is his reputation of having a high temper. They carry a chip on their shoulders; they're a proud people. Unfortunately, however, they're the one ethnic group that has lost their heritage in terms of knowing who they were, and who they are, largely because they were the first large ethnic group to come in who were not Anglo-Saxon. They settled in the frontier where they didn't interact with very many people and by the time the Frontier moved on, many of them moved on with the Frontier. They're scattered all the way clear to the west coast.

Family, Kin, and Home

Equal Inheritance

Their family system was one in which all the children inherited equally including the girls, and this was highly unusual in most parts of the world at the time the Celts had this pattern. This is largely responsible for the pattern that has developed in Appalachia since. When a couple gets married, the son gets his inheritance right then; the daughter likewise, and that's how they set up housekeeping. Each time the farm moves through the generations it gets split up into smaller farms and so you have a characteristic in this region of many farms too small to raise a family on simply because of this pattern. Now the Anglo-Saxon pattern was the eldest inherited and the others had to do something else. That's a device for keeping the farm, the land, together. The Scotch-Irish who came, came wanting land. Many of them squatted on some of William Penn's land that he'd set aside for his own family and he finally let them keep it without cost.

Equality of Women

Another of the characteristics of the family pattern in Appalachia, and it's Celtic, is that women have as high a status as the man. The women are independent and the couples choose each other; the parents had little or no voice in choosing who the kids married and it's still the pattern to this day.

They didn't have the honeymoon pattern which is now a prominent one; they had the "shivaree" if you've ever heard of the "shivaree" or "bell crowd", some of you know it as the "bell crowd". And the kind of humor that the Celts had in this region is exhibited in this. Of course the "bell crowd" was one in which neighbors got together and located where the couple was the first night they were married so everybody came with all the noise makers they could to keep them awake all night long and keep them from going to bed. The expected pattern was the young husband had to come out and bribe them to get them to go home and leave him alone if he had the money, and of course he knew this was coming so he'd better have some resources. His pattern was to try to not be there, and the joke on everybody was whenever they'd "bell" a house for hours and finally go in and get him and his bride and they'd not be there because they'd left and hid somewhere else. This exhibits the kind of humor you have in this area; it's a practical joking kind of humor that you still find in the region, particularly in the rural areas.

Love of Homeplace

They have a strong attachment to the land and the old "homeplace". They love the hills and every holiday is marked by the number of cars with out-of-state license plates back in the community returning to visit home and kin. They just get lonesome for home. They gotta go back and see the old "homeplace". They seem to be tied to the hills long after they leave the area. I used to tell my students at Marshall that many of them had to leave in the last twenty years but they always want to come back, and they're like most of the immigrants who came to this country who wanted to come here and making a "killing" and go back. Most of them never get back because there's no jobs here. So they come back every chance they get and visit. And whenever they die they want to be buried back here. If you don't believe me just stand on the 6th Street bridge at Huntington and watch. Watch the hearses come over. You'll find there's a much bigger traffic of hearses coming to West Virginia on the 6th street bridge than there is going the other way. If they can't die here they want to be buried here. You watch the newspapers and you'll know they're people from far off and they bring them back here to bury them. Cause they've got some kind of love for these hills. They don't boast about it and make a big noise about it, it's just there. And this is characteristic of so much of the culture. They are not selfconscious about it as many other groups are because they've never been aware that they are an ethnic group until they get outside the area.

44

Clan System

The Celts still had a clan system while the Anglo-Saxons had long since lost the clan system. Incidentally the Irish had it up until about 400 years ago. The Highland Scots had it up until 1745 when it was outlawed by the English. The clan still exists in Appalachia, they don't call it that but it's still here. I've got proof of it. It determines what kinship system you marry into, what church you go to, who you swap work with, who you get drunk with, who you help in times of crisis and so on, so the clan still exists, they just call it "set". Have you ever heard that term? When somebody dies they sit up with the body until burial, though they don't use the word "wake". They depend very heavily on kinsmen and neighbors, the "kith and kin". Kith incidentally is an old English word, I think it's English, meaning neighbors. And "kin", of course, is kinfolk.

Self-Government

Independent

Their attitude toward civil authority dates back to the days when the Anglo-Saxons pushed the Celtic peoples back into the rough mountain country of Western England and Lowland Scotland. For two thousand years these people have been set upon by tax collectors who always want to tell them what to do and how to do it. They have developed an attitude towards law, towards authority, which you find still in this region today, more so than practically any other area of the country.

They were rather disgusted with the British Crown when they came to this country. And so most of George Washington's troops who stayed with him were Scotch-Irish. At one time, and I won't give you the exact quote because I can't, he made a statement about give me men such as these and let me stay in the hills of West Augusta, and in effect he said I can fight the British off till hell freezes over. West Augusta was Washington's name for West Virginia. That wasn't his expression because he wasn't supposed to curse you know. They hated the British and so they fought very hard against the British in the revolutionary war. As a matter of fact the first declaration of independence or the first independent constitution—the Mecklenberg declaration in North Carolina—was developed by the Scotch-Irish. The state of Franklin in Tennessee, an abortive attempt to set off a new state, was developed largely by the Scotch-Irish. And of course many of them got land in the Appalachian area and eastern Kentucky particularly, for fighting in the revolutionary war. That was the "G I Bill" of those days. So if you look into some of the family histories of the region particularly over in eastern Kentucky, you'll find they first got a grant of land shortly after the revolution in eastern Kentucky for services in the Revolutionary War.

Personal Politics

They take their politics personally. A bureaucratic city politician doesn't have a chance in the mountains. That's why nearly every politician in Appalachia publicizes the families he is kin to.

Community Action

They developed an unofficial, an informal, I guess is the best word, means of getting together in groups. Whenever a problem came up the people in the community got together and solved the problem. And did it themselves. They didn't wait for the government to do it. The Anglo-Saxons would go to the mayor of the town. They always had official government. Celtic government was informal, virtually nothing, and they settled disputes by physical means. If you got in a quarrel with somebody, you fought it out.

Fightin', Feudin', Fussin'

Another pattern in Appalachia is, you settle disputes by fighting it out. If you'd get in a quarrel with another family and one fight didn't settle it - of course whoever got licked would go home and get some recruits and he'd come back. So this is why you'd have the fightin', feudin', fussin' pattern in the region that died out in the late 1880's or thereabouts. You have that in mountainous areas all over the world where there's little law enforcement. You still have somethin' of this same pattern in the area. They don't actually go at each other with guns and whole families get involved, but you do get into disputes and incidentally, they like to use knives on each other. Every good Appalachian just like every Celt (incidentally the word Celt comes from the kind of weapons they used), you know, the Scotsman whenever he was dressed up, always had a knife, a Dirk, that's what they called it, stuck in his sock. So every good Appalachian carries a Barlow, when you get in a fight, you use your trusty Barlow.

Food And Drink

Ovenless Bread

Another difference between the Anglo-Saxons and the Celts was the Anglo-Saxons made bread in ovens; they baked bread in ovens and they used yeast and the Germans did too and so did the people around the Mediterranean. The Celts didn't. If you'll notice, all the standard Appalachian breads are all made in such a way that you can make them on top of the stove because they were not an oven using people until some time after the Civil War. From the Pennsylvania Dutch, who were really German, the Appalachians took over the Dutch oven. They were Deutsch or low German which meant they were from the northern part of Germany and in their dialect their names of themselves was Deutsch. You take any English-speaking

46

person and he's met some Deutschman and he comes home and tells his neighbors I met a Deutschman today what's he going to call him? He's going to say a Dutchman. Deutsch is not a word in English. It sounds odd, it doesn't sound like it's English or something. That's how they got the name, "Pennsylvania Dutch". The Appalachian people got the Dutch oven, that was their first oven, from the Pennsylvania Dutch. They cooked in the open fireplace until they discovered the Dutch oven.

Milk Drinking Men

Another characteristic of the Celts is they were one of the few people that grown men can drink fresh milk because fresh milk was one of their basic foodstuffs. And that's the reason why many American men today can drink fresh milk without being called a sissy. Most parts of the world men don't drink milk and there are parts of this country where no Scotch-Irish settled and the men there don't drink milk either, it's for kids and sissies. Now they never had any preserved kinds of meats like the Germans and Anglo-Saxons did. The Celts invented bacon, that's the only one they really had, along with fresh pork sausage which you can't keep very long. They did not develop any cheese, they drank their milk fresh or they used it in their cooking. The Germans and the Anglo-Saxons, they made cheese out of their milk, they didn't drink it raw. They took their meat and they preserved it, and if you'll notice most of the names of sausages and cheeses are from Germany or Northern France. The Appalachians even got cottage cheese from the Pennsylvania Dutch. The only sausage of any kind that they really developed, outside of fresh pork sausage which is not really preserved, was souse or head cheese. They eat their meat fresh, they drink their milk fresh or clabbered.

Hearty Thirst

Now there's another characteristic of Celtic culture that mention should be made of. The basic drink (you know practically every culture has a basic drink - alcoholic if they can figure out a way to get it) of the Celts originally was cider because wherever in Europe you find crab apples growing that's the area the Celts settled, and the people that live there today are basically of Celtic ancestry. Of course from apples, you get cider. Now it wasn't the cider that you know as cider, it was what we know as hard cider, but they had a way of making it even harder. They put it out in shallow pans in the winter time since they lived in a temperate zone, and they'd let it freeze, and you know water freezes in a pure form; so they'd let it freeze and they'd lift that thin sheet of ice off and that left a double strength cider, hard cider about 20 percent alcohol or 40 proof. I've tried it and it works. You'll notice the stress on apples in the region. Apples is one of their favorite foods and still is to this day. Apple pie, applesauce, and all that sort of thing, and incidentally, Johnny Appleseed was a Scotch-Irishman. His name was Chapman.

While in Ireland, the Scotch-Irish picked up a drink. They learned to make Irish Whiskey. The Irish had picked it up from the Arabs in North Africa and Spain when Spain was Moslem. It was made out of rye, and when they got to the new world they kept on making their rye. In the early days of the frontier, the early days of the history of the Ohio River and the Southern area, the most famous drink was Monongahela rye. It was rye whiskey made by the Scotch-Irish in western Pennsylvania; and after the United States was founded, they're the only ethnic group that ever rebelled against the United States Government. That was the Whiskey Rebellion. When the government needed some money to pay off the Revolutionary War debt, they levied taxes on whiskey. The Scotch-Irish weren't going to pay it and George Washington had to send out ten thousand troops into the area to calm things down. Well, by the time they got down into Kentucky they discovered that rye doesn't grow too well in this area, not like it does in Scotland or Ireland. It's too wet here, or too dry, or too cold, or something. They gradually slacked off growing rye.

Then somebody discovered (and there's an argument over where it was discovered, some say in North Carolina, some say in Bourbon County, Kentucky) they could make whiskey out of Indian corn, maize. And you know to this day, American whiskey made with corn is known as bourbon—it's different from Scotch.

Religious Faith

Calvinistic Creed

Now the Presbyterian church is a church that has always insisted on an educated ministry. So when these people came into the mountains the Presbyterian church did not follow them. First of all there were no seminaries in the mountains and the educated ministry didn't want to come in—they were townspeople. So they had to develop their own religion and the pattern largely developed in the great revival period in the last century. And they developed into the Baptists and the Methodists and the Holiness. Of course, the Methodist Church was really founded in England, but when it came to this country it readily adapted to the frontier. And if you'll look today at the creed or ideology, whatever you want to term it, of the Baptist and Methodist and the Holiness, it's all based on a Presbyterian pattern - a Calvinistic pattern, not on a Puritan pattern, in this region. The Scotch-Irish also were very instrumental in getting the Congregational Church started up in New England. They moved into the ''out back'' country of New England, in New Hampshire, Vermont, in that area. The Puritans didn't like them; they didn't welcome the Scotch-Irish. That's one of the reasons why they moved in the ''out-back'' country.

48

Cultural Absorption

Scotch-Irish ancestry and its tradition can usually be found in anywhere from 60 to 85 percent of the folks in any gathering in the region. That doesn't necessarily mean a person is of Scotch-Irish descent. It's a characteristic of Celtic culture to absorb other people and make them Celts culturally, not biologically. West Virginia is like this. The Dutch people, and some of you probably have names that are derived from Dutch, are just as hillbilly as some of the Celts are. The English became hillbilly because they had to in order to live here. Up in Raleigh county there is a group of Spanish people who speak with a hillbilly accent and they think like a hillbilly and act like a hillbilly because they are hillbilly, yet they're Spanish. In some of the coal mining areas where a number of the blacks settled, they have a hillbilly accent not a southern black accent. So the important thing I'm stressing here is the culture not the biological ancestry. The biological ancestry of one is just as good as another. But the pattern was set by the Scotch-Irish and many of the characteristics of Appalachia today are due to this characteristic along with being in a remote isolated area, and being farmers. And they will keep this pattern for two or three generations after they move to a city. And here's the reason.

You develop the kind of personality you have through the way you're reared, and you get your personality pretty much set by the time you get to school. Now what the new government policy of getting the kids into kindergarten and even getting them into the early childhood education is going to do this I don't know. But by the time you get these kids in school their personality is set and remember you tend to raise your children the way you were raised, not the way Dr. Spock said for you to do it. And this is why it will carry on for two - three generations before it gradually weakens and Spock begins to have some influence, if he's still around by that time.

CONCLUSION

Over the years, the blending of many cultural strains, Celtic, Anglo-Saxon, Germanic, Southern European, African and others in this mountain environment have combined to produce a rich heritage of which every native son and daughter can be justly proud - a cultural endowment well fitted to answer every man's question as posed by John Steinbeck "How do we know its us without our past?"

With the inroads of mass media upon isolation, highway networks opening up the back hollows, spreading urbanizing influences, and a rising level of living, the cultural heritage is rapidly fading into the past and in danger of being lost. It has much to say to the needs of man today. By careful study, to develop understanding and recapture something of its love of life, wisdom and ingenuity, and independent spirit to shed light on the present and the future,

49

it could well be that the desired rise in level of living may not be at the cost of man's humanity, but enrich and deepen insights into the Wonder of Life for all.

Adapted from Dr. Simpkins'
address at the Huntington Galleries
Mountain Heritage Week June 19-24, 1972
by B. B. Maurer

Arts and Crafts

JOHN H RANDOLPH is Associate Professor of Art at Salem College and Director of the Heritage Arts Curriculum and Program. A native of Harrison County, Mr. Randolph received his BA degree from Salem College and his MA degree from West Virginia University. Before returning to Salem College as a member of its faculty, Mr. Randolph taught in Cabell and Harrison County, West Virginia schools, in the U. S. Army Dependent Schools in Italy, and was Dean of Students at the Columbus Boy Choir School, Princeton, New Jersey.

His love of his hill country heritage and his native creativity and ingenuity have come to flower in the conception and development of Fort New Salem, a pioneer village recreating early life in the hills during the period 1750-1850.

The developing village now consists of more than twenty original log structures from throughout West Virginia which have been moved and reassembled on the campus hill site. Here native artists and craftsmen ply their crafts and share the pioneer way of life as a part of the college cultural education program.

Fort New Salem has received national recognition as a feature in the 1975 National Geographic publication, *The American Craftsman.* In recognition of Professor Randolph's work as Director of this growing educational attraction, the Mountaineer Country Travel Council of northern West Virginia made his the first recipient of its Tourism Award.

52

THE MOUNTAIN ARTS OF WEST VIRGINIA

In the 1790's, the Randolph family drove across Pennsylvania into the western hills of Virginia in their ox pulled wagon. They carried with them all of their earthly possessions. The wagon was loaded with the items that were the necessary tools to start a new life.

I am taking the liberty to extract from the diary of an early settler, notes that prove how the frontiersman established himself into a new life in the mountains of what was to later become West Virginia.

Joel Bond is a single man with no family ties and has asked to travel with this small band. He works with, and for, these people with the hope of earning enough money to have his own property.

He tells of the mundane tasks necessary for the existence and sustenance of the frontier way of life. He helps us to understand that this early life is filled with the creativity that so often we consider the luxury arts and crafts of our mountains; however, they were commonplace to him. So as we read Joel's account, we find a new dimension of the arts; that of survival. These are the most important art forms of the mountains. There are no plastic, no plaster of paris, no kit forms or ready made items for assembly and most of all, nothing is instant. Some of the crafts today, that are called Heritage Crafts, were not known to our ancestors and in turn we have not the patience nor the willingness in many cases to practice the true Mountain Arts. I hope that Joel's story will make people more aware of their true heritage and they will explore his way of creativity.

Feb. 1, 1790: Has rained all day, everyone is wet, tired and anxious to get over the hills. We have been told we are only three days from New Salem.

Feb. 2: Have seen tall oaks today and yellow poplars that reach to what looks like a hundred feet high. House building will be easy enough with this kind of timber. Weather is clearing.

Feb. 3: Have followed a good stream of water all day, seems to be plenty of game and the soil is rich. We are all anxious to stop traveling and settle in our new land. It looks like snow as we stop for the night, along Tenmile Creek.

Feb. 4: Have arrived at New Salem. Tolerable warm today.

Feb. 5: Started cutting trees today for cabins. Have had help from folks who are already here. There are more people here than I had expected. Everyone offers help. The older boys are hunting and the women are cooking for everyone.

We are going to build a log cabin instead of a house. It will take less time. We want to finish the cabins in short order, for the land has to be cleared for planting. All this has to be done in two months. Without a good crop we cannot endure the next winter.

Logs are stripped of bark and set together with a round saddle notch.

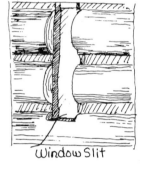

Window Slit

The cabin has no windows, only slits covered with translucent skins to let in the light.

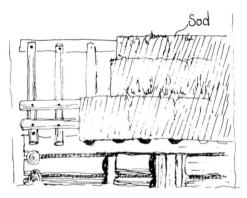

Sod

The roof is made of poles pinned to rafters and squares of sod to keep out the weather.

The cabin has a dirt floor which is higher than the outside ground level. There is no fire place only a pit in the middle of the room and a hole in the roof to let out the smoke. Sometimes the smoke becomes a problem. The space between the logs is chinked with wood chips which holds the clay used to plug up the holes.

Clay is easy to find on any creek bank.

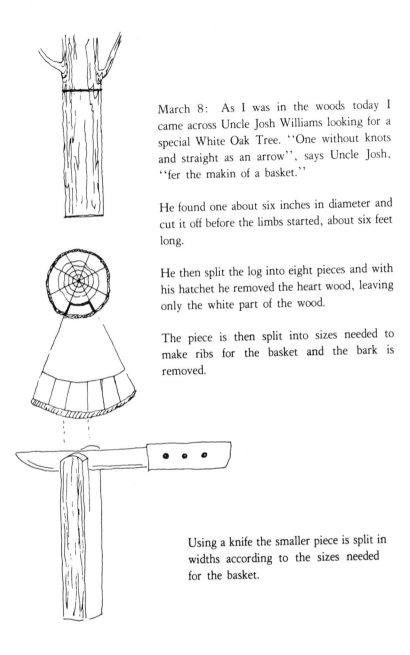

March 8: As I was in the woods today I came across Uncle Josh Williams looking for a special White Oak Tree. "One without knots and straight as an arrow", says Uncle Josh, "fer the makin of a basket."

He found one about six inches in diameter and cut it off before the limbs started, about six feet long.

He then split the log into eight pieces and with his hatchet he removed the heart wood, leaving only the white part of the wood.

The piece is then split into sizes needed to make ribs for the basket and the bark is removed.

Using a knife the smaller piece is split in widths according to the sizes needed for the basket.

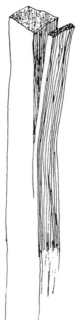

The ribbons are pulled by dividing the stick in half until the desired width is reached.

The ribbons are then shaved to make them even and smooth before weaving. Uncle Josh says that making a basket from a tree is somewhat of a miracle, and to me, too. Especially when I see his busy fingers taking the wood strips and producing a very important item needed for every home in the settlement.

There seems to be three baskets that are being made here, the Appalachian or hip basket, the square cornered, and the double bottomed round. All of these baskets are made of white oak.

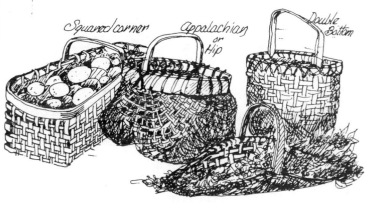

Squared corner   Appalachian or Hip   Double Bottom

March 9: When I related today about meeting up with Uncle Josh yesterday, I was reminded that two of the chairs needed new bottoms and maybe it would be possible to have him replace them with his white oak splints. I'll stop by tomorrow and see.

Other types of chair bottoms typical of the time period consisted of rush and cane. Rush was made from twisted creek rush while cane was a more elegant form of weaving using processed tree barks or finely graded ash, oak, and in rare cases bamboo. Cane bottoms were not common on the frontier.

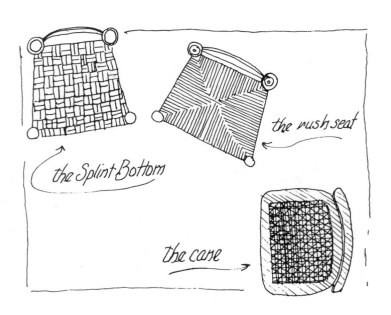

the rush seat

the Splint Bottom

the cane

April 5: While drawing logs this morning with the young oxen, I broke the chain. So this afternoon I took it to the blacksmith shop. I'll have to pick it up in the morning, for Mr. Davis seems to be very busy. He has two young apprentices. Mr. Davis has been in New Salem almost a year and is the only blacksmith for miles. His work today consisted of hinges and fireplace cranes. Seems with so many people building homes, he has more orders than he can fill. Fair this morning, rained this afternoon.

This is Mr. Davis' shop.

April 6: My chain was not ready today, I used my leather chain. It stretches when wet, but will pull along as it dries out. I loop one end to the log and the other to a near-by tree. It doesn't move far, fast, but helps get it to the skid. Weather tolerable warm.

April 15: Today Mrs. Randolph and the girls are dipping candles from beef tallow.

The tallow is rendered in an iron kettle over a low fire, skimmed off the top and strained. It is reheated in a smaller pot just to the point of being melted. The girls then take a length of wick the depth of the pot and double it and attach the

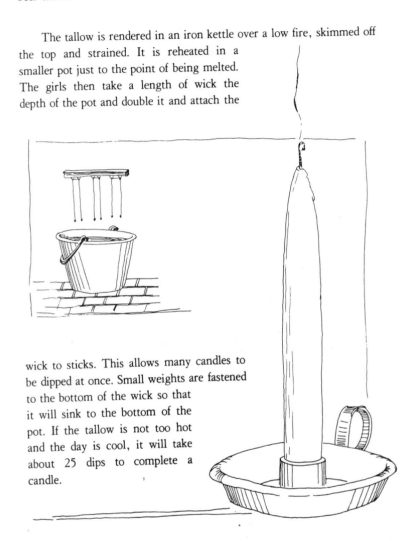

wick to sticks. This allows many candles to be dipped at once. Small weights are fastened to the bottom of the wick so that it will sink to the bottom of the pot. If the tallow is not too hot and the day is cool, it will take about 25 dips to complete a candle.

May 14: Mr. Simons, the local wood craftsman, and his apprentice, delivered a new loom today. Everyone was happy to see it work as it will weave the spun wool and flax into yardage cloth so badly needed for new clothes for the family. It is a two-harness loom. Mrs. Randolph does not attempt to weave patterns. Keeping the house takes too much time.

Being the only furniture builder in the settlement, he spends much time building the items most needed by the people, looms, spinning wheels, tables, beds and coffins. (Matter-of-fact many furniture dealers and builders turned full-time to the undertaker trade because it was the better paying business).

May 20: We have a house guest tonite, a Mr. Jarvis is here. He is a traveling weaver and will weave bedcovers, (coverlets) for the family. He has his loom in the back of a wagon and trades his skill for board and room. He will use the thread that Mrs. Randolph has spun and dyed with her plant dyes.

May 18: Mrs. Randolph had me to pick up her spinning wheel from Mr. Simons' shop. It was broken in our move to New Salem. She and the children will spend many hours picking and carding the wool before it will be spun into thread.

Much of the thread will be used for weaving while another portion will be plyed and used for knitting. The small wheel or Saxony wheel is used for spinning flax and finer wool thread. It is operated with a foot treadle and since the spinner is seated, she had both hands free to work with the fiber. The high or great wheel, however, is sometimes called the walking wheel and is used for only the spinning of wool.

It is said that a good spinner would walk as many as twenty miles a day. The yarn is removed from the wheel to the yarn winder, measured into hanks and dyed with the tree roots, tree bark, nut hulls, berries, plant stems, roots or flowers depending upon the color desired.

May 24: Tomorrow is Buddy's birthday and I have been whittling him a wooden toy. I will make toys for the other children for their birthdays as well. (For Christmas, the children received other kinds of homemade toys as well).

Whistle Flute

Limber Jack

Corn husk Doll

Apple head Doll

Rag Doll

Doll Cart

Top

Chain from one piece of wood

Doll Furniture

June 5: Quilting bee.

Today the church ladies gathered for a quilting bee. (A bee is any gathering where people come to socialize and work on one project).

They worked on Mrs. Jones Diamond Quilt.

I understand that after she got it home that she was displeased with some of the work by the other women and took out the stitches and did them over.

I have heard the women talk about bouncing the cat on their new quilt. All unmarried women would gather around the quilt and toss the cat in the air, which ever woman the cat came to was the next to marry. I suspect its' more superstition than truth.

The pieced quilt is truly American, for the quilter could use all her scrap material. As a wedding gift other women would give her their favorite quilt pattern, thus she accumulated a quilting catalog. Below are a few of the most popular patterns used. There are hundreds. The same pattern might be called by another name on the other side of the hill.

July 2: The boys tell me that a peddler is in the town tonite selling pottery and is looking for a place to settle and set up his shop. They say he makes jugs, jars and many kinds of bowls. The clay here is of good quality and I am sure he will be successful in securing materials for his trade. It would be nice if he also makes brick. With plans for the new house, I would be most pleased to be able to build a brick chimney. Stormy tonite, have had showers all day.

Aug. 3: I saw a man enter the clearing today, traveling in his overloaded wagon of kettles, pots, pans, buckets, and many other items needed by local housewives. I realized that he was a tinker. Not only will he sell his wagon load of merchandise but he will be able to make repairs on pots and kettles. Although he is a tinsmith, and has a shop over next to Morgantown, he travels through the country side peddling his wares and making repairs. His pay may be in money but more often it will be a smoked ham, eggs, a woven coverlet or other bartered items. In turn, he also became a peddler of many goods trading and selling according to his needs.

Sept. 30: Was clear and cool today. Went hunting over in the Indian Run area. Saw one of the biggest turkeys I ever saw, but he got away. Sure are a lot of signs, I can understand how the run got its' name. The Indians must have found it a paradise.

As I sat down at noon time to eat journey cake, I noticed a wild bee tree not far off. I marked it and only hope no one else beats me to it before colder weather. We need honey and the girls will be happy to add the wax to their candle fat. It will make the candles last longer and smell better. I have tracked bees before; it takes a keen eye and a great deal of patience. I have spent many hours sitting by a waterhole waiting for a bee to come for a drink and then track him to his gum tree. Sometimes I have watched the bigger part of a day. Has turned tolerable cold this evening. Fear it may frost.

this is the
bee tree

Oct. 20: For the longest time we have had to grind our meal on a small hand-mill called a quern, or haul our grist to Clarksburg to be ground. This took all day. I saw Mr. Simes this afternoon and he tells me that a mill is being built down on Ten Mile Creek. He is real happy since his family has had to pound his every day meal, Indian style, in a mortar made from a carved hickory log and a hard or maul.

With the new mill we will be able to leave our grist and pick it up when it is finished. I really look forward to having wheat flour for bread. I sure like corn bread, but reckon a change would surely be good. I think Mr. Simes and I will ride down there tomorrow and see if we can lend a hand. We've had frost three nights in a row and is cold again tonight.

Nov. 15: The Randolph family has been able to get their farm and home in a livable condition that has assured them that they will be able to survive the frontier. So now it is time to consider improving our way of life. Mr. Randolph has approached me to help him build the new house. It is to be a hewed log house with plank floors, glass windows, (small panes of glass were used. They could not ship large panes) a white oak shingle roof, a cut stone fireplace, and a front porch. It should be quite an imposing structure.

This is the "V-Saddle" notch. It is a very common log house style notch. Notice how the top of the log is cut to fit into the bottom of the next.

This is the "Dovetail" notch, and according to some authorities the "Chamfer and Notch". This seems to be the most secure for it locks the logs together, so the building should be stronger and more square.

The logs are hewed with a foot adze and smoothed with a heavy broad axe. It is amazing to see the ease with which a good craftsman can execute what would appear to be a difficult task. But with a keen eye and a sharp tool it becomes the mark of a master.

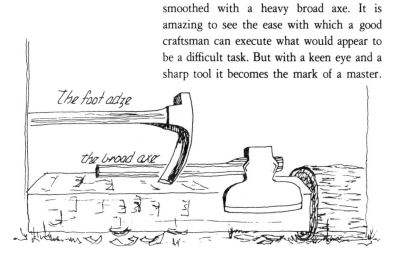

The foot adze

the broad axe

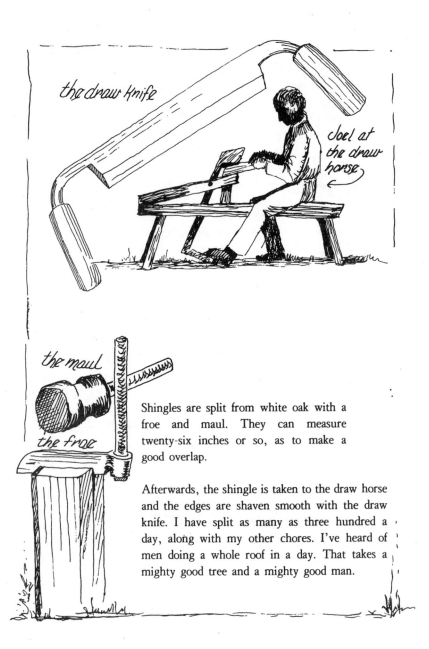

the draw knife

Joel at the draw horse ←

the maul

the froe

Shingles are split from white oak with a froe and maul. They can measure twenty-six inches or so, as to make a good overlap.

Afterwards, the shingle is taken to the draw horse and the edges are shaven smooth with the draw knife. I have split as many as three hundred a day, along with my other chores. I've heard of men doing a whole roof in a day. That takes a mighty good tree and a mighty good man.

From the early times of Josh Bond and his settler companions, the arts of the mountains have perpetuated into a beautiful array of collector items as well as practical items used in homes across our nation.

There are other arts and skills that have been practiced over these nearly two hundred years that we don't find in Joshs' accounts. To be sure, there are those that have been lost for all times, however, the revival of the old ways leave many of these crafts for the enjoyment of the present and future generations.

Terms, names of tools, patterns and names of other items in this survey are the results of research in the Central West Virginia area as told to the author by older citizens in the region. Other names can be found in other areas, as there seems to be a difference in opinions by authorities in this field of study.

In recent years there has been the revival of an ancient musical instrument called the Dulcimer. It would appear that this wooden instrument was brought to the mountains by the English settlers and sometimes referred to as the "Rebec" or "plucked dulcimer". It traditionally has three strings and is plucked with a quill while on the lap of the player.

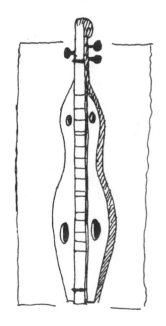

There, too, is a trapezoid shaped "hammered dulcimer", reminiscent of the xylophone or the primitive psaltry. It is played with two small wooden hammers while placed on a table or on its' own stand. Another popular instrument is the frettless banjo.

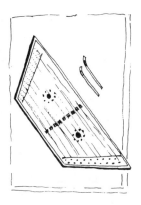

The drying of herbs and flowers in the eighteenth and nineteenth centuries was common place. Herbs were used for medicinal and savory purposes. The Apothecary Shop was the home of the local druggest who knew the latin names and the concoctions for the illnesses suffered by the settlers. The latin names prevented the uneducated from collecting the same herbs and ruining a good business.

Flowers were collected and dried by the women and girls giving a touch of summer in the drab winter months.

The hooked, crocheted, and woven rug served two purposes in the home. They covered the cold floors and added decoration to a sometimes drab room. It is not uncommon to hear about wall-to-wall rag carpet laid over straw or corn husks for warmth.

After the chores were done and a time came for relaxing, the homemaker sat down and worked on her sampler, crochet, knitting or other fancy work. This "pick-up" work could become gloves, mittens, socks, lace or items to "fancy-up" the house. A very special lace made by the mountain women is called tatting. Pictured at the right is the special shuttle and lace as it is being prepared for an edging for pillow cases, dresser scarfs or maybe a new Sunday dress.

Women pride themselves on doing this type of "fancy work".

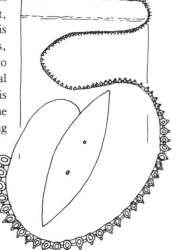

Most buckskin and leather clothing was made in the home, but as the need for saddles, harness, bags, pouches and other leather items arose the leather craftsman found a hearty business. He worked with the blacksmith where often his shop would be located.

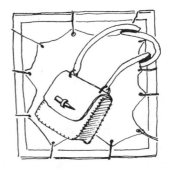

The cobbler, too, handled much of the leather business. However, shoes and their repairs were done in the home until it was easier to go to the cobbler's shop and be more properly fitted.

The Western Virginian living below the Mason-Dixon Line is sometimes referred to as "a hoopie", this nick name came from his trade of barrel making. With an abundance of white oak, the most desired wood, barrels were made for house and farm use along with being the most important container for shipping merchandise.

Other items produced by the cooper include buckets, tubs and measures. This art form is very rare and nearly a lost art in the American Mountains.

The mountain handcraft is not just a necessity of the past, or a luxury of the present, but a historical recording for the future. The ingenius product of the primitive carft becomes a work of art in today's craft revival.

Most native handcrafts were derived from the necessities of homemaking and farming. Each family had to create items to maintain a way of life and each person became an inventor and a skilled workman. The simplicity of the handcraft was due to the fact that there was not time to be elaborate; functionalism was the first need. As time passed and the way of life became more comfortable, decoration of the primitive object established the craftman as an artist. As in painting and sculpture, the native handcrafts reveal the creators' knowledge of materials which is the relationship of the materials to the particular object being created. The cabinet maker found in making a chest of drawers that certain woods could stand the wear needed for drawers, while other parts of the chest could be made of wood of a more desirable grain; therefore, he had to have a basic knowledge of the local woods. He was concerned with tools, many of which he made himself; thus, the cabinet maker became a blacksmith. He needed to know how to temper and work the metal that would be used in a particular tool.

The intelligence of the early craftsman cannot be questioned. He had to be a superior being to be able to survive in a world where he had to create his own machinery. From him comes the information that has led to the mechanical discoveries of today. Our mechanical world has lessened the need for the primitive craft, and because the need has disappeared many of the crafts have been lost. There is no necessity for a woman to spend hours at the spinning wheel, when she can acquire all the yarn she needs with little effort.

The simplicity of the primitive craft has excited craftmen who feel a need to explore early methods and develop them into a profitable avocation. The crafts that stimulate the craftsman are those that have been a part of his inherited environment. The revival of the crafts is desirable. West Virginia citizens are beginning to realize that the crafts they have produced and lived with for generations are wanted by a buying public.

It is difficult to find patterns and tools which are authentic. Directions and procedures have been lost. There are few people living today who know how the early crafts were done. The author has often found that differences exist in methods and materials recorded in books and in those suggested by the craftsman. The most interesting material comes from the craftsmen. The major difficulty in interesting or training new craftsmen is obtaining information that can be easily understood and executed.

The public expects to see the primitive crafts being worked in the traditional manner and shows disappointment when modern methods are used.

West Virginia's best crafts reflect the pride of the people in their unique creations which comes from the individual style of each craft. Each person has methods and ideas that he prefers. Because ideas and theories vary, disputes arise over best wood to use for making a broom, or the time of year the wood should be cut. This is also true of weaving designs and of quilt patterns; one discovers that some quilt patterns will have as many as four different names. This indicates that diversity is a quality that would always exist in handcraft.

Language

Yesterday's language

WYLENE P. DIAL has become an authority on the dialect of the Appalachian people as an avocation. When she became a West Virginian in 1945, she was fascinated by the lively and expressive speech which she heard among her neighbors in Lincoln County. Her many years of listening and collecting and study have resulted in a refreshing insight into familiar language which we now hear differently through her ears.

Mrs. Dial was born in Washington, D. C., earned her AB degree at Brenau College, Gainesville, Georgia, and her MA degree at Marshall University. She taught for eight years in the Lincoln County schools and since then has been on the staff of the West Virginia University Appalachian Center, as 4-H Agent, Area Program Coordinator for Extension Education and now Extension Specialist - Aging.

As one of the originators of the innovative Mountain Heritage Program of the Appalachian Center, Mrs. Dial seeks to help West Virginians understand and appreciate their rich cultural background. She has served on the Governor's Task Force on Health, the State Comprehensive Health Planning Advisory Committee, and been a consultant to the VISTA Program, the Headstart Program, and the West Virginia Department of Mental Health.

She is the author of the Extension Series on the Aging: *Your Choice of a Retirement Home, Staying Healthy, How to Avoid the Retirement Blahs, Preventicare*, and *A Guide for Friendly Visitors*.

CONTENTS

THE DIALECT OF THE APPALACHIAN PEOPLE

The dialect spoken by Appalachian people has been given a variety of names ranging all the way from "pure Chaucerian" to "debased and ignorant." The more opprobrious the term, the more likely it is to have come from some earnest soul from outside the area who knows considerably less about the English language than he thinks he does.

Instead of calling the folk speech of the region corrupt, it ought to be classified as archaic. Many expressions current in Appalachia today can be found in the writings of English authors of other centuries, beginning with Anglo-Saxon times.

Most editors who work with older materials have long assumed the role of officious busybodies: never so happy, apparently, as when engaged in tidying up spelling, modernizing grammar, and generally rendering whatever was written by various Britons in ages past into a colorless conformity with today's Standard English.

To this single characteristic of the editorial mind must be ascribed the almost total lack of knowledge on the part of most Americans that the language they speak was ever any different than it is right now. How many people know, for example, that when the poet Gray composed his famous "Elegy" his title for it was "An Elegy *Wrote* in a Country Churchyard"?

Southern Mountain dialect (as the Appalachian folk speech is called by linguists) is certainly archaic, but the general historical period it represents can be narrowed down to the days of the first Queen Elizabeth and can be further particularized by saying that what is heard today is actually a sort of Scottish flavored Elizabethan English. This is not to say that Chaucerian forms will not be heard in everyday use and even an occasional Anglo-Saxon one as well.

When we remember that the first European settlers in what is today Appalachia were the so-called Scotch-Irish along with Germans (chiefly from the Palatinate) there is small wonder that the language has a Scottish tinge; the remarkable thing is that, except in areas where they settled thickly--the Pennsylvania "Dutch" (Deutsch) country, for instance--the Germans appear to have influenced it so little. Expressions such as "*Hit wonders me* how they manage to get along," and words like *schmearcase* (cottage cheese) occur in the Pennsylvania Dutch dialect and are found in parts of Appalachia too. So are *briggity* and *wamus* (a heavy woolen jacket), but some authorities attribute these last two words to the Dutch rather than to the Germans, and there are very few others in general use to add to the list.

The Scots, on the other hand, appear to have had it all their own way, linguistically speaking. When I first came to Lincoln County, West Virginia, as a bride, it used to seem to me that everything that didn't *pooch out, booved up*. *Pooch* is a Scottish variant of the word *pouch* that was in use in the

1600's. Numerous objects can pooch out, including pregnant women and gentlemen with bay windows. *Hoove* is a very old past participle of the verb *to heave* and was apparently in use on both sides of the border by 1601. The top of an old-fashioned trunk may be said to hoove up. Another word heard in the back country is *ingerns*. *Ingerns* are onions. In Scots dialect the word is *inguns;* however, if our people are permitted the intrusive *r* in *potaters, tomaters, tobaccer,* and so on, there seems to be no reason why they should not use it in *ingerns* as well.

It is possible to compile a long list of these Scots words and phrases. I will give only a few more for illustration and will wait to mention some points on Scottish pronunciation and grammar a little further on.

Fornenst is a word that has many variants. It generally means "next to" as in "Look at that rattler quiled up *fornenst* the fence post!" but I have also heard it used to mean "opposite to." (*Quiled* is an Elizabethan pronunciation of *coiled*.) "I was getting better but now I've done took a *backset* from the flu." "When I woke up this morning, there was a little *skift* of snow on the ground." "He dropped the dish and busted it all to *flinders*." "Law, I hope *how soon* we get some rain!" (*How soon* is supposed to be obsolete, but it enjoys excellent health in Lincoln County.) "That trifling old *fixin* ain't worth a *haet!* " *Haet* means the smallest thing that can be conceived and comes from *Deil hae 't* (Devil hate it). *Fixin* is the Old English or Anglo-Saxon word for *she-fox* as used in the northern dialect. In the south of England you would have heard *vixen*, the word used today in Standard English.

It is interesting to note that, until recently, it has been primarily the linguistic historians who have pointed out the predominately Scottish heritage of the Southern Mountain people. Perhaps I may be allowed to digress for a moment to trace these people back to their beginnings.

Early in his English reign, James I decided to try to control the Irish by putting a Protestant population into Ireland. To do this he confiscated the lands of the earls of Ulster and bestowed them upon Scottish and English lords on the condition that they settle the territory with tenants from Scotland and England. This was known as the "Great Settlement," or the "King's Plantation," and was begun in 1610.

Most of the Scots who moved into Ulster came from the lowlands [1] and thus they would have spoken the Scots variety of the Northumbrian or Northern English dialect. (Most highland Scots at that time still spoke Gaelic.)

While in Ulster the Scots multiplied, but after roughly 100 years they became dissatisfied with the unreasonable trade and religious restrictions imposed by England, and numbers of them began emigrating to the English colonies in America. The first wave came into New England, but thereafter many of these Scots who now called themselves the "Scotch-Irish" came into

Pennsylvania where, finding the better lands already settled by the English, they began to move south and west. "Their enterprise and pioneering spirit made them the most important element in the vigorous frontiersmen who opened up this part of the South and later other territories farther West into which they pushed."[2]

Besides the Scots who arrived from Ireland, more came directly from Scotland to America, particularly after "the '45," the final Jacobite uprising in support of "Bonnie Prince Charlie" the Young Pretender, which ended disastrously for the Scottish clans that supported him. By the time of the American Revolution there were about 200,000 Scots in this country.

But to get back to the dialect, let me quote two more linguistic authorities to prove my point about the Scottish influence on the local speech. Raven I. McDavid notes, "The speech of the hill people is quite different from both dialects of the Southern lowlands for it is basically derived from the Scotch-Irish of western Pennsylvania."[3] H. L. Mencken said of Appalachian folk speech, "The persons who speak it undiluted are often called by the southern publicists 'the purest Anglo-Saxons in the United States,' but less romantic ethnologists describe them as predominately Celtic in blood, though there has been a large infiltration of English and even German strains."[4]

The reason our people still speak as they do is that when these early Scots and English and Germans (and some Irish and Welsh, too) came into the Appalachian area and settled, they virtually isolated themselves from the mainstream of American life for generations to come because of the hills and mountains, and so they kept the old speech forms that have long since fallen out of fashion elsewhere.

Things in our area are not always what they seem, linguistically speaking. Someone may tell you that "Almety ain't got sense enough to come in outen the rain, but she sure is *clever*." *Clever*, you see, back in the 1600's meant "neighborly or accommodating." Also, if you ask someone how he is, and he replies that he is "*very well*," you are not necessarily to rejoice with him on the state of his health. Our people are accustomed to using a speech so vividly colorful and virile that his "*very well*" only means that he is feeling "*so-so*." If you are informed that "*several*" people came to a meeting, your informant does not mean what you do by *several*—he is using it in its older sense of anywhere from about 20 to 100 people. If you hear a person or an animal referred to as *ill*, that person or animal is not sick but bad tempered, and this adjective has been so used since the 1300's. (Incidentally, good English used *sick* to refer to bad health long, long before our forebearers ever started saying *ill* for the same connotation.)

Many of our people refer to sour milk as *blinked* milk. This usage goes back at least to the early 1600's when people still believed in witches and the power of the evil eye. One of the meanings of the word *blink* back in those days was "to glance at"; if you glanced at something, you *blinked* at it, and thus sour milk came to be called *blinked* due to the evil machinations of the witch. There is another phrase that occurs from time to time, "Man, did he ever *feather into him*!" This used to carry a fairly murderous connotation, having gotten its start back in the days when the English long bow was the ultimate word in destructive power. Back then if you drew your bow with sufficient strength to cause your arrow to penetrate your enemy up to the feathers on its shaft, you had *feathered into him*. Nowadays, the expression has weakened in meaning until it merely indicates a bit of fisticuffs.

One of the most baffling expressions our people use (baffling to "Furriners," at least) is, "*I don't care to...*" To outlanders this seems to mean a definite "no," whereas in truth it actually means, "Thank you so much; I'd love to." One is forevermore hearing a tale of mutual bewilderment in which a gentleman driving an out-of-state car sees a young fellow standing alongside the road thumbing. When the gentleman stops and asks if he wants a lift, the boy very properly replies, "I don't *keer* to," using *care* in the Elizabethan sense of the word. On hearing this, the man drives off considerably puzzled leaving an equally baffled young man behind. (Even the word *foreigner* itself is used here in its Elizabethan sense of someone who is the same nationality as the speaker, but not from the speaker's immediate home area.)

Reverend is generally used to address preachers, but it is a pretty versatile word, and full-strength whiskey, or even the full-strength scent of a skunk, are also called *reverend*. In these latter instances, its meaning has nothing to do with reverence, but with the fact that their strength is as the strength of ten because they are undiluted.

In the dialect, the word *allow* more often means "think, say, or suppose" than "permit." "He *'lowed* he'd git it done tomorrow."

A neighbor may take you into her confidence and announce that she has heard that the preacher's daughter *should have been* running after the mailman. These are deep waters to the uninitiated. What she really means is that she has heard a juicy bit of gossip: the preacher's daughter is chasing the local mail carrier. However, she takes the precaution of using the phrase *should have been* to show that this statement is not vouched for by the speaker. This same phrase is used in the same way in the Paston Letters in the 1400's and also occurs in the dialect of the Pennsylvania "Dutch."

Almost all the so-called "bad English" used by natives of Appalachia was once employed by the highest ranking nobles of the realms of England and Scotland.

Few humans are really passionately interested in grammar so I'll skim as lightly over this section as possible, but let's consider the following bit of dialogue briefly: "I've been *a-studying* about how to say this, till I've *nigh wearried* myself to death. I *reckon hit* don't never do nobody no good to beat about the bush, so I'll just tell *ye*. Your man's *hippoed*. There's nothing ails him, but he spends more time *using* around the doctor's office than he does *a-working*.''

The only criticism that even a linguistic purist might offer here is that, in the eighteenth century, *hippoed* was considered by some, Jonathan Swift, among others, to be slangy even though it was used by the English society of the day. (To say someone is *hippoed* is to say he is hypochondriac.)

Words like *a-studying* and *a-working* are verbal nouns and go back to Anglo-Saxon times; and from the 1300's on, people who *studied* about something, deliberated or reflected on it. *Nigh* is the older word for *near*, and *weary* was the pronunciation of *worry* in the 1300 and 1400's. The Scots also used this pronunciation. *Reckon* was current in Tudor England in the sense of *consider* or *suppose*. *Hit* is the Old English third person singular neuter pronoun for *it* and has come ringing down through the centuries for over a thousand years. All those multiple negatives were perfectly proper until some English mathematician in the eighteenth century decided that two negatives make a positive instead of simply intensifying the negative quality of some statement. Shakespeare loved to use them. *Ye* was once used accusatively, and *man* has been employed since early times to mean *husband*. And, finally, *to use* means to frequent or loiter.

Certain grammatical forms occuring in the dialect have caused it to be regarded with pious horror by school marms. Prominent among the offenders, they would be almost sure to list these: ''Bring *them* books over here.'' In the 1500's this was good English. ''I found three bird's *nestes* on the way to school.'' This disyllabic ending for the plural goes back to the Middle Ages. ''That pencil's not mine; it's *her'n*.'' Possessive forms like *his'n, our'n*, and *your'n* evolved in the Middle Ages on the model of *mine* and *thine*. In the revision of the Wycliffe Bible, which appeared shortly after 1380, we find phrases such as ''...restore to hir alle things that ben *hern*,'' and ''some of *our'n* went in to the grave.'' ''*He don't* scare me none.'' In the sixteenth and seventeenth centuries *do* was used with *he, she*, and *it*. *Don't* is simply *do not*, of course. ''*You wasn't* scared, *was you?*'' During the seventeenth and eighteenth centuries many people were careful to distinguish between singular *you was* and plural *you were*. It became unfashionable in the early nineteenth century although Noah Webster stoutly defended it. ''My brother *come* in from the army last night.'' This usage goes back to late Anglo-Saxon times. You find it in the Paston Letters and in Scottish poetry. ''I *done finished* my lessons,'' also has many echoes in the Pastons' correspondence and the Scots poets. From the late Middle Ages on up the Northern dialect of English used formations like this: ''*guiltless persons is condemned*,'' and so do our people. And, finally, in times past, participial forms like these abounded: *has beat, has bore with it, has chose*.

Preterite forms were varied: *blowed, growed, catched,* and for *climbed* you can find *clum, clome, clim,* all of which are locally used.

Pronunciation of many words has changed considerably, too. *Deef* for *deaf, arn* for *iron, heered* for *heard, afeared* for *afraid, cowcumber* for *cucumber, bammy* for *balmy, holp* for *helped, yaller* for *yellow, and cheer* for *chair* are a very few. Several distinct characteristics of the language of Elizabeth's day are still preserved. Words that had *oi* in them were given a long *i* pronunciation: *pizen, jine, bile, pint,* and so on. Words with *er* were frequently pronounced as if the letters were *ar: sarvice, sartin, narvous.* It is from this time that we get our pronunciation of *sergeant* and the word *varsity* which is a clipping of the word *university* given the *ar* sound. Another Elizabethan characteristic was the substitution of an *i* sound for an *e* sound. You hear this tendency today when people say *miny, kittle, chist, git,* and so on. It has caused such confusion with the words *pen* and *pin* (which our people pronounce alike as *pin*) that they are regularly accompanied by a qualifying word--*stick pin* for the pin and *ink pin* for the pen.

You can hear many characteristic Scottish pronunciations. *Whar, thar,* and *dar* (*where, there,* and *dare*] are typical. So also are *poosh, boosh, eetch, deesh, feesh* (*push, bush, itch, dish,* and *fish*).

So if you were told as I was in my youth, "No dear, it doesn't rhyme; the writer was just taking poetic license," you may see that it might once have rhymed after all.

One of the accusations frequently leveled at speakers of Southern Mountain dialect is that they use "outlandish, made-up words," and we should consider a few of these: "I'm going to *redd up* the kitchen." This word, used in the sense of "to set in order," goes back to Anglo-Saxon times and was still being used in the sixteenth century by the Scots according to the OED. If you are "bee-stung" in my part of the country, someone will be sure to commiserate with you on your *whelks* (and this word goes back at least to Chaucer). If a neighbor tells you, "I got so mad I wanted to pick up a board and *warp* (worp) him along-side the head," he is using another word that goes back to Anglo-Saxon days. When your friend catches "a whole *slue* of fish," he is using a word current in Elizabeth's day, and he may tell you "there was a *sight* of folks at the baptizing" using another very old word to indicate a large number.

Two words that I hear in my state and parts of Virginia that are both supposed to be obsolete according to some lexicographers (although both are listed in Webster's 3rd) are *airish,* "I reckon we better git on into the house, it's right *airish* (chilly) out;" and *mizzling,* a word used to describe a misty day that has a very fine drizzle of rain falling.

In some ways this vintage English reflects the outlook and spirit of the people who speak it; and we find that not only is the language Elizabethan, but that some of the ways these people look at things are Elizabethan too.

Numbers of our people plant by the "signs" (the stars) and conduct other activities according to the signs. Many other superstitions still exist here. In some homes, when a death occurs all the mirrors and pictures are turned to the wall. Now, I don't know if today the people still know why they do this, or if they just go through the actions because it's the thing to do, but this belief goes far back into history. It was once thought that the mirror reflected the soul of the person looking into it, and if the soul of the dead person saw the soul of one of his beloved relatives reflected in the mirror, he might take it with him, so his relatives were taking no chances.

The belief that if a bird accidentally flies into a house, a member of the household will die, is also very old and is still current in the region. Cedar trees are in a good deal of disfavor in Lincoln County, and the reason seems to stem from the conviction held by a number of people that if someone plants a cedar, he will die when it grows large enough to shade his coffin.

Aside from its antiquity, the most outstanding feature of the dialect is its masculine flavor--robust and virile. This is a language spoken by a red-blooded people who have colorful phraseology born in their bones. They tend to call a spade a spade in no uncertain terms. "No, the baby didn't come early, the weddin' came late," remarked one proud grandpa. Such people have small patience with the pallid descriptive limitations of standard English. They are not about to be put off with the rather insipid remark, "My, it's hot!" or "Isn't it cold out today?" They want to know just how hot or cold: "It's hotter 'n the hinges of hell," or "Hit's blue cold out thar!" Other common descriptive phrases for cold are (freely) translated, "It's colder 'n a witch's bosom," or "It's colder 'n a well-digger's backside."

Speakers of Southern Mountain dialect are past masters of the art of coining vivid descriptions. Their everyday conversation is liberally sprinkled with such gems as: "That man is so contrary, if you throwed him in a river he'd float upstream!" "She walks so slow they have to set stakes to see if she's a-movin.'!" "That lad's an awkward size--too big for a man and not big enough for a horse." "Zeke, he come bustin' outten thar and hit it for the road quick as double-geared lightnin' a-mentionin' hell-fire at ever breath!" "That pore boy's so cross-eyed he could stand in the middle of the week and see both Sundays!"

Nudity is frowned upon in Appalachia, but for some reason there are numerous "nekkid as..." phrases. Any casual sampling would probably contain these three: "Nekkid as a jaybird," "bare-nekkid as a hound dog's rump," and "start-nekkid." Start nekkid comes directly from the Anglo-Saxons, so it's been around for more than a thousand years. Originally "start" was steort which meant "tail." Hence, if you were start-nekkid you were nekkid to the tail. A similar phrase, stark-naked is a Johnny-come-lately, not even appearing in print until around 1530.

If a lady tends to be gossipy, her friends may say that "her tongue's a mile long," or else that it "wags at both ends." Such ladies are a great trial to young dating couples. Incidentally, there is a formal terminology to indicate exactly how serious the intentions of these couples are, ranging from *sparking* which is simply dating, to *courting* which is dating with a more serious intent, on up to *talking* which means the couple is seriously contemplating matrimony. Shakespeare uses *talking* in this sense in *King Lear*.

If a man has imbibed too much of who-shot-John, his neighbor may describe him as "so drunk he couldn't hit the ground with his hat," or, as Vance Randolph tells us, on the morning-after, the sufferer may admit that "I was so dang dizzy I had to hold on to the grass afore I could lean ag'in the ground." The farmer who was having a lot of trouble with a weasel killing his chickens complained, "He jest grabs 'em afore they can git word to God."

Someone who has a disheveled or bedraggled appearance may be described in any one of several ways: "You look like you've been chewed up and spit out," or "You look like you've been a-sortin wildcats," or "You look like the hindquarters of hard luck," or, simply, "You look like somethin' the cat drug in that the dog wouldn't eat!"

"My belly thinks my throat is cut" means "I'm hungry," and seems to have a venerable history of several hundred years. I found a citation for it dated in the early 1500's.

A man may be "bad to drink" or "wicked to swear," but these descriptive adjectives are never reversed.

You ought not to be shocked if you hear a saintly looking grandmother admit she likes to hear a coarse-talking man; she means a man with a deep bass voice. (This can also refer to a singing voice, and in this case, if grandma prefers a tenor, she'd talk about someone who sings "shallow.") Nor ought you leap to the conclusion that a *"hard girl"* is one who lacks the finer feminine sensibilities. *Hard* is the dialectal pronunciation of *hired* and seems to stem from the same source as do "far" engines that run on rubber "tars."

This language is vivid and virile, but so was Elizabethan English. However, some of the things you say may be shocking the folk as much as their combined lexicons may be shocking you. For instance, in the stratum of society in which I was raised, it was considered acceptable for a lady to say either *damn* or *hell* if strongly moved. Most Appalachian ladies would rather be caught dead than uttering either of these words, but many very proper ladies of the region are pretty free with their use of a four letter word for manure which I don't use. I have heard it described as everything from bug ——— to bull ———.

Along with a propensity for calling a spade a spade, the dialect has a strange mid-victorian streak in it, too. Until recently, it was considered brash to use either the word *bull* or *stallion*. If it was necessary to refer to a bull, he was known variously as a *father cow* or a *gentleman cow* or an *ox* or a *mas-cu-line*, or the *male beast*, while a stallion was either a *stable horse* or else rather ominously, *The Animal*.

It is from this general period that the pronunciation *pie-ano* or *pie-anner* for *piano* seems to have evolved, people feeling that the first syllable of *piano* was indelicate.

Only *waspers* fly around Lincoln County; I don't think I've ever heard of a *wasp* there, and I've never been able to trace the reason for that usage, but I do know why *cockleburrs* are called *cuckleburrs.'* The first part of the word cockleburr carried an objectionable connotation to the folk. However, if one balks at that, it seems somewhat hilarious to find nothing objectionable about *cuckle*.

I read somewhere of a Tennessee sheriff who was testifying at a trial and who declared modestly that he *roostered* his pistol because there were ladies present in the courtroom. I have even heard this usage carried over to the cockroach, it being delicately referred to as a *rooster-roach*.

One little old lady once told me of an embarrassing incident that had occurred to her father in his youth. It seems he had gone to the general store for some asafetida (to wear in a bag around his neck) and discovered, to his horror, that the only clerk in the whole store was a young lady. He decided he couldn't possibly ask for it by its right name since the first syllable didn't sound proper to him, so (after thinking it over) he requested some *rumpifidity*. A mountain sculptor was so tickled by this tale that he broke down and told me about a friend of his who had suffered in a similar cause. His friend, he informed me, was a fiddler and he broke one of the cat-gut strings on his fiddle. So he, too, went to a general store for a replacement, and again, the only available clerks in the store were ladies. This gave him a shock, and he had to consider seriously how best to request the type of fiddle strings he wanted. He came up with what he felt to be a masterpiece of delicacy and asked for a *pussy bowel* string!

A friend of mine who has a beauty parlor now, used to have a small store on the banks of the Guyan River. She told me about a little old lady who trotted into the store one day with a request for "some of the *strumpet candy*." My friend said she was very sorry they didn't have any. But, she added gamely, what kind was it, and she would try to order some. The little lady glanced around to see if she could be overheard, lowered her voice and said, "Well, it's *horehound*, but I don't like to use that word!"

The dialect today is a watered down thing compared to what it was a generation ago, but our people are still the best talkers in the world, and I think we should listen to them with more appreciation.

FOOTNOTES

[1] Thomas Pyles, *The Origins and Development of the English Language.* New York, Harcourt, Brace & World, Inc., 1964, page 35. "It is not surprising that those lowland Scotsmen who colonized the'King's Plantation' in Ulster and whose descendants crossed the Atlantic and settled the Blue Ridge, the Appalachians, and the Ozarks should have been so little affected by the classical culture of the Renaissance."

[2] Albert Baugh, *A History of the English Language,* 2nd ed. New York, 1957, p. 409.

[3] H. L. Mencken, *The American Language,* ed. Raven I, McDavid, Jr., the 4th ed. and the two supplements abridged, with annotations and new material. New York, 1963, p. 455.

[4] Ibid., p. 459.

APPALACHIAN SPEECH - YESTERDAY'S LANGUAGE

People from outside Appalachia frequently think the folk speech sounds strange or even downright uncultured. This is because they don't realize that what they are hearing is antique English.

In the days of the first Queen Elizabeth, the highest ranking nobles of the realms of England and Scotland employed many of the same words, expressions and grammatical forms that can be heard today on the lips of living West Virginians.

All of the following "samples" are at least Elizabethan; many are considerably older:

a sight of - a lot of. "There was *a sight of* folks come to the funeral."

all fire and tow - said of a high tempered person. "Man! She's *all fire and tow!*"

brickle - brittle. "She's not very work-*brickle*." (She's not a very good worker.)

board - table. "The food's on the *board*."

bum - the buttocks. "She's getting so fat she's a regular *fatty-bum*."

clean - completely. "I *clean* forgot."

fox fire - the phosphorescent light emitted by decaying timber.

heard tell - "I *heard tell* of that two weeks ago."

fit - "Them two fellers *fit* for nigh onto an hour."

git shed of - get rid of. "I cain't *git shed of* these old cats nohow."

least - smallest. "He's my *least* 'un." (My smallest child.)

pair of beads - a string of beads.

plumb - shows degree. "He lives *plumb* to the head of the holler."

poke - a paper bag. "Be sure to put my groceries in a *poke*."

peart - feeling well; to be sprightly or lively. (Not the same word as *pert*.) "Mamaw's feelin' right *peart* today."

press - a clothes closet or wardrobe. "Hang my clothes in the press."

quietus - death, or something that quiets or oppresses. "There, that'll put the *quietus* on him!"

right - very. "I'm getting *right* hungry."

smouch - to kiss. Another old word meaning the same thing is *buss*.

tole - to lure. "Get an ear of corn and *tole* the cow into the shed."

There is a Scottish flavoring to the dialect because of the predominantly Scotch-Irish heritage of the region, and pronunciations such as *whaur* (where), *daur* (dare), *deestrict* schools (district schools), *Commeesioner* of Agriculture (Commissioner of Agriculture), *feesh, eetch* and *deesh* (fish, itch, and dish), *poosh* and *boosh* (push and bush) and the like abound. So, of course, do Scottish words. In the previous section *backset, flinders, haet, inguns, skift,* and *how soon* are all of Scots extraction. So far other very old words such as:

again (frequently written "agin") - means against. "I'm *again* the whole durn thing."

craps - crops. "This hail won't do the *craps* any good."

drap - drop. "I've sware off--I haven't touched a *drap* all month."

handwrite - handwriting. "It was right there in his own *handwrite*."

let on - pretend. "You *let on* like you don't know nothin' about it."

my lone - "I've been sitting here all by *my lone* the live long day."

residenter - a resident, usually one who has resided in a locality for a long time.

skutching - a whipping. "He give me a proper *skutching*." This is used in other parts of Britain as well.

Southern Mountain Dialect (as it is known by linguists) has a distinctly masculine flavor--robust and virile. It is spoken by a red-blooded people who have colorful phraseology born in their bones, and who are undoubtedly the best talkers in the world.

Their conversation abounds with such gems as, "Awkard? That gal was eighteen afore she could walk and chew gum at the same time!" "We went so fast we burned the wind." Aunt Jenny Wilson said to me, "Gini, I want you to look at that feller. You could take his face and a jug of buttermilk and stand off judgment thirty days!" And a doctor from Philippi told me of an old gentleman who used to say, gently, "She can't help bein' ugly, but she *could* stay home!"

OVERVIEW OF EARLY MODERN ENGLISH

The literature and language of any people is best understood if it is studied against the backdrop of the historical and cultural development of that people. This brief overview will be an amalgam of both history and language, since to study one, you really must study the other; unless, God forbid, it is your misfortune to fall into the hands of some desiccated old pantaloon who presents the facts to you in a dry-as-dust third-hand style instead of letting you read the proper sources for yourself.

When you begin to study the English language you will go quite a ways back into the past; just how far will depend on which historical linguist you are reading. Some begin around 200,000 B.C. when the earliest known human beings in the British Isles were busy roaming the tundra during the last interglacial period hunting for food (the mastodon and the wooly rhinoceros, for instance.) This seems to be stretching things a little since no one has the faintest idea what form of language these people used.

Other linguists begin more reasonably in approximately the third millenium B.C. and discuss the start of a vast migration of nomadic peoples from somewhere in northern Europe; the exact location is conjectural. These people drove their herds of cattle before them, wielded great battle axes to settle the hash of any who wished to dispute their right of passage, and carried their language, called Indo-European, as far as the borders of China to the east, India and Persia to the south, and most of Europe to the west.

Indo-European can get rather complicated, and we haven't time to go into all that now, so we will simply note that many European languages are descended from it (Greek, Roman, German, French, English, and Gaelic among others); also it was divided into six main branches, Indic, Iranian, Celtic, Gracco-Latin, Germanic, and Slavonic. Of these, two especially are of interest to us because from Germanic finally evolved English and from Celtic the languages spoken in parts of Ireland, Scotland, and Wales.

"Mist-shrouded Britain, rising sheer and white from the waves of the stormy North Sea, has always cast a spell over visitors approaching it from the European mainland. The visitors must have liked what they found, because often the visits turned into invasions or attempted invasions."[1] Each invasion brought with it a different language to surge over the face of the land. Some of these tongues stamped indelible imprints across English speech as we know it today; while others, for the very paucity of their lasting contributions, might almost as well have ebbed back into the sea from whence they came.

Celtic people had been in Britain for many centuries before Julius Caesar invaded the island in 55 B.C. in a series of raids really not much more than reconnaissance thrusts. It was not until almost a century later that the Romans began to occupy the island in earnest.

Despite the fact that the Romans remained in residence for roughly 400 years, the British Celts continued to speak their own language, although many of them who wished "to get on in the world" learned to speak and write the language of the Roman conquerors as well.

While the Romans were still occupying Britain they were plagued by raiding parties of savage Picts from what is now Scotland, by the Scots from Ireland who came across the Irish Sea, also to raid, and by piratical forays of the Germanic tribes who sailed across the North Sea to pillage the eastern part of Britain, which came to be called the Saxon Shore. The homeland of these Germanic tribes was located in what is now Schleswig-Holstein—an area partly in northern Germany and partly in Denmark.

When the barbarian invasions on the continent of Europe forced the Roman legions to withdraw from Britain in order to defend their home front, we find that the language situation in the British Isles was this: The British Celts were still speaking Brythonic; Pictish was spoken by the Picts in the northwestern part of Britain; Gaelic (Irish Celtic) was spoken in Ireland and was a somewhat different type from British Celtic.

After the last Roman troops were pulled out of the island, the British Celts found themselves unprotected from the increasingly savage attacks of the Picts and Scots. This was truly a case of Celt eat Celt for Picts, Scots and Britons were all Celtic people. [2]

Exactly what happened next is a little cloudy. One account (that of the Venerable Bede) insists that the Britons, in desperation, hired the "Saxons" to come to their rescue and fight off the Picts and Scots.

If this account is true, it would be understating the case to say that the Britons were guilty of an error in judgment. In response to the appeal, the Germanic warrior-adventurers began to arrive by the shipload, the first landing (according to Bede) being in A.D. 449 when a ship arrived with a group of Jutes (or more properly *Iutes*) under the leadership of two brothers, Hengest and Horsa, both of whose names meant "Horse." Other long ships were not slow in arriving with more Jutes and Angles, Saxons, and Fresians as well.

These ancestors of the English dealt out poetic justice to the Picts and Scots who prudently retired to the north leaving the Germanic visitors with leisure time in which to look around the country a bit. Then the fat was really in the fire. Having looked, they sent back an archaic version of "Having a wonderful time. . .wish you were here. . ." to all their friends and relatives at home. Thus the kinfolk proceeded to journey over to see for themselves. They were so pleased with what they found that for the next hundred and fifty years or so these different tribes kept coming to seek their fortunes in the new land.

The British Celts, in the meantime, were forced into the mountainous corners of the island, chiefly into Cornwall and Wales, also up into northwestern England and southern Scotland. Some took ships to Christian Ireland, some to the Isle of Man, and some to the French coast where they settled Brittany.

When the Germanic invasion came to an end, the Jutes had settled the lands of Kent (the southeastern part of the island). The Saxons occupied the rest of the region south of the Thames as far as Cornwall, and the Angles settled the large area stretching from the Thames northward to the Scottish Highlands (excepting Wales).

When these Germanic Tribes came to Britain they were all speaking dialects of Low German, and it is probably accurate to say that the different tribes had no real difficulty in communicating with each other. After they had come to roost in the different parts of the island, four principle dialects were spoken: Kentish, the speech of the Jutes who settled in Kent; West Saxon, spoken in the rest of the region south of the Thames; Mercian, spoken from the Thames to the Humber (excluding Wales); and Northumbrian (which means "North of the Humber River) reached up into Scotland as far as the Fifth of Forth.

With the passage of time, these dialects—spoken in the different small kingdoms which the Anglo-Saxons set up—became more and more dissimilar.

During the period of the Germanic invasions into Britain, the Christian Scots from the Irish shore crossed over the 12 miles of sea into northern Britain and formed the kingdom of Dalriada. (These Irish Celts eventually gave their name to all of Scotland.)

By around A.D. 600 the land that comprises present-day Scotland was peopled by these races: The Irish Scots settled their kingdom on the long peninsula of Kintyre in the southwest, Picts in the Highlands, Celtic Britons in the western part of the Lowlands, and Germanic Angles in the eastern part. "The Celtic language which spread from Ireland, called Gaelic or Goidelic, was of a type somewhat different from that of the Britons. It was ultimately adopted by the Picts and survives in Scots Gaelic, sometimes called Erse, a word which is simply a variant of *Irish*. Scots Gaelic is spoken in the remoter parts of the Scottish Highlands..."[3]

For a time the Scots and Picts fought each other, but the slaughter abated in 563 when St. Columba arrived from Ireland and the Picts began to be converted to Christianity. The Britons and the Angles in the Lowlands united sometime in the early six-hundreds.

The Anglo-Saxons were a pagan people when they conquered Britain, worshipping the rugged Norse gods. They continued this practice until the arrival of missionaries—some from Ireland, some from the church at Rome. The Irish had already developed a remarkable Christian culture with exquisitely beautiful religious art. The Irish church differed somewhat in ritual and symbolism with the Roman church, disclaiming papal authority as well as permitting its clergy to marry.

In 579 St. Augustine (not the famous North African Bishop of Hippo) arrival of missionaries—some from Ireland, some from the church at Rome. Northumbria from Ireland to convert the northern Anglo-Saxons to Christianity. For several decades it was not clear which division of Christianity the English would follow, and it was not until the synod of Whitby in 664 that they decided for the Roman Church.

There then followed a period of learning, of increased trade, and at least a tempering of the battle-hardened Anglo-Saxons.

Into this period of comparative peace burst another invasion of the island of Britain. During the 9th and 10th centuries a few thousand men called Vikings swarmed out of the wild fijords of Scandinavia and came close to conquering the world. Hamburg, Antwerp, London, Paris, the Rhone, Bordeaux, Seville, Morroco, settlements on the Volga River and the Caspian Sea, even Constantinople itself felt the terror inspired by these pagans. Before 1016 they had added Iceland and Greenland to their possessions. They had also landed upon the shores of North America.

"...Western civilization trembled before the ferocious pagans who tossed Christian infants from pike to pike and cut the 'blood eagle' onto the quivering backs of their prisoners. Wherever they went in their shallow-draft, dragon-prowed vessels, they brought violent and unexpected death. The church added to its regular prayers the plea: 'God spare us from the wrath of the Northmen.' "[4]

England was hard hit, first by raids and then by a large and professionally organized army which landed in East Anglia under the command of Ivar the Boneless and his brother Halfdan.

Intermittent warfare continued until Alfred, the young king of Wessex who had been hunted like a fugitive through the marshes of Somerset, was able to struggle to victory over the invaders in one of the world's greatest military reverses. England was then divided in half. One part was ruled by Alfred (who has since been known as Alfred the Great), and the other half, the Danelaw, was under the dominion of the "Danes," as the English called the Vikings (although there were also Norwegians and, later, Swedes among them).

After Alfred's death, trouble with the Vikings began anew for his weak successors. Finally in 1017 the disgusted English witan (a sort of pre-parlimentary body of wise men advisors) passed over the English descendants of Alfred and chose the ablest monarch they could find—the Danish King Canute—who, ironically enough, became the first true ruler of a fully unified England.

The Vikings, before they finally settled down and became a part of England, caused great misery and terror through much of the land. But, the worst of all their deeds was the vast destruction they wrought on the English church and the almost complete annihilation of learning. Along the entire east coast of the island and as far inland as a day's ride would take you, almost every church was destroyed, and monasteries and schools were obliterated and the occupants enslaved or slain. Soon most of the English nobility and clergy were illiterate. One reason Alfred is called "The Great" is because of the effort he made toward the reeducation of his people.

Most conquerors bring at least some new things to add to the culture of the people they overcome; it is hard to assess exactly the extent of the Viking's contribution. Basically they were of the same Norse culture to which the Anglo-Saxons once belonged, and they had, therefore, nothing that was radically new to add to the English vocabularies, and they are given credit for having caused complex, highly inflectional Old English (the term applied to all Anglo-Saxon speech in England until roughly A.D. 1100) to become somewhat simplified by sloughing off inflectional endings and softening the harsh consonants. Our modern pronouns—*they, them,* and *their*—are also of Norse origin.

The Vikings' influence on the language of the time appears to have been strongest in the north of England and the Lowlands of Scotland where the largest number settled. The fact that the people were already speaking the Anglian dialect of Old English, the closest of the Anglo-Saxon dialects to the tongue of the Danes, did nothing to impede the influence. It is certain that the Viking conquerors did bequeath to Ireland, southern Scotland, the Shetland Islands, the Orkney Islands, and much of northern England, a strain of vigorous people.

When the wild Norsemen finally settled and Christianized, the people had scant time to enjoy peace before the last successful invasion ever to be staged against England was begun. This was, of course, the Norman Conquest. It came from the shores of France, but oddly enough these Norman-French were yet another set of Vikings whose ancestors had invaded the northern French coast in the 9th and 10th centuries. The French called them Normans (Northmen), and the area they settled is still called Normandy today.

During the five generations that the Normans had been in France they had become Frenchmen culturally and linguistically; thus they were very different from other Norse invaders of England.

The invasion came about in this way: Edward the Confessor was the last English king in the direct male line of descent from Alfred the Great. When he died without issue, William, Duke of Normandy, who was distantly related to him, laid claim to the English throne. The English turned a deaf ear to this outlander and proceeded to elect Harold, son of the great Earl Godwin, to the kingship.

Duke William (later to be called the Conqueror) came of a line of men who were not about to be put aside by a snub like that. His father had gone to great pains to earn his name of Robert the Devil, and his son William,

98

although born on the wrong side of the blanket, proved himself to be a worthy son of such a father. He gathered his men about him, crossed the channel and proceeded to defeat the English in the Battle of Hastings in 1066. Harold was killed by an arrow which pierced his eye; his two brothers were also slain, and the English, deprived of their effective leadership, were defeated.

William, now the Conqueror, wasted no time in pursuing his advantage, and after five years the English nobles who continued to resist him had all been vanquished. He rewarded his followers with the spoils of the land.

This time the invasion of England did not involve a large migration of people. The total admixture of Norman French blood of the population of England was relatively small, but the economic and political power of the land was, however, settled firmly in Norman hands.

It would be inaccurate during this Norman era to refer to the kings of England as English kings. They were in actuality, the French dukes of Normandy, who regarded the throne of England as one of the choicest plums of their domain, and who found it very handy to use English soldiers in their ceaseless warfare on the continent.

For a period of about 300 years the English language, as such, was relegated to a very low place on the totem pole. French was the language of the royal court and of chivalry; Latin was the language of the law courts and the church, and English was the language of the common man. The "degeneration" that English underwent during the Viking period was accelerated during these 300 years; the complicated forms of Old English were much simplified, and we find that we have arrived at the stage of the language known as Middle English--the dates for which are roughly A.D. 1100 - 1500.

There were still several dialects of English in Middle English Times. "Northern English was spoken north of the Humber River; it had an important subdivision in Scots, spoken originally in Lowland Scotland but extending itself farther north in Middle English Times..."[5]

Midlands was the dialect spoken in the mid-part of England (it was divided into Eastern and Western Midland), and the Southern dialect was spoken, reasonably enough, south of the Thames.

I imagine that long since you have been muttering darkly to yourself about "Why on earth doesn't she get on with it and stop driveling about the dialects? Who Cares?!!" Actually, there has been a certain amount of method in my madness. I wanted to be very certain that you have gotten it firmly fixed in your mind that "original English" did not come in just one style but in several, each equally good.

From Roman times, London had been an established center. By the Middle English Period it was the capital of the nation. As such it was the site of the royal court; the great law tribunals met there, and it was in London that Parliament convened; then, as now, London was the largest and wealthiest city of England. It was the center of commerce and of social life. Even the two great universities of Oxford and Cambridge were close enough to influence the city.

To this center flocked men from all the corners of the island—nobles, merchants, lawyers, scholars, students—anyone who had business in London or at court, or who wished to advance his fortune. From a city populated with such a mixture as this there grew up yet another type of speech. Called simply the London dialect, it was, as you might suppose, a mixture of several others. London was located in that part of the country that spoke the East Midland dialect and it was speech with essentially East Midland characteristics, though showing Northern, and to a lesser extent Southern influences that began to emerge as the dialect spoken in London. It is from the London dialect that modern standard English (both British and American) eventually descended.

Until the late fifteenth century, however, authors wrote in the dialect of their native regions. So did many noble lords and ladies of the court; even so late as the days of Queen Elizabeth many courtiers spoke in their "native tongue." It was said of Walter Raleigh that "He spake broad Devon to the day he died."

Since we have shown that a considerable part of Scotland was speaking a form of northern English dialect, and since we will show that Appalachia was largely populated by Celts, particularly Scots, we ought to go back now to the Scots whom we left in the seventh century and bring their history up to date.

As the continued Norse attacks on the Northern island and shores weakened the Picts, they turned more and more to the Scots. In 843 Kenneth MacAlpin, half Scot and half Pict, merged the two peoples and became the first king of Gaelic Alba (for Scotland was not yet the name of the country).

The Vikings have been mentioned previously, though the emphasis was laid on their activities in England. At one time they had conquered Caithness, Southerland, Ross, and more than half of Alba. Before the end of the ninth century they were the masters of the Orkney, Shetland, and the Western Isles. In 915 the Danes occupied northern England so that at one period or another the greater part of Scotland was either surrounded by, or in the hands of, the Norsemen. With periods of varying success the Norse occupation continued until about 1264 when they were finally expelled, except from Orkney and Shetland.

During this period there were still Scottish kings, of course, among them Macbeth. It was during the 35-year reign of Malcolm Ceanmore that the rise of the Scottish Clan system can be seen.

In 1018, Malcolm married a Saxon princess, Margaret (later known as St. Margaret), and under her influence and that of her sons, Saxon speech and customs became general in the Scottish Lowlands. Malcolm encouraged the immigration from England of a large number of Saxon and Norman nobles to whom he made feudal grants. Although this feudalism was broken up and the nobles expelled from Scotland by Donald Ban when he succeeded his brother to the throne, the Saxon speech and the flavor of Saxon custom remained in the Lowlands.

For the next hundred years or so the kings of Scotland were concerned with consolidating the kingdom and extending the boundaries of the central government.

For long years the kingdoms of England and Scotland had dwelt in amity. This was now to change. In 1286, Alexander III of Scotland rode his horse over a cliff in the darkness and left as his heir Margaret, his granddaughter, known as the Maid of Norway. The Scottish nobles agreed to accept Margaret who was fourteen, and they planned to have her not only succeed to the throne of Scotland but also to marry Edward, son to the king of England, in an effort to secure continued peace between the two kingdoms. The maid of Norway embarked in 1290 and died before she reached the shores of Scotland.

The Scottish nobility were allied at many points with the English royal family. The English took an active hand in trying to influence the disputed succession.

There were a dozen claimants to the Scottish throne, but the choice narrowed down to two men--John Balliol and Robert Bruce. Edward I of England put himself forward as the arbitrator of the dispute and announced in favor of John Balliol who soon became his puppet. A large faction in Scotland disagreed violently with this decision and a struggle for power continued. Scotland, in time, allied itself with France to resist England.

Battles followed, and Robert the Bruce (grandson of the other Robert Bruce) was the new champion of Scotland, when, in 1314, Edward II of England set forth with an army to conquer the land. There ensued the Battle of Bannockburn and "No more grievous slaughter of English chivalry ever took place in a single day," according to Winston Churchill.

After the death of the Bruce, the throne of Scotland passed on to his son, Davis II, a child of six. There then ensued one of those disastrous minorities which were the curse of Scotland. David reigned for forty-two years, but eighteen of them were spent outside his kingdom as a refugee or captive.

David II was succeeded by his nephew, Robert, the High Steward; the first in the line of Stuart kings who were to reign in Scotland and eventually in England as well.

For much of the 14th century and most of the 15th, Scotland was too deeply divided by opposing factions to have overmuch to do with either England or France. Few Scottish kings seemed to die peacefully. Indeed, of six successive monarchs from Robert III to James VI, no one king died a natural death, and infants or young children inherited from their abruptly deceased fathers. A minority always meant that some regent must rule in the king's place until he came of age, and the time of regency generally saw much striving for power and position among the powerful nobles.

It will suffice here to skim over the Stuart kings until we come to James VI of Scotland, son of the famous Mary, Queen of Scots. Mary was related to

Queen Elizabeth of England, and on Elizabeth's death, her throne went to James, who became James I of England.

It was early in his English reign that James decided to try to control the Irish by putting a Protestant population into Ireland. To do this he confiscated the lands of the earls of Ulster and bestowed them upon Scottish and English lords on condition that they settle the territory with tenants from Scotland and England. This was known as the "Great Settlement" or the "King's Plantation," and it was begun in 1610.

Many of the Scots who moved into Ulster apparently came from the Lowlands (at least they bear Lowland surnames),[7] and thus they would have spoken the Scot's variety of the Northumbrian or Northern English dialect. This particular dialect would have been kept intact if the Scots had had no dealings with the Irish, and this, according to records, was the case.

While in Ulster the Scots multiplied, but after roughly 100 years they became dissatisfied with conditions imposed upon them by the English and began emigrating in large numbers to the English colonies in America. With them, of course, they brought their language.

Many of them came into Pennsylvania where, finding better lands already settled by the English, they began to move south and west into what is now Appalachia; some Palatine Germans came along with them. They called themselves the "Scotch-Irish" but were, in actuality, Scots. By the time of the Revolutionary War, there were about 200,000 Scots in the country. "Their enterprise and pioneering spirit made them the most important element in the vigorous frontiersmen who opened up this part of the South and later other territories farther west into which they pushed."[8]

Besides the Scots who arrived from Ireland, more came directly from Scotland to the American colonies after "the '45"—the final Jacobite uprising in support of "Bonny Prince Charlie," the Young Pretender—which ended disastrously for the Scottish clans that supported him.

Some English, Irish, and Welch families joined the Scots on the frontier (which Appalachia then was), and it is from their descendants that many of you are sprung. Because of the isolation of the area, families who settled here tended to keep the type of speech they had brought with them. Thus what is heard in our country today is a Scottish flavored Elizabethan English.

It is interesting to note that it has been primarily the linguistic historians who have pointed out the predominately Scottish heritage of the Southern mountain (Appalachian) people. Pyles and Baugh have already been cited. Raven I. McDavid notes, "The speech of the hill people is quite different from both dialects of the Southern lowlands for it is basically derived from the Scotch-Irish of western Pennsylvania."[9] And H. L. Mencken said of Appalachian folk speech, "The persons who speak it undiluted are often called by the Southern publicists, 'the purest Anglo-Saxons in the United States,' but less romantic ethnologists describe them as predominately Celtic in blood; though there has been a large infiltration of English and even German strains."

FOOTNOTES

[1] Mario Pei, *The Story of English.* New York, Fawcett World Library, 1962, p. 8.

[2] There is a lively academic dispute over whether the Picts were or were not Celts.

[3] Thomas Pyles, *The Origins and Development of the English Language.* New York, Harcourt, Brace & World, Inc., 1964, p. 87.

Martin S. Day, *History of English Literature to 1600.* Garden City, N. Y., Doubleday & Company, Inc., 1963, p. 31.

[5] Ibid., p. 44.

[6] Winston S. Churchill, *The Birth of Britain.* New York, Bantam Books, Inc., 1963, p. 230. This is an excellent book to read to find out about the colorfully turbulent days of early Britain.

[7] Pyles, p. 36. "It is not surprising that those lowland Scotsmen who colonized the 'King's Plantation' in Ulster and whose descendants crossed the Atlantic and settled the Blue Ridge, the Appalachians, and the Ozarks should have been little affected by the classical culture of the Renaissance."

[8] Albert C. Baugh, *A History of the English Language,* 2nd ed., New York, 1957, p. 409.

[9] H. L. Mencken, *The American Language*, ed. Raven I. McDavid, Jr., the 4th ed. and the two supplements abridged, with annotations and new material. New York, 1963, p. 455.

[10] Ibid., p. 459.

Folklore and Literature

The Mysterious Horseshoe   Ruth A. Musick

JUDY PROZZILLO BYERS, a native West Virginian, is both a student and a teacher of Appalachian folklore and folk literature. She has traveled extensively in the north central part of the State giving "tale-telling programs" and is an experienced collector of folklore, particularly ethnic folk tales of West Virginia.

A teacher of English in the secondary schools of Marion County and at Fairmont State College, Mrs. Byers was named West Virginia's Teacher of the Year for 1977. She received her AB degree from Fairmont State College and her MA degree from West Virginia University, and has done post graduate work at West Virginia University and the Folklore Institute of Indiana University.

Mrs. Byers and her family were long-time friends and contributors of Italian ethnic tales and lore to Dr. Ruth Ann Musick, some of which Dr. Musick published in *Green Hills of Magic* and *Coffin Hollow and Other Ghost Tales.* Having been an assistant to Dr. Musick while in graduate school, she later worked with Dr. Musick and Dr. Patrick Gainer (q.v.) in the revival of the West Virginia Folklore Society and now serves as treasurer of the Society and associate editor of its *West Virginia Folklore Journal.*

At her death in 1974, Dr. Musick bequeathed her unpublished collections to Judy who is now engaged in their editing and publication in Dr. Musick's memory. She recently contributed a biographical sketch on Dr. Musick and her works to *The West Virginia Heritage Encyclopedia.*

106

CONTENTS

WEST VIRGINIA LITERATURE:

ORAL AND WRITTEN EXPERIENCES

"The June morning is freshly cool and damp. Over the horizon fleecy white clouds sway gently amid the deep blue dawn just as if they are being rocked in the arms of the rolling hills, green with maple and oak. In the still dark valley, ribbons of gray fog rise slowly from a meandering river that peek-a-boos around the skirts of the hills. Wild rhododendron spread their pale pink blossoms near the river edges, making delicate petticoats for the bottom land. Not far away, an old dirt road follows the river's course, laced on its north side by split log fencing. Suddenly, the sun transforms the scene into gold. A young cardinal adds a hint of crimson, singing its good morning to the earth. Somewhere over the hills, hidden from my limited vision, the sun's gold is also touching a coal tipple facing the sky, a newly plowed corn field, and a small industry in a valley."

On I-79 North between Fairmont and Morgantown one early morning last summer, I paused at a car rest and experienced the above crystal moment of Appalachian beauty—an experience about my West Virginia put into narrative words.

Narrative words become the seeds for poetry and prose. Thus, literature is created. Between the seeds and creation, however, lays the germination of imagination, atmosphere, and setting. West Virginia, its people, topography, and climate, is this necessary germination that has produced a rich and varied literature, both oral and written.

ORAL LITERATURE

Oral literature consists of poetry and prose created in the mind, transmitted from one person to another or from one grouping of people to another by word of mouth, and preserved in this oral form instead of the written form. Oral literature is usually created earlier than written genres in any culture of people, for it is representative of talking, a basic means of communication. Oral literature is often labelled under folklore as folk literature because most of the literary pieces have no single authorship but are created collectively by the folk or people, transmitted by the folk as delineations of the folk life, and preserved by the folk. Oral poetry in the forms of chants and songs, with sparse or no instrumental accompaniment, generally develop before oral prose because of the melodies fitting the natural rhythm of the sung voice patterns, the easiness in which a poetic piece is memorized with the conventional usage of stock characters and popular expressions, commonplace themes and verbal repetitions, and the usual shortness in the length of the piece. Oral prose types follow with longer lengths, more complicated structures, and individualized dramatic presentations.

West Virginia is nestled in the heart of the Appalachians, an ancient mountain range, once more towering and massive than the Rockies but now chiselled to rolling hills by centuries of temperate climatic forces. Varieties of green vegetation and timber cover a curious blend of rock and fertile earth that more deeply houses rich deposits of coal, oil, and gas.

Long before the white men came to these hills, sometime between 10,000 and 20,000 years ago, the Mound Builders or Adena People, migrated from Mexico or Central America seeking the big game. They maintained a highly developed society as the first agriculturists and industrialists into the Ohio Valley. Yet, true to other prehistoric cultures, the Mound Builders disappeared, leaving no oral literature but evidences of inspirations to literary imagination in remnants of burial mounds housing artifacts.

Their cousins, various tribes of Indians, such as the Iroquois and Cherokees (two of the more important tribes into West Virginia), and to a lesser extent, Tuscaroras, Shawnees, Delawares, and Mingoes used West Virginia as a common hunting ground and burial ground instead of a permanent living area. The lure of game animals, fish, and salt springs brought many tribes into deadly combat with each other and later with the white settlers. However, these nomadic scouts left a figurative permanence upon West Virginia by marking many trails, rivers, and valleys with Indian names.

The Indians also often left reasons why these sites were so named, and around their campfires chants and tales evolved verbalizing this reasoning. Landmarks were explained in physical imagery and qualities, such as bravery and beauty, and were glorified in story and legend. Two explicit examples are "The Legend of Seneca Rock" and "The Legend of Monongahela" in which the tone of love is the catalyst in the courageous but imaginative existence of young Indian warriors. Songs and chants equally echoed boasts of brave hunting feats. The more curious sought answers to the questions of the workings of natural phenomena by creating myths, such as "The Iroquois Myth of Creation" in which man first originated on the earth by falling out of a hole in the sky and landing on a substance that became the back of a huge earth turtle. Both vegetable and animal symbolism, native to the land area, were embodied into the Indian mythology to enhance the explanations.

Indian oral literature, then, was created from daily living situations and needs, weaving human emotional themes of love, hate, fear, and pride. It was not only transmitted by word of mouth among and between tribes from generation to generation, but also was heard by the first white men to journey into these mountains, who were receptive to the oral recordings because of the humanistic, self-identifying tones, entertaining quality, and useful knowledge. In turn, with curiosity and vigor they often transmitted the literature among themselves, thus perpetuating and solidifying Indian lore in West Virginia.

During the latter 1600's and early 1700's white settlers began to move away from the tidewater regions across the piedmonts and plateaus into these western mountains which became the first "western frontier." A variety of tales and stories emerged out of the early Anglo-Celtic (English, Irish, and Scotch) and Germanic migrations into the hills. These people became coined as the pioneer farmers, the wilderness explorers, the raisers of hogs, cattle, and horses, and the rugged often ruthless hunters, trappers, Indian traders, and Indian fighters.

They were strong, fearless, and rugged individualists who prized courage and independence akin to family loyalty and a fierce love of God. With a stoic self-reliance as stubborn and rugged as the untamed land surrounding them, these mountaineers, both men and women with children by their sides, cleared the dense vegetation, built their cabins and communities, planted their hill crops, raised their farm animals, hunted, trapped, fished, and survived.

Besides a grangerized foresight, these first Anglo-Celtic and Germanic settlers also possessed a romantic insight characterized by an imaginative nature, wit, and humor, verbosity, and vivid humanism. Often educated, many of these immigrants brought with them into the mountains such books as the Bible, ancient history—and selections of world literature. They, likewise, conveyed a rich folklore of culture and tradition, of which the oral literature or folk literature was most prominent.

Embraced by the secure arms of the Appalachians that graced the horizons, the early mountaineers were lodged in the valleys, or hillsides, on ridges, and along river banks—protected by the mountains that served to keep them secure from the outside world but, too, removed and unchanged. Here, then, among and between families and communities the oral traditions of the Anglo-Celtic ancestors were remembered, transmitted, perpetuated, and, thus, preserved.

The oral literature flourished for a number of domestic reasons. The various oral poetic and prose types were expedient and nostalgic instruments to convey to the young and among the adults memories of a romanticized life across the ocean, so long ago. These oral presentations served as a basic means of entertainment in the calamity ridden lives of the first frontiersmen. After the evening meal, the family members would gather around the open hearth on winter nights or outside under the stars in the summertime to hear old world tales and sing ballads and folk songs. The art of storytelling was a clever and important talent to learn, for a great part of family happiness was weighed on how well kinsmen could entertain and communicate with each other in story and song. Thirdly, during the day as the mountaineer was "going about" his daily and often weary chores, cooking and cleaning and canning and sewing for the women folk while gardening and milking and sawing and hunting for the male kin, oral literature was sung or told to make the hard family work more bearable and enjoyable. A sad love song, a humorous tale, or a mysterious legend seemed "to pass away the time" and the work, too.

Even though most of the first oral white man's literature into the mountains was European in origin, collectively it began to wear a new flavor of rugged quality as it interspersed into the, now, rugged life styles of the people, the wild, free, natural environment, and the rich already existing examples of oral Indian literature. The Old World variants, therefore, that survived were slowly transformed by oral transmission to fit the mores and needs of the mountaineers. Unlike written literature whose printed work is permanent as soon as the ink dries, the oral word is as changeable as the individual personality of the storyteller or singer. Many of the flamboyant themes of affluence and sovereign powers were substituted for literary examples dealing with human conditions and human emotions of which the mountaineer could identify: the trials and tribulations of the family and of daily frontier living (The family was proud, close, loyal, clannish, brave, and long suffering. Many of the actual family chores and labors were dramatized in tales and songs, along with a variety of community activities, such as a spelling bee or a corn huskin'.); the sensitive inner emotions of the people (young love, marriage, childbirth, lamented love, sickness, death, laughter, and war to name a few examples); and the world of the unknown and adventurous. The people were sharp-eyed and curious. Examples of the unknown, strange, suspenseful, or unexplainable intrigued and whetted their imaginations. Tales of both the supernatural and preternatural were popular; however, from time to time different religious sects and

111

itinerant ministers traveling through the mountains preached against the vices of various characteristics in examples of these unearthly tale typings. In time, some examples of the fairy tale motifs became extinct in the oral literature along with many accounts of witchcraft.

Later, as the mountaineers became more established in their wilderness homes, they slowly but consistently began to add to the rich repertoire of existing oral literature, much of it already in numerous variants of the Old World originals, by creating their own oral examples from daily events and happenings based on truths but stretched and romanticized to suit their frontier imagination and delight. The humid, misty climate with its patchy valley fogs rising from the river beds into the silenced dawns were often inspirations for spirits and will-o'-the-wisps seen against the morning light or graying dusk. The rolling topography ever changing against the four seasons held mystery in the deep valleys that always reflected the sun's shadow but never the sun. Could that shadow really be the face of an old man or the strange witch lady up the hollow? Dense wooded areas contained hidden secrets, bewilderment, and sometimes fear! Also, some oral literature was created by copying and parodying stories from the Bible and precious few other books that the mountaineer families prized and used for home learning. As a youngin' learned to read the Biblical and ancient literary selections, he often imagined himself on similar exotic adventures which became inspirations for such authentic oral prose pieces as exemplified in the tall tale, yarn, and jest. Oral transmission was the most desirable means of enjoying literature for a people who daily were many times too busy to sit down and read a written selection. And, of course, for the mountaineer who could not read, oral literature was a necessary communicative process.

Time, however, continued to pass and with it were created subtle changes in the people and physical characteristics of the mountains, ramifications of which affected all modes of mountain life including its oral literature. Toward the middle of the 1800's the drum beats of America's industrial revolution in the making was beginning to be heard across the mountains into western Virginia. In the aftermath of the Civil War and West Virginia's statehood, swiftly the area that had isolated the Anglo-Celtic and Germanic migrants for generations was presented to the outside world by the laying of railroad tracks across the mountainous paths. Soon churning steam engines winded their way among the hills, opening the industrial age to West Virginia and taking from the mountains the rich coal and abundant timber that it had kept untouched for centuries. Amid supple coal beds were soon to be discovered opulent veins of natural gas and oil, two other booms for the mountainous development in the making.

Since a massive surplus of manpower was needed to mine these natural resources, much more brawn than the native granger sons could possibly provide, the timing was right for the introduction of cheap labor into the mountains from western and southern Europe, immigrants who had recently flocked to America in great numbers to escape the crop famines that had plagued these agricultural sections of Europe. Like the Anglo-Celtic and Germans before them, these people represented many walks of life styles to settle into these mountains. Yet, similarly they further characterized stoic qualities, as being the most courageous and independent of their Old World families and communities, by displaying enough faith and individualism to cross an ocean, seeking a new life in a strange and relatively untamed land.

Under the direction of wealthy natural resources' barons, these immigrants helped to build the railways, man the trains, cut the timber, mine the coal, and tap the rich natural gas and oil deposits. They were native to such countries as Hungary, Czechslovakia, Poland, Yugoslavia, southern Ireland, Austria, Russia, and many others, of which thirty percent of the people were from Italy. For security and expediency they lived in nationality communities close to the natural resources deposits. In the valleys, along the river beds, and nestled beside ridges small coal camps that later became coal towns, began to develop.

Each new nationality group brought a rich culture and folklore that became perpetuated and preserved between and among the segregated nationality communities. Both the oral and written literatures were important contributors to the adjustment of these people to the mountains, with the oral literary typings, as usual, taking precedence. The oral literature showed themes of family loyalty, family dominance, pride, a deep love and fear of God, yet a curious blending of superstition with Christianity, to mention just a few, coupled with a deep sensitivity toward human emotions. The oral transmission of Old World tales through storytelling was often given a more honored reverence than oral verse typings because the best storytellers were usually the oldest members of a family who had learned the tales directly from the European source. Also, the tales were generally retold in the native speech of the nationality, allowing many of the immigrants one of the few means to keep in direct oral contact with their native language since they were learning English in order to adjust to their new industrial life mode. Many of the mining bosses immediately Americanized the foreign names for less complicated bookkeeping, forcing the immigrants to conform more explicitly. Thus, for these varied nationalities whose fierce cultural loyalties mixed with a stubborn pride were difficult to bend, two separate life styles began to develop and to become perpetuated. During the working hours on the job whether it was in a coal mine or on a railroad, the typical immigrant compromised his individualism, but within the security of his community and home he often lived his native culture, depending on the oral literature as a strong part of that culture.

The black people who settled in these western mountains also contributed a culture and folklore to the already overflowing pot of heritages. Their oral literature was rich with songs and chants, created to subdue the drudgeries of field work and house chores. Their themes generally showed a longing for a better life even if this dream could only be answered in the after life of heaven. Fear of the night, the unknown, and the devil that always tried to block the actualization of reaching heaven triggered in the black storyteller's imagination a powerful narrative sensitivity for the supernatural and preternatural, inspiring a harvest of superstitious tales. On clear summer nights the black communities would leave the shanties and masters' homes to gather around a huge fire for a perpetuation of Christianity interpreted in vivid mixtures of oral poetry and prose, displaying a rural language endowed with earth imagery, tones of God's fiery love but terrible wrath on sin and vice, and moralistic themes of the evils of the strange and mystic in contrast to the glories of the good and spiritual. Like the wild geography surrounding them, these black people did not generally feel the suppression of their black brothers in the rich tidewater and piedmont areas, for poor Appalachia because of a harsher climate, poor cotton and tobacco soil, and no capital to warrant slavery as an important business did not have much slavery. An abundance of cheap black labor from the deep South, however, came to West Virginia after the Civil War to aid in the building of the railroads. They were treated poorly, receiving commissionary food and one dollar a day with shacks in the "niggertown" sections of coal camps and towns. Their oral literature contained the same tones of paganistic fears amid an everlasting hope in God and His Kingdom; yet, they often immortalized the brave working deeds of their brothers on the railroads, such as John Henry at the Big Bend Tunnel at Talcott, in legendary song and story. Similar, then, to all the other inhabitants of these western hills, their oral literature, too, gave them strength and hope, contiguous with an entertaining escape and joy from the many trials of daily living in the mountains.

CATEGORIES OF ORAL LITERATURE

In addition to the two major categories of poetry and prose, oral literature can also be divided more specifically into three categories:

(1.) folk songs (the first verse of poetry)
(2.) tales (the first short stories and other prose accounts)
(3.) verbal lore (the colorful, stock usage of language, words, and phrases that accompany both the oral poetry and prose)

I. FOLK SONGS

There are a variety of folk songs, fashioned and perpetuated by the human experience of the mountaineers:

A. Ballad   (a narrative song, telling a story; a wide variety of subjects ranging from reverence to comedy and from gloom to gaiety; stock characters; impersonality of oral dramatization; subtle presentation since some situations are left in doubt or in question; the usage of conventional diction; incremental repetition; the leaping and lingering of the narrative episodes; the ballad stanza is predominantly iambic; and the usual presence of a refrain)

The other types of oral poetry contain themes and tones that are demonstrative in the ballad; yet, these songs do not tell a story:

B. Lullaby (a cradlesong of good night to lull a baby to sleep; also a song of good-by or farewell)

C. Carol   (a song of joy or praise, especially in honor of a special religious event, such as Christmas)

D. Lament (a song presenting a situation of lost or unrequited love)

E. Religious Songs   (verses and praises to the love of God)

F. Black Spirituals and Blues   (Religious praises and emotional verse reactions; the Negro oral poetry was one of the greatest contributions to American folklore)

G. Work Songs   (created and chanted chorally by both the rural agricultural and industrial workers, depicting their toils and sufferings)

H. Game Songs   (songs and chants inspired by the sharp wit and humor of the mountaineers, often called "play party games" that substituted for the dancing that was

often condemned under the watchful eyes of certain
fundamentalist itinerant ministers who preached in
the mountains)

II. TALES

The narrative prose inspired by Appalachian living is as unique
and as varied as the oral poetry:

A. Fairy Tale: deals with "little people" of the supernatural
world, such as fairies, elves, spirits, pixies, gnomes,
dwarfs, brownies, and leprechauns; they are usually
helpful to the human hero in the tale by performing an
act of magic that resolves a human problem or conflict;
many of these tales were lost or disregarded in time
through oral transmission, being condemned as evil by
some fundamental religious sects in the hills who
judged any form of magic as a trait of the devil.

In Ruth Ann Musick's *Green Hills of Magic,* a section entitled "Little People" is devoted to the supernatural world of the helpful fairies, displayed in such
tales as "Peggy O'Leary and the Leprechauns" and
"Friendship of the Wee People."

B. Legend: a story that distinguishes a person, place, or event,
such as those collected and presented by Margaret
Prescott Montague in her book *Up Eel River.* Tony
Beaver, one of the characters, is the legendary Paul
Bunyon in the lumber camps of West Virginia.

C. Fable: a short tale, usually involving animal characters,
which expressed, either implicitly or explicitly, a moral
principle.

D. Myth: a tale that explains natural situations, such as the creation of the world, the origins of vegetation, animals,
and people and the characteristics of the physical elements. Examples of these can be found in the *West
Virginia Folklore Journal* especially dealing with Indian lore depicting both the fable and the myth; also,
Richard Chase's folklore collections are excellent.

E. Tall Tale: an exaggerated account, often a "down right lie" a
situation or event, depicting humor and satire. An excellent source for this type of tale is B. A. Botkin's *A
Treasury of American Folklore,* in which he categorized the Tall Tale into Jesters, Yarns, Liars, and

116

Boasters. *The West Virginia Folklore Journal* also contains examples of Tall Tales.

F. Supernatural Tale: a folk tale involving a situation beyond the normal experience or knowledge of man, characterized by ghosts, spirits, and misty apparitions who haunt the earth for a number of reasons: to aid a loved one who is still alive, to seek revenge among the living, and to find peace and solace among the living; usually this spirit has died in a tragic manner before his or her time. All four of Dr. Musick's folk tale collections represent the various types of ghost tales in West Virginia.

G. Preternatural Tale: a folk tale of the supernatural that involves instead of ghosts and spirits, the dark and diabolical sides of the unknown; witches and witchcraft; demons and devils; and incantations of magic, spells, sorcery, and curses; many of these tales were banned during oral transmission by sects of the itinerant missionaries into the mountains, along with fairy tale motifs. Dr. Gainer's *Witches, Ghosts, and Signs* and Dr. Musick's *Green Hills of Magic* reveal the witch and demonlore of the hills.

III. VERBAL LORE

Within the structural content of both the oral poetry and prose, laid building blocks of verbal, narrative expressions and cliches, patterns of words that added to the richness of the oral selections. This verbal lore was not only common among the mountaineers but also served as further proof that the oral and domestic traditions were really one. These expressions, one linked to another and another, inspired much of the substance for the oral creations.

Examples of this lore:

A. Proverbs: expressions which contain some element of wisdom or commonly accepted beliefs, such as the Italian saying that "the fish stinks from the head on down."

B. Riddles: a problem or puzzle placed in the form of a question that takes some thought to answer, such as "What has eyes but can not see?" (a potato)

C. Beliefs and Superstitions: a statement considered true if it is labeled a belief or speculated as a truth if it is considered a superstition; to leave an empty rocking chair rocking is an omen of bad luck to the believer but only questionable and curious to the superstitious.

D. Joke: an amusing remark or short narrative.

Much verbal discourse concerning weather and nature lore, remedies, tokens, omens, family customs, and cookery, all pertaining to the oral domestic tradition were accepted as either beliefs or superstitions of the people and became woven into the oral poetry and prose.

SELECTED ORAL LITERATURE COLLECTIONS

A more enduring preservation was given to the oral literature of West Virginia as folklorists and literary scholars began to capture and record these oral examples in written form and later on tapes. Serving as editors of this literature that had been collectively authored by the folk or people, many of whom were native West Virginians, have compiled and passed along collections of an oral tradition that otherwise would have been eventually lost in the fast pace of our computerized life. Apparently one of the prices of progress is that modern mountaineers can not or will not take the time to entertain each other with intriguing storytelling or common song, to orally transmit pieces of knowledge growing from narration instead of equation, and to communicate using narrative motifs and expressions. Below is a selected bibliography, briefly annotated, that exemplifies a college of oral literature that has been preserved in these salient collections:

Botkins, B. A., ed., *A Treasury of American Folklore,* New York: Crown Publishers, Inc.

This is a huge volume of stories, ballads, and traditions of the Appalachian people, including West Virginia, of course. As a well-known folklorist, Mr. Botkin categorized the kind of folk tales, making direct reference to John Harrington Cox's *Negro Tales From West Virginia.*

Brown, Stephen D., ed., *Haunted Houses of Harpers Ferry: Regional Ghost Stories,* Harpers Ferry, West Virginia: The Little Brown House.

Harpers Ferry is an area rich in history with Civil War battlefields, old homes, and even older legends. This is a collection of tales about ghosts and phantom figures that roam where the gently rolling hills of Western Maryland and Northern Virginia meet West Virginia's craggy eastern borders at Harpers Ferry.

Bush, Michael E., ed., *Folk Songs of Central West Virginia,* Custom Printing.

This is a picturesque handbook of folk songs from central West Virginia.

Chappell, Louis W., ed., *John Henry,* Kennikat Press.

A nationally known folklorist, Professor Chappell traces the history of the legendary oral literature hero, John Henry, the black steel driver who died with a hammer in his hand proving the strength of man power over machine power on the Big Bend Tunnel, at Talcott, West Virginia.

Chase, Richard, ed., *American Folk Tales and Songs and Other Examples of English-American Tradition as Preserved in the Appalachian Mountains and Elsewhere in the United States.* Signet Key Books.

Chase, Richard, ed., *Grandfather Tales.*

Mr. Chase is another basic folklore scholar who is recognized for his classifying of oral prose.

Child, Francis James, ed., *English and Scottish Popular Ballads,* 5 vols., London: Sampson, Law, Son and Company, 1882-1898.

Professor Child was the first scholar to collect and classify the famous English-Scottish ballads, 305 in number, many variants of which were orally transmitted over the ocean into the mountains by the Anglo-Celtic pioneers who first settled here.

Cober, Mary E., ed., *The Remarkable History of Tony Beaver, West Virginian,* New York: McKay.

There are seventeen separate folk tales in this collection, about Tony Beaver.

Cox, John Harrington, ed., *Folksongs of the South,* Folklore Association, Inc.

This entertaining collection of historic folk songs leaves a lasting impression of what life was like in the pioneering days of West Virginia. Professor Cox was a member of the West Virginia University English faculty for many years where he founded The West Virginia Folklore Society in 1915. The collected oral poetry, verse, and music from the student members of this, at the time, young society became the fruits for this book.

Donnelly, Shirley, ed., *The Hatfield-McCoy Feud Reader*, McClain Printing.

This edition is a series of stories and newspaper clippings dealing with the famous family feud along the shores of the Tug River in Mingo County, West Virginia, and Pike County, Kentucky, which was legendized in oral prose.

Gainer, Patrick W., ed., *Folk Songs From the West Virginia Hills*, Grantsville, West Virginia: Seneca Books.

This annotated collection is one of the most authentic and major in the study of the West Virginia oral poetry in folk song and music. Dr. Gainer, a nationally known folklorist, taught folklore and English for many years at West Virginia University, collected folklore among the hills, established folk festivals throughout the state, and led The West Virginia Folklore Society. This book represents a major sampling of the people's songs that have survived through the oral tradition: ballads of adventure and derring-do; songs of romance and unrequited love; play-party songs and nonsense rhymes; Negro spirituals, church chorals, and fiddle-tune songs; and the Child ballad variations of which Dr. Gainer has collected more in West Virginia than any other folk scholar.

Gainer, Patrick W., ed., *Witches, Ghosts and Signs*, Grantsville, West Virginia: Seneca Books.

A second authentic and basic text for folk study, this book contains tales of strange events and witchery, collected over the years. There are also sections on superstitions, folk remedies, and the language of the mountaineers. This edition deals mainly with the preternatural motif in oral mountain literature.

Gainer, Patrick W., ed., *The West Virginia Centennial Book of 100 Songs*.

This book contains not only many of the folk songs that Dr. Gainer has collected down through the years but also tunes accompany the words. Sixteen of these songs have been recorded in the record album, *Patrick Gainer Sings Folk Songs of the Allegheny Mountains*, in which Dr. Gainer displays his rich Irish tenor voice and the sparse accompaniment of mountain instruments.

Gainer, Patrick, W., ed., *The West Virginia Folklore Journal*, Fairmont, West Virginia: P.O. Box 446.

This biannually published journal is the official publication of The West Virginia Folklore Society, containing a variety of examples of oral folk poetry and prose, representative of the state of West Virginia which has been and is continuing to be collected.

Jabbour, Alan and Carl Fleischhauer, ed., *The Hammons Family, A Study of a West Virginia Family's Tradition*, Washington, D.C.: Archive of Folk Song, Library of Congress, AFS L65-L66.

This is an album containing oral recordings of members of the Hammons Family remembering songs, tales, riddles, and proverbs, from their Anglo-Celtic ancestry in the mountains.

Jones, James Gay, ed., *Appalachian Ghost Stories and Other Tales*, Parsons, West Virginia: McClain.

Jones is a professor at Glenville State College. His collection consists of an introductory essay on the Appalachian setting and a choice selection of folk stories about ghosts, true experiences, and tall tales.

Jones, James Gay, ed., *Haunted Valley and More Folk Tales*, Parsons, West Virginia: McClain.

Most of these tales have authentic historical settings dating from the early days of settlement in Appalachia to recent times.

Montague, Margaret Prescott, ed., *Up Eel River*.

This is a collection of the Tony Beaver tales as created in the lumber camps of West Virginia, legendizing a strong hero by the name of Tony Beaver who becomes the Paul Bunyan of the Appalachians and who lives in his wonderful lumber camp called Up Eel River.

Musick, Ruth Ann, ed., *Ballads, Folk Songs, and Folk Tales from West Virginia*, Morgantown, West Virginia: West Virginia University Library.

This is the first book to have been published by Dr. Musick, one of the most eminent folklore scholars to have collected in West Virginia. A native of Iowa, Dr. Musick came to West Virginia in 1946 to teach English and folklore at Fairmont State College, where she was a professor for many years and collected folklore from among her student and community informants. She was a leader in The West Virginia Folklore Society for many years, serving among other roles as the originator and editor of the society's official publication, *The West Virginia Folklore Journal*. This first book is especially rich in the superstitions of the people.

Musick, Ruth Ann, ed., *The Telltale Lilac Bush*, Lexington: University Press of Kentucky.

One hundred ghost tales collected in the hills of West Virginia are contained in this volume. Mostly, from north central West Virginia, these tales represent the supernatural motif in oral prose.

Musick, Ruth Ann, ed., *The Green Hills of Magic, West Virginia Folk Tales from Europe*, Lexington: University Press of Kentucky.

This is the most complete study available of a gathering of tales collected from the numerous immigrants of western and southern Europe who during the early 1900's sought employment in the great coal fields of northern West Virginia. Dr. Musick's main folk literature contribution has been in the area of oral prose, such as the folk-tale, of which this edition deals mainly with the strange preternatural tales of these immigrant cultures.

Musick, Ruth Ann, ed., *Coffin Hollow and Other Ghost Tales*, Lexington: University Press of Kentucky.

This collection contains ninety-six ghost tales set in coal mines and remote farm cabins, in hidden hollows, and on mountain tops in West Virginia. Some of the stories hark back to the days when the mountains and valleys of the state were first settled and Indians still threatened; many are set in slave times and reflect the Civil War bitterness of a divided state. But, most are told as the experiences of the immediate family or the friends of the informants themselves, and one story is as recent as the war in Vietnam.

Price, William B., ed., *Tales and Lore of the Mountaineers*, Salem, West Virginia: Quest Publishing Company.

Oral literary typings as pronounced as legends of Indians, tales of haunted houses, stories of the early Baltimore and Ohio Railroad, and superstitions concerning old inns and taverns are among this collection of Mr. Price, a native West Virginian, school teacher, and Salem College Professor.

Preble, John W., ed., *Land of Canaan: Plain Tales From the Mountains of West Virginia*, Parsons, West Virginia: McClain.

This is a collection of tales from the mountains that run the gamut from searching for a snake bite cure to stilling tomato juice.

Written literature also consists of poetry and prose, but, unlike its oral relative, written literature is usually created by one person who individually gives permanence and preservation to his creation by transmitting his imaginative thoughts into a written form.

West Virginia written literature, as any regional literature, is basically reflective of the people and the influences affecting them, such as the physical environment, personal and collective psychological trends, and sociological encounters—to mention just a few. Also, similar to other regional writings, the creative written literature of the hills is inspired and often controlled by the powerful oral traditions demonstrative in folklore, that have dominated the mountain atmosphere for centuries. Thus, from mother oral literature has been born written offsprings, so identically characteristic to the parent that the same themes, emotionally humanistic tones, domestic and work settings, Appalachian physical imagery, and narrative expressions are to be found; in both the fiction structure where imaginative situations are based on reality and the nonfiction, based on true situations.

CATEGORIES AND CHARACTERISTICS OF WRITTEN LITERATURE

In addition to the major categories of poetry and prose, existent in either the fiction or nonfiction structure, written literature can also be divided into genres of poetry, drama, novel, and short story, each of which is related to the other through common representatives of mountain character.

A variety of traits typify this mountain character from which both poetry and prose plot lines develop:

Appalachian characteristics as reflected in the written literature are a smorgasbord of paradox, comparison, and contrast—as multifaceted as the numerous nationalities who have settled in this region, each bringing its own wealth of folklore and culture; the temperate climate and seasons; and the rolling green topography ever changing and mysterious. In this written literature, then, a variety of these settings can be mirrored with two distinct settings overshadowing the others: the hill Appalachian and the valley Appalachian.

The hill Appalachians, akin to the Anglo-Celtic and Germanic mountaineers who first settled the land, are representative of the characters in the poetry of Louise McNeill's *Gauley Mountain* who molded themselves to the land either for individual farming of crops, raising of livestock, and gathering of orchards, or for collective living in small communities nestled in the hills. Here lived the men who worked the coal mines and were housed in the coal camps as discussed in *Coal Camp Girl* by Lois Lenski, an adolescent children's novel that gives deep insight into the mores of life in a coal community of today. Also, this coal-hill life is displayed in Ray House's *A Handful of Stars.*

Then, there is the valley Appalachian—the newer mountaineer who lives in the small metropolises, such as Charleston, Clarksburg, Fairmont, Morgantown, and Wheeling. Many of these people have ancestors who had lived and worked in the coal camps and towns; many of them still labor in the mines, in the lumber yards, and on the railroads. But, many of these newer mountaineers have "moved into town," the county seats, some of which were once just hill communities themselves. A variety of these people manage labor in the small industries that outline the towns and are central exponents to the many natural resources in the hill above. Another variety of these valley people own the small businesses and groceries within the cities or represent the line of professions (doctors, lawyers, teachers) necessary to the hub of activity.

A lively selection of written literature portrays this movement of valley society, in small town West Virginia. B. Wees, an Elkins merchant who had a yen for preserving the past by holding on to the customs and ways of how a small town lived during the early 1900's, has collected his memories in a volume of poetry about downtown Elkins; the dress shops, dry good stores, groceries, and the churches and school, and of course, the stately little liberal arts school, Davis and Elkins College, which adds a poise to the community life. Davis Grubb's *Fool's Parade* takes the reader to downtown Moundsville during the stifling and wild depression era, while John P. Bishop reveals life in the Eastern Panhandle community of Charles Town, embraced by small farms and orchards, as seen through the eyes of a boy whose metamorphosis into manhood is dramatic and haunting.

The young acting and reacting to valley Appalachian life becomes a common theme in such works as Jack Welch's novel *Decision in Paris* and Betsy Byars' *Summer of the Swans.* However, Mr. Welch in his work leaves the world of the adolescent to portray a young college woman from a valley town who confronts through a trial of love, a testing ground for her strong religious convictions which is a dominant Appalachian trait.

Margaret McDowell also takes a deep look into the characteristics of the Appalachian college student. From her apartment house on College Avenue, Morgantown, she has had the opportunity to observe

124

at West Virginia University the young products from both the hills and valleys, displaying them in her first volume of poetry, *View From College Avenue.*

Valley Appalachian life is not just collected in the interior small towns and cities of the state, but holds a different facade in the small towns that line the Ohio River. In Stella Morgan's novel, *Again the River* and James Wright's collection of poetry, *Shall We Gather at the River,* the Ohio River and its influence upon the people is unfolded: the traffic, means of livelihood for industries that feed into the river channels; and the pollution from the river plants.

Mountain Heritage is displayed in several historical dramas about West Virginia: Julia Davis' *The Anvil,* the trial of John Brown; and *Honey in the Rock,* John Brown's raid on Harpers Ferry. Plus a touch of the more common but exciting life of the pioneer mountaineer and his kin has been disclosed in Billy Edd Wheeler's play, *Hatfields and McCoys,* and Clyde Ware's cinematic production of a Civil War pacifist in *No Drums, No Bugles.*

Amid these settings, also, a vast display of tones and themes emerge, further reflecting Appalachian values of traditionalism (a love for the past, heritage, the tried and proven); familism (the family is the central focus of life, clannish, and isolated); religion (emotional and fundamental, sincere and loving); individualism (often modest and unassuming but independent); love of home place (a deep love for the land and home place); sense of humor; neighborliness; personalism; modesty; loyalty to country and government but an inborn distrust for much politicking. These values control the plots and structural analyses of West Virginia's written literature as much as they once formulated the basis for the oral literature.

SELECTIONS OF WRITTEN LITERATURE

Under the structural format of fiction, West Virginia literature can be subdivided into various genres: poetry, short stories, novels, and drama. Examples of children and adolescent selections have also been added since their youthful attitudes equally represent the Appalachian atmosphere.

I have, however, deliberately omitted subdivisions of nonfiction because many of these examples are listed under other categories, such as history and sociology. A few exceptional selections, nevertheless, are worth noting:

Comstock, Jim, ed., The *West Virginia Hillbilly* newspaper, Richwood, West Virginia.

(This weekly newspaper is an excellent example of mountain journalism, which contains the news, events to come, attitudes, beliefs, features on special people in the state, humor, and anything else that would typify the Appalachian way of life.)

Comstock, Jim, *Best of Hillbilly* (compiled and edited by Otto Whittaker).

(This is a rich collection of the journalistic wit and wisdom from the writings of Jim Comstock that have appeared in his The *West Virginia Hillbilly* newspaper, which show the colorful and independent news reporter at his best.

Comstock, Jim, ed., *The West Virginia Heritage Encyclopedia* (50 vols.) Richwood, West Virginia: Jim Comstock, 1974.

(This series of books gives information on all branches of knowledge pertaining to West Virginia and its people, written in article form and categorized in alphabetical order. Many nonfiction writers are featured in the different volumes as are fiction writers. One interesting nonfiction writer is Mary Harris Jones who appears in Volume 25, "West Virginia Women." Affectionately labelled "Mother Jones" by the thousands of coal miners in West Virginia whose cause she supported at the turn of the century for better working conditions and higher wages, she wrote an autobiography and a set of personal essays entitled *Thoughts of Mother Jones*, in which she vividly describes the United Mine Workers' stoic struggle for leadership in the nation's coal fields, particularly southern West Virginia.)

Listed below is a selected bibliography, briefly annotated, of a variety of West Virginia written literature, categorized according to genre. This bibliography is in no way complete but, hopefully, is representative of the rich reservoir of written creation inspired by the mountain environment. References to an assortment of these examples have already been made in the previous discussion of the characteristics of Appalachian written literature.

Poetry

Dressler, Muriel, *Appalachia, My Land*, Morris Harvey College, Charleston, West Virginia: MHC Publication.

This is poetry from and about Appalachia. A visiting poet with the Arts in the Classroom Program, developed by the West Virginia

Arts and Humanities Council as an enrichment program for the schools of West Virginia, she has also done reading for professional organizations, publications in national magazines, and has been the recipient of West Virginia awards in poetry, specializing in Appalachian culture and heritage poetry.

McDowell, Margaret, *View From College Avenue*, available—Mountainlair Book Store, West Virginia University.

Margaret McDowell as a poet of the Appalachian valley, small town and city variety has presented in her volume of poetry a multi-faceted glimpse at one woman's reality in a West Virginia college town.

McDowell, Margaret, *Our Song, Too*, available—Mountainlair Book Store, West Virginia University.

In her second collection of poetry, Margaret McDowell captures the heritage, rhythm, and change of the people of Appalachia who she feels are still moving, growing and developing. Her poems contain many character sketches of the voices of people singing out their hill life and existence.

McNeill, Louise, *Gauley Mountain*, Parsons, West Virginia: McClain Printing Company.

Within this verse-history of Gauley and its people is silhouetted the black mountains, the river, and the pioneers who came to conquer both. Louise McNeill, whose family has lived in West Virginia since the 1700's, possesses immense poetic inspiration as proven by her technique in showing these settlers and their offspring, some of them around today. She is poet laureate of West Virginia.

McNeill, Louise, *Paradox Hill*, Morgantown, West Virginia: West Virginia University Library.

This is Louise McNeill's second volume that traces through ballad and lyric stanzas the life forces, struggles, thoughts, and emotions of the mountaineers both yesterday and today, reflecting their growth into tomorrow.

Plumley, William, ed., *Poems From the Hills*, Morris Harvey College, Charleston, West Virginia: MHC Publication.

This is the first anthology, basically of poetry and verse, in the Morris Harvey literary series. Also, a visiting poet with the Arts in the Classroom Program, William Plumley is the director of the Morris Harvey College Arts Festival.

Plumley, William and Barbara Yeager, eds., *From the Hills*, 1972, Morris Harvey College, Charleston, West Virginia.

From the Appalachian people has been gathered a collection of prose, verse, and graphics containing a forward and selections by Jesse Stuart. Other contributors to this volume include such poets as Muriel Dressler, Louise McNeill, and William Stafford. Another popular West Virginia poet listed is Peter D. Zivkovic, an English professor and poet/writer from Fairmont State College. He also serves as a visiting poet with the Arts in the Classroom Program. Over 150 poems have appeared in literary and national magazines, numerous of which have won West Virginia poetry awards.

Now *From the Hills* has changed its title to *The Wooden Tower*, edited by Lorena Anderson, Supervisor of Language Arts, West Virginia Department of Education; Marjorie Warner, Program Specialist, Language Arts, West Virginia Department of Education; and Barbara Yeager, Executive Editor, MHC Publications. The West Virginia Department of Education is in association with MHC Publications.

(It is still an anthology of Appalachian literature.)

Price, Walter Willard, *Sing, O Mountaineer!*

A collection of verse written by one of the passing generations of true mountaineers, the author was reared in Preston County and has lived in other West Virginia counties and in some other states.

Wheeler, Billy Edd, *Song of a Woods Colt.*

This young poet has been described as West Virginia's answer to New England's Robert Frost. This collection of his poems is intensely unique and honest, reflecting a passionate heart and sensitivity to his love for the mysteries of Appalachian nature.

Wright, James, *Shall We Gather at the River*, Middleton, Connecticut: Wesleyan University Press.

This selection of poetry presents the life of the valley Appalachian along the Ohio River of West Virginia and Ohio. Mr. Wright's poetry has earned him many honors in addition to a Fullbright Fellowship; he has been widely published in journals and magazines.

Davis, Julia, *The Anvil.*

This is a play about the trial of John Brown that took place in the old court house in Charles Town, written from notes said to have been thrown away by Porte Crayon (David Hunter Strother) after the article he had written from them had been rejected by *Harper's Monthly.* The play was given in the very courthouse as the author's own salute to the West Virginia Centennial. Julia Davis is the daughter of John W. Davis, former ambassador to England, and a native of Clarksburg.

Hunter, Kermit, *Honey in the Rock.*

This play is shown summerly at the Grandview State Park Outdoor Theatre, Beckley, West Virginia; it is a take-off on the historical Civil War event of John Brown's raid on Harpers Ferry.

Richardson, Howard and William Berney, *Dark of the Moon*, New York, Theatre Arts.

An excellent "folk fantasy drama that uses as its plot the version of the 'Barbara Allen' ballad in which Barbara marries a witch boy. It also makes use of other familiar folk songs."

Ware, Clyde, *No Drums, No Bugles.*

Clyde Ware, a West Virginia native who was born in West Union, presents his first cinematic production in *No Drums, No Bugles,* a story based on a West Virginia folk tale of an archetypal isolationistic who rejects his family life, comforts of home, and his community, to defend his beliefs about war and death. Instead of fighting on either side in the Civil War, he hides in a cave. The strong character, Ashby Gattrel, is played by actor Martin Sheen.

Ware, Clyde, *When the Line Goes Through.*

This is Clyde Ware's second cinematic production in which he takes a mountain situation, this time a family is isolated in an area that no longer has a railroad running through it, and actually does the filming in West Virginia. In this cinema he uses his home town of West Union. In the first production, *No Drums, No Bugles,* he uses areas of Doddridge County, the actual setting for the folk tale.

Wheeler, Billy Edd, *Hatfields and McCoys.*

A play based on the famous West Virginia family feud between the Hatfields and the McCoys, that plays every summer at the Grandview State Park Outdoor Theatre.

Short Stories and Short Narratives

Blackhurst, W. E., *Afterglow,* McClain Printing Company.

This is a collection of poems and short stories spun from philosophies, thoughts, and memories of the people and places this West Virginia lover has experienced.

Caudill, Harry, *Dark Hills to Westward: The Saga of Jennie Wylie.*

This is a fictionalized tale of a real-life heroine who lived among the Indians and pioneers of the area of Appalachia during the terrible times of "our first and bloodiest frontier."

Comstock, Jim, ed., *The West Virginia Heritage Encyclopedia,* Volume 24, Supplemental Series, Stories and Verse of West Virginia, Richwood, West Virginia: Jim Comstock.

Jim Comstock was so moved and intrigued with the work of Ella May Turner that he named this volume after her and gives in it examples of works from selected authors of West Virginia 1935. He has a sweeping introduction to the volume in which he gives a panorama view of each of the writers and when possible traces a linkage in theme, atmosphere, and attitude from one to the other.

Among his selected writers is Pearl Buck who, even though she was a West Virginian who wrote primarily about the Far East, wrote before her death a personal essay entitled, "My Mother's House" about her birthplace, especially for Mr. Comstock in the hopes that the writing would financially aid in the restoring of this West Virginia landmark. Thus, Mr. Comstock has edited a unique selection of West Virginia literature in this volume, mostly fiction but also some nonfiction, such as the above discussed essay. He has equally chosen many still obscure writers whose contributions are limited but rich. It is an anthology of "just a taste" of some West Virginia writers from 1935 to the present.

Pierson, Edna Church, *The Witch of Turner's Bald.*

"A man's death and other ominous incidents shrouds a young, mountain girl's life. The arrival of a minister to the mountain community starts events moving as he seeks to dispel the mystery of

The Witch of Turner's Bald. . . ." The author and her family live in Bridgeport, West Virginia.

Turner, Ella May, ed., *Stories and Verse of West Virginia.*

She was a gentle schoolteacher who has presented in this anthology some of the earliest examples of written literature in West Virginia from the Civil War up until 1935.

Novels

Bishop, John P., *Act of Darkness,* Avon Books.

Using the real setting of Charles Town, West Virginia, this novel presents the struggles of a young man growing up in an Appalachian town, and how he not only wants to escape the town but also the southern culture in the town. It is a book about the loss of innocence, a universal theme.

D'Ariano, Regina and Roy, *I'll Strike It Rich: A Novel of an Italian-American Family,* Vintage Press, New York.

Adventure, land, a better life, all were the dreams of immigrants to America. Timothy Salvati was one of these dreamers. Leaving Italy in 1884 and hoping to "strike it rich," he found himself eating out of garbage cans, living in cellars, building railroads, and battling strikes, swamps, and sadistic foremen. Then he met Elizabeth Armenth, an American farm girl. Settling in the coal mining town of Monongah, West Virginia, they try to make the American dream come true. A novel of hardship and suffering, but also of hope.

Grubb, Davis, *Fool's Parade,* New American Library.

This is a novel displaying valley Appalachian life during the 1930's. Later, Columbia Pictures put the novel in cinema version, starring James Stewart.

Hall, Granville Davisson, *The Daughter of the Elm.*

This is a work of fiction based upon events which occurred in the middle of the nineteenth century, using the settings of Marion and Harrison counties. The book has been of special interest to people in this section of the state.

Hannum, Alberta Pierson, *Look Back With Love, A Recollection of the Blue Ridge.*

This is a personalized novel of Appalachian life and reflections, by a productive West Virginia writer who has also written such works as *Thursday April, The Hills Step Lightly, Roseanna McCoy,* and *The Mountain People*—all representative of the hills and its people.

House, Ray, *A Handful of Stars.*

The author is a Fairmont man and was for many years a professor of English at Fairmont State College. This is his nostalgic recollection of an Appalachian boyhood/manhood, revealing both the spirit and the temperment of our mountain folk in the coal mines today.

Knowles, John, *A Vein of Riches.*

A Fairmont native and author of the best seller, *A Separate Peace,* Knowles uses the setting of Fairmont during the coal boom in the first quarter of this century to give a fictitious account of the lives of two actual coal baron families in the area.

Morgan, Stella, *Again the River.*

This author is another Fairmont writer whose setting for this novel is an imaginary scene called "Lowtown" which Mrs. Morgan locates on the West Virginia side of the Ohio River. Here she describes the trials of the valley Appalachians against and with the river.

Skidmore, Hubert, *River Rising.*

A novel with a central West Virginia setting, this is a fine piece of writing in the modern manner and will appeal to young people as well as to adults.

Smith, William Dale, *Multitude of Men,* New York: Simon and Schuster.

A young man returns to West Virginia after serving in the army and takes a job in a steel mill. There are conflicts between the company union and an outside labor group.

Welch, Jack, *Decision in Paris,* Firm Foundation Pub.

Professor Welch, an Appalachian Literature instructor at WVU, is a young creative writer. In this moving novel he depicts Appalachian character in which a young girl is torn between a strong Christian faith and her love for a boy who is indifferent to that which is most vital to her.

Blackhurst, Warren E., *Of Men and a Mighty Mountain,* Parsons, West Virginia: McClain Printing.

This is a description of one of the greatest lumber operations in the eastern United States on Cheat Mountain.

Blackhurst, Warren E., *Riders of the Flood,* Parsons, West Virginia: McClain Printing.

This is a story of driving logs down the Greenbrier River during the period of 1884-1900.

Blackhurst, Warren E., *Sawdust in Your Eyes,* Parsons, West Virginia: McClain Printing.

This is an account of the opening of the Appalachian forests for lumbering and about a town full of interesting people.

Byars, Betsy, *Summer of the Swans,* The Viking Press.

An adolescent children's book (grades seven up), this is an example of Betsy Byars' style which is about young people at odds with themselves and the world. Here, amid a West Virginia setting, of a small city in the valley, is the warm, humorous, poignant story of a difficult fourteenth summer for Sara. As a distinguished author of juvenile literature, Mrs. Byars received the Newberry Medal Award in 1971 for this book.

Mrs. Byars and her family live in Morgantown, West Virginia, where her husband is a professor of engineering at WVU.

Davis, Julia, *Ride With The Eagle; A Valley and a Song;* and *Mount Up.*

These books are essentially written for older boys and girls, capitalizing on Appalachian atmosphere and feelings. The first title is a story about a river for young people. Last on the list is her latest book for young people, *Mount Up,* taken from a true story of the Civil War that appeared in the journal of her grandfather's experiences as a Confederate cavalry officer. This is the same author who wrote the play, *The Anvil.*

Lenski, Lois, *Coal Camp Girl.*

One of the American Regional Series, this fine book for children is a picture of life in a "coal camp" in southern West Virginia. Even illustrated by the author, it is a Newberry Medal winner.

Oakley, Helen, *Freedom's Daughter,* New York: Norton.

A high spirited girl begs her father to take her to the Wheeling convention, where she argues for the creation of a new state, West Virginia.

O'Dell, Scott, *Journey to Jericho,* Boston: Houghton.

This is a story of a family reunion, which describes vividly the ever present anxiety hanging over a mining community in West Virginia.

Smith, Agnes, *An Edge of the Forest,* New York: The Viking Press.

Agnes Smith is a Fairmont writer who has pieced together a fantasy using animal personification, telling children what can be found at the edge of the forest. The oldness and enchantment of the Appalachian topography and animal life are typified.

West, Jerry, Bill Libby, *Mr. Clutch: The Jerry West Story.*

A juvenile book plus enjoyed by adults, this writing portrays the pleasure, glory, and sadness which makes basketball what it is today. Jerry West was one of the most exciting players on the court. Here, in a warm, personal style, he tells his own story. Not only does he delve into his entrance in the world of pros, but he lends insight into the life of a star off the courts.

Thus, from these hills has been produced and will continue to be produced a rich and varied display of literature, both oral and written. It is my hope that this article has revealed some of this literary richness to the reader. Several scholars first opened my eyes to our mountainous literary wealth, and it is to their inspiration and teaching that I dedicate the contents of this paper:

Dr. Ruth Ann Musick, eminent folk literature scholar and folklorist; Professor Jack Welch, Appalachian literature scholar and writer; Dr. Patrick Gainer, West Virginia's finest folklorist.

An unpublished paper, entitled "A Folklore Model: An Oral and Dramatics Approach for the Teaching of Literature," is available to educators by writing the author: Judy Prozzillo Byers, 804 Coleman Avenue, Fairmont, West Virginia 26554.

Music

PATRICK W. GAINER, professor emeritus of English at West Virginia University, has a long and distinguished career in preserving the folk traditions of West Virginia. He has recorded the songs, stories, fiddle tunes and other oral traditions which are a part of the folk culture of West Virginia and is an accomplished singer in the old styles.

Born in Parkersburg and raised on a farm in Gilmer County, Dr. Gainer attended.Glenville State College and received his AB and MA degrees from West Virginia University. He did graduate work at the University of Chicago and at St. Louis University, where he received his PhD degree. During the fourteen years he was a member of the English Department of St. Louis University, he returned to West Virginia each summer to continue his work of collecting folklore.

Dr. Gainer served in the U.S.O. during World War II as director of training in New York and as director in Brazil and in the South Atlantic. He came home to West Virginia, joining the West Virginia University faculty in 1946, where he remained until his retirement in 1972.

In order to make people aware of our folk culture, Dr. Gainer organized the West Virginia State Folk Festival at Glenville in 1950 and directed it for ten years. He also organized and directed folk festivals at Logan and Beckley.

The State of West Virginia awarded Dr. Gainer the Order of the Thirty-fifth Star during the 1963 centennial year for his work in preserving our folk culture. He compiled and edited *The West Virginia Centennial Book of 100 Songs*. His record album, ''Folksongs of the Allegheny Mountains,'' is widely known.

134

CONTENTS

TRADITIONAL MUSIC IN THE HOME OF THE
WEST VIRGINIA MOUNTAINEER

An important part of our cultural heritage which has come down to us through the oral tradition of many generations -- in some cases for centuries -- is the folk music preserved mostly through the traditions of the home. This consists largely of all kinds of song, but also of music played on such instruments as the rebec, fiddle, banjo, guitar, zither, parlor organ, harmonica, and certain other instruments not common -- such as the dulcimer (now sometimes called the "hammered dulcimer.")

The songs that have been preserved in oral tradition for at least several generations are called "folk songs." They are called folk songs because they belong to the people and not to any one individual. One cannot compose a folk song. Many composers have written imitations of folk songs, but these imitations cannot correctly be called folk songs. One cannot obtain a copyright for a real folk song, for it belongs to all of the people. Today there are many pseudo-folk songs being sung and many of them are very popular, but they are only imitations of real folk songs.

Many people think that folk songs are always sung to the accompaniment of the guitar or other string instrument. However, the folk songs that have been preserved in the oral tradition of the home were almost never sung to any accompaniment. This has always been true of folk songs in any part of the world. There are two good reasons why this is true: (1) The songs are largely cast in ancient modal structures which are very difficult to accompany with an instrument such as a guitar; (2) A greater reason why the songs were sung without accompaniment is that there were very few instruments. If people would have to use an instrument to accompany the singing, there would have been very little singing in the home.

Singing was part of the daily lives of the people, and they sang as they went about their work. Mother and grandmother sang as they worked at the spinning wheel or loom or as they went about the many chores of the household. Father and grandfather sang as they fed the stock, sharpened an axe, or as they sat before the fireplace. They sang not to entertain anyone but because it made them feel good to sing. Sometimes on the long winter evenings the children were entertained by songs and stories told by parents and grandparents.

There were songs to express all kinds of feelings and sentiments. There were old ballads that told stories of knights and ladies, of love and adventure, thus enabling the singer to escape for the moment to another land far from his own environment. There were ballads that told how persons were motivated by evil emotions and driven to a tragic end by wrong doing. There were songs that expressed religious feeling or told stories from the Bible. There were funny songs that brought a good laugh to the singer and the listeners. There were songs to amuse the children especially at those fireside family gatherings on long winter evenings. Even the lullaby which the mother sang to her baby was probably a folk song which she had learned from her mother.

These songs that were sung in the home and the stories that were told were the literature of the people. The songs were their poetry, and the tales were their prose literature handed down by word of mouth from one generation to another and "touched up" by the imagination of each story teller. This is an important part of our cultural heritage which tends to become lost in our time. There is no longer the family circle in which every member of the family participated. The television set is now the center of attention, and we have for the most part become watchers and listeners instead of participants.

At this point I wish to bring to your attention the false conception which many people have about West Virginians, especially about the people who live in the hills and mountains of our state. Many people who live in other parts of our country look upon the people of West Virginia as "Hillbillies." "Hillbilly" is a derogatory term, the original of which is billygoat. To those of us who have grown up in the hills, the term is utterly contemptuous. We are proud to be called "Mountaineers," just as were our ancestors who founded the state and chose as our motto: "Mountaineers always free."

I was once told by a person from a middle-western state that when he thought of West Virginia he thought of "depression, loneliness, and poverty." I explained that my own boyhood was spent on a farm near a little village in the foothills of the West Virginia mountains. In this little village the center of community activity was the school. Each month of the year a night at the school was called "Literary Night." People came from miles around to listen and participate as the school children and adults of the entire community took part in debates, readings, dramas, recitations and poetry, and story telling.

Each year the "Singing Master" came to the community and taught a singing school for ten days or two weeks, teaching young and old to read music by the shape-note method, so that everyone in the community learned to read music. After the singing school was concluded we met once a week to sing in excellent harmony. Once a week people came to our home to sing. The community had a brass band with a band wagon in which the band traveled to other communities. On County Fair days the band joined with the bands of other communities to form an all-county band. The little village had a good hotel, two good general stores, a hardware store, and two blacksmith shops. There were box suppers and pie socials where food was sold by auction, and the money was used to buy books for the library at the school. When there was work to be done, such as bean stringing, apple peeling, corn husking, threshing, or molasses boiling, people gathered in to help with the work, and after work was done there was a play-party.

It is true that we did not have much cash money, but we didn't need it, for most of our household needs were obtained at the store by bartering eggs, butter, chickens, and other farm commodities. There was no such thing as purchasing milk, bread, or meat, and even sweetening was often supplied by home-grown sorghum.

There was a time, not many years ago, when singing could be heard in the home at almost any time of the day. For many years I have made an effort to preserve this part of our heritage by writing down or recording with a tape recorder the songs which the people sang to me. Much of the material I wrote down long before tape recorders were in use, and I was able to write down both words and tunes. The question is often asked me, "How did you find these people?" For the most part I have depended on clues given me by many people, most of whom have been my students. Following one of these clues one day in Webster County, I walked up a hollow, and as I approached a beautiful large log house I heard the voice of a woman singing an old lover's lament:

LOVER'S LAMENT

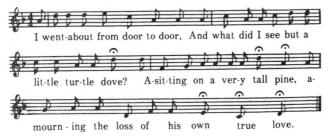

I went-about from door to door, And what did I see but a lit-tle tur-tle dove? A-sit-ting on a ver-y tall pine, a-mourn-ing the loss of his own true love.

-2-
Oh, fare you well, my own true love,
For I must leave you for a while,
And never more will I return
Till I have gone ten thousand miles.

-3-
Oh who will shoe your bonny feet,
And who will glove your little hands,
And who will kiss your ruby lips,
When I am gone to a foreign land?

-4-
My father will shoe my bonny feet,
My mother will glove my little hands,
And you may kiss these ruby lips
When you return from the foreign land.

138

The lady was alone in the house, not singing to anyone, but just singing because she felt like it. It made her feel good. The song was a very old one, a lament of the lover who must leave the girl he loves.

An old-world ballad that was brought to America long ago by our ancestors and preserved as a part of our heritage of song tells a story of love and adventure. It take us away from our environment to a foreign land of knights and ladies. It is called "Lord Bateman." Note that the first stanza is repeated exactly for each succeeding stanza. The words are important, for they tell a good story. Since there was never any instrumental accompaniment, the words were always distinct in traditional singing.

LORD BATEMAN

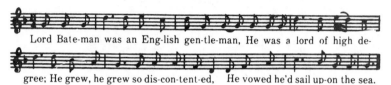

Lord Bate-man was an Eng-lish gen-tle-man, He was a lord of high de-gree; He grew, he grew so dis-con-tent-ed, He vowed he'd sail up-on the sea.

-2-
Oh, he sailed east, and he sailed west,
He sailed across the northern sea,
Until he came to a Turkish country,
Where he was put in slavery.

-3-
The Turkish king had a lovely daughter,
Oh, she was of a high degree,
She stole the keys from her father's dwelling,
And out of prison set him free.

-4-
"Let's make a vow unto each other,
Let's make it seven long years to stand,
If you'll not marry another woman,
I'll never marry another man."

-5-
Oh, seven long years had passed and gone,
Seven long years and almost three,
She gathered up all her fine clothing,
And vowed Lord Bateman she go see.

-6-
Oh, she sailed east, and she sailed west,
Until she came to the English shore,
And there she went to see Lord Bateman,
She'd vowed she'd love forevermore.

139

"Oh, is this Lord Bateman's hall,
And is he in there all alone?"
"Oh, no, oh no," cried the proud porter,
"Today a bride he's just brought home."

-8-

"Remind him of the Turkish prison,
Remind him of the raging sea,
Remind him of the Turkish lady,
Who out of prison set me free."

-9-

"There is a lady at your gate,
And she is of a high degree,
She wears a ring on her left forefinger,
And on the others she wears three."

-10-

Lord Bateman rose up from his table,
And broke it into pieces three,
Saying, "I'll give my love to the Turkish lady
Who out of prison set me free."

-11-

"Oh, Lady, take back home your daughter,
For she is none the worse by me,
For I will marry the Turkish lady
Who out of prison set me free."

Note that the tune of "Lord Bateman" does not end on "do" of the scale but on "re". There is a simple explanation. Most of the old-world songs which we have found in West Virginia still retain the ancient character of their music, a system which dates back before the middle ages. Instead of being in our modern scale, in which the half-steps occur between the third and fourth and the seventh and eighth notes of the scale, this song uses the Dorian mode, with the half-steps between the second and third and the sixth and seventh notes. Thus it does not end on "do" but on "re". It is remarkable that more than eighty percent of the old-world songs surviving in our West Virginia traditions retain their ancient modal structures. It is remarkable too that the words have not been changed significantly through centuries of oral tradition.

Chiefly because radio and television have practically destroyed our oral traditions, it is now difficult to find anyone singing the old ballads in the home. In rare instances one may find some elderly person who can sing some of the ancient old-world ballads if the story is suggested. Not long ago I was in Pocahontas County, where I met an elderly lady who sang several of these old ballads. I was astonished when she said, "Here's one I haven't sung for a long time; it's called "In Scotland Town Where I Was Born." When she began to

140

sing I realized that she was singing an old ballad centuries old in tradition, going back even to the thirteenth century. The only collector who had ever found this ballad surviving in the whole of the United States was Phillips Barry, who found it in Maine.

Here is the way she sang the old ballad of *Hind Horn*:

HIND HORN

In Scot-land town where I was born, A la-dy gave to me a ring. And if this ring stays bright and fair, You'll know that your true love is true, my dear. But if this ring grows old and worn, You'll know that your true love is with some other one.

-2-
Well, he went on board, and away sailed he,
He sailed till he came to some foreign country.
He looked at his ring, and his ring was worn,
He knew that his true love was with some other one.

-3-
So he went on board, and back sailed he,
He sailed and he sailed to his own country.
One morning as he was a-riding along,
He met with a poor old beggar man.

-4-
"Old man, old man, old man, I say,
What news have you got for me today?"
"Sad news, sad news to you I say,
Tomorrow is your true love's wedding day."

-5-
"So you can take my riding steed,
And the beggar's rig I will put on."
"Well, the riding steed hain't fit for me,
And the beggar's rig hain't fit for thee."

141

-6-

Well, whether it be right or whether it be wrong,
The beggar's rig he did put on.
So he begged from the rich, he begged from the poor,
He begged from the highest to the lowest of 'em all.

-7-

So he went on at an old man's rate,
Till he came to the steps of yonder's gate.
When the bride came trippling down the stair,
With rings on her fingers and gold in her hair.

-8-

And a glass of wine to hold in her hand,
To give to the poor old beggar man,
He took the glass and drank the wine,
And in that glass he placed this ring.

-9-

"O where did you get it, from sea or land,
Or did you get it from a drownded man's hand?"
"Neither did I get it from sea or land,
Nor neither did I steal it from a drownded man's hand."

-10-

"You gave it to me on our courting day,
I'll give it back to you on your wedding day."
Well, off of her fingers the rings she put,
Off of her hair the gold did fall.

-11-

"I'll follow my true-love wherever he may go,
If I have to beg my food from door to door."
Between the kitchen and the hall,
The beggar's rig he did let fall.

-12-

His gold a-showing out more fairer than them all,
He was the fairest of the young men in that hall.
"I'll follow my true-love wherever he may go,
If I have to beg my food from door to door."

Sometimes the songs tell stories of tragedies, and the story lives because it teaches a good lesson. One of the most popular of all the old-world tragic ballads is "Barbara Allen." Three hundred years ago Samuel Pepys wrote a note in his diary that he had that day heard a woman sing the little Scotch song of Barbara Allen. There are many tunes to which the ballad is sung, but here is probably the oldest tune in existence.

142

BARBARA ALLEN

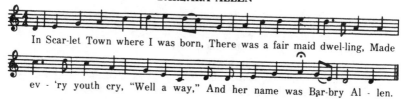

In Scar-let Town where I was born, There was a fair maid dwel-ling, Made ev - 'ry youth cry, "Well a way," And her name was Bar-bry Al - len.

-2-
'Twas early in the month of May,
When the green buds were a-swellin',
Young Johnny Green on his death-bed lay
For the love of Barbry Allen.

-3-
He sent his servant to the town
Where his love was a-dwellin'
Saying, "Follow me to my master dear,
If your name be Barbry Allen."

-4-
So slowly, slowly she got up,
And slowly she went nigh him,
But all she said when she got there,
"Young man, I think you're dyin'."

-5-
"O don't you remember the other night,
When you were at the tavern?
You drank a health to the ladies round,
But slighted Barbry Allen."

-6-
"O yes, I remember the other night,
When I was at the tavern,
I drank a health to the ladies round,
But gave my love to Barbry Allen."

-7-
As she was walking through the town,
She heard the death bell tollin'
And ev'ry toll it seemed to say,
"Hard-hearted Barbry Allen."

-8-
"O Mother, O Mother, go make my bed,
Go make it soft and narrow,
Young Johnny Green died for me today,
And I'll die for him tomorrow."

-9-
O she was buried in the old churchyard.
And he was buried a-nigh her,
And out of her grave grew a red, red rose,
And out of his a green briar.

143

And they grew till they reached to the top of the church,
And they couldn't grow any higher;
And there they met in a true-lover's knot,
The red rose and the green briar.

Sometimes the songs are funny, for there was often the need for a good laugh. Here is one that came from Scotland long ago that tells of a man and wife who are so stubborn that they will suffer all kinds of inconveniences because of their stubbornness. It is called "Get Up and Bar the Door."

GET UP AND BAR THE DOOR

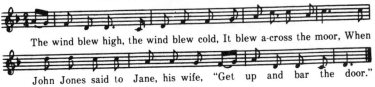

The wind blew high, the wind blew cold, It blew a-cross the moor, When John Jones said to Jane, his wife, "Get up and bar the door."

-2-
"Oh, I have worked all day," said she,
"I've washed and scrubbed the floor,
You lazy man, get up, I say,
Get up and bar the door."

-3-
"Oh, I have worked so hard," said he,
"I know I can't do more;
So come, my own, my dearest wife,
Get up and bar the door."

-4-
Then they agreed between the two,
A solemn oath they swore,
That the one who spoke the very first word
Would have to bar the door.

-5-
The wind blew east, the wind blew west,
It blew all over the floor,
But neither one would say a word
For barrin' of the door.

-6-
Three robbers came along that way,
They came across the moor;
They saw a light and walked right in,
Right in through the open door.

-7-
"Oh, is the owner of this house
A rich man or a poor?"
But neither one would say a word
For barrin' of the door.

-8-
They ate the bread, they drank the ale,
Then said, "Come, give us more."
But neither one would say a word
For barrin' of the door.

-9-
"Let's pull the old man's beard," said one,
"Let's beat him till he's sore,"
But still the old man wouldn't speak
For barrin' of the door.

-10-
"I'll kiss his pretty wife," said one,
"Oh, her I could adore."
And then the old man shook his fist
And gave a mighty roar.

-11-
"Oh, you'll not kiss my wife," said he,
"I'll throw you on the floor."
Said she, "Now, John, you've spoken first,
So get up and bar the door."

Some of the songs are religious in character. Some of the old-world ballads tell stories that are biblical, such as the ballad of "The Rich Man and Lazarus." Some of them deal with biblical characters, but are not in fact biblical stories. Such is the ballad which tells the story of the miracle of the cherry tree. It is not in the Gospel, but it is a beautiful story.

THE CHERRY TREE

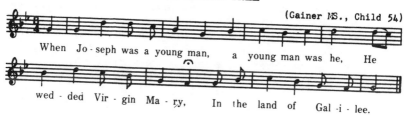

(Gainer MS., Child 54)

When Jo-seph was a young man, a young man was he, He wed-ded Vir-gin Ma-ry, In the land of Gal-i-lee.

-2-
When Joseph and Mary were walking one day,
They walked through an orchard where was cherries to behold.

-3-
Said Mary to Joseph, so meek and so mild,
"Please gather me some cherries, for I am with child."

-4-
Then Joseph flew in anger, in anger he flew,
"Let the father of that baby gather cherries for you."

145

Then the cherry tree bowed down, low down to the ground,
And Mary gathered cherries while Joseph stood around.

Then Joseph took Mary all on his right knee,
"Pray tell me, little baby, when your birthday will be?"

"On the fifth day of January my birthday will be,
When high in the heavens my star you will see."

The fifth day of January is the Eve of the Epiphany, which used to be called "Old Christmas," and which is still celebrated by some churches as the Nativity.

There were many religious songs that first appeared in hymn books. Many of the older people would hear them in church but could not read them. Thus many of these old hymns passed into oral tradition, were passed on from one singer to another, and became real folk songs. Such was true of the old hymn "Amazing Grace."

In the early days of our mountain settlement, even before churches were built, people often met in a clearing to have religious meetings. Since they had no songbooks, they learned to sing hymns by a method which was called "lining out." The itinerant preacher would often bring with him a little book of words and hymns, with the indication of the metrical pattern of the lines of the hymns. These indications of the metrical pattern are still printed in your hymn books, especially for some of the old songs. L.M. meant long meter; S.M. meant short meter; and C.M. meant common meter. The leader would select a tune that would fit the metrical pattern, and would then have the people repeat after him each line of the hymn as he sang it.

Around the year 1800 a new system of writing music was devised in New York, called the "shape-note" method. Each note of the scale was shaped so that one could easily know just which note of the scale it was by the shape of the note. Harrisonburg, Virginia, became the center for this kind of singing, and the first books were published there.

Shortly after the Civil War this method of singing spread over the Allegheny Mountains into West Virginia and through the South. A man who could teach this method of reading music, whom we called "the singing master," came into the community each year and taught a "subscription school" for ten days or two weeks, to which the people came for miles around to learn to read music and to sing hymns. Thus almost everyone in the community, young and old, learned to read music. After the singing master went on to another community, we had singing once a week in the little church. It was the usual thing for people to gather at our home once a week, where we sang and had a good social evening. Never did we use any accompaniment for this singing, and consequently the tonal quality and diction were much better and clearer than is true of the present-day singing called "Gospel Singing," where almost invariably a piano or some string instrument covers up the voices.

Sometimes a song is very dear to my memory because of the circumstances in which I first heard it. Someone said to me, "Why don't you go to see Uncle Frank Kennedy? He used to sing a lot, and he might sing for you." It was twilight time when I arrived at his house and found him sitting outside alone. I sat down with him and told him how I was trying to write down the old songs so that they would not be lost. He agreed with me that the young people were not learning the old songs. I asked him to sing "A Few More Months," the song which I had been told was his favorite. He said, "Well, I can't sing the way I used to, but I'd like for you to hear the song. He then sang softly there in the twilight:

A FEW MORE MONTHS

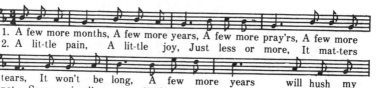

1. A few more months, A few more years, A few more pray'rs, A few more
2. A lit-tle pain, A lit-tle joy, Just less or more, It mat-ters

tears, It won't be long, A few more years will hush my
not, Some ming-ling yet With earth's al - loy, And then for-

song, My earth-ly song, When they shall lay me in the val-ley.
got, Oh, soon for-got, When they shall lay me in the val-ley.

Sometimes a singer will say, "Now here's a song which was made up about some people I knew Here's one about a young man who went to call on a girl and she gave him poison. These people lived over the mountain. The young man's name was John Randal." The old man then sang the ancient ballad which came from Scotland long ago, "Lord Randal."

Of course I did not tell him that the ballad could not have been made up about the poisoning of the John Randal who lived over the mountain, for I was the one who came to learn from him. This adaptation of an old-world ballad to an incident which took place in America is unusual, but it does sometimes occur. Local names of people and places will sometimes take the place of the old-world names.

The old gentleman's name for the song is "Johnny Randal."

147

JOHNNY RANDAL
[Lord Randal]

(Gainer MS., Child 12)

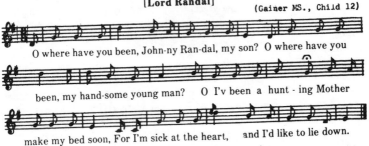

O where have you been, John-ny Ran-dal, my son? O where have you
been, my hand-some young man?   O I'v been a hunt - ing Mother
make my bed soon, For I'm sick at the heart, and I'd like to lie down.

-2-
Where got you your dinner, Johnny Randal, my son?
Where got you your dinner, my handsome young man?
O I got it at my true-love's, Mother make my bed soon,
For I'm sick at the heart, and I'd like to lie down.

-3-
What did you have for your dinner, Johnny Randal, my son?
What did you have for your dinner, my handsome young man?
Fried eels in fresh butter, Mother, make by bed soon,
For I'm sick at the heart, and I'd like to lie down.

-4-
O I fear you are poisoned, Johnny Randal, my son,
O I fear you are poisoned, my handsome young man.
O yes, I am poisoned, Mother make my bed soon,
For I'm sick at the heart, and I'd like to lie down.

-5-
What will you leave to your true-love, Johnny Randal, my son?
What will you leave to your true-love, my handsome young man?
A rope for to hang her, Mother, make my bed soon,
For I'm sick at the heart, and I'd like to lie down.

An old lady told me a story of witchcraft and sang a song which she said was sung by a girl who was put under the spell of a witch. She said that one day Mary Fisher and her mother were in the front room of their house, when Mrs. Fisher saw the old witch woman coming up the path through the meadow. "Mary," said Mrs. Fisher, "There comes that old witch. Now don't let her pick up anything and take it away from here, for she can put a spell on us.'" When the old woman came to the door, Mrs. Fisher insulted her and told her she wasn't wanted in their house. The old woman went down by the garden, and as she passed a lettuce bed which Mary had planted, she picked a leaf, turned around and waved it at them, and left. Mary immediately became ill and nothing could be done for her.

Mary had an instrument that had three strings that she sometimes played, and there was one song that she sang most before she died, called "What Shall I Give to Thee?"

WHAT SHALL I GIVE TO THEE

(Gainer MS.)

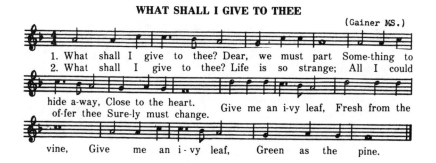

1. What shall I give to thee? Dear, we must part Some-thing to hide a-way, Close to the heart. Give me an i-vy leaf, Fresh from the vine, Give me an i-vy leaf, Green as the pine.

2. What shall I give to thee? Life is so strange; All I could of-fer thee Sure-ly must change.

There were many songs that were sung at the fireside when the family gathered on the long winter evenings. This was true until television came, and the family became watchers and listeners instead of participants. How well I remember those evenings when Great-Grandmother -- we called her "Granny" -- came to stay with us. She would get us in a half-circle and entertain us with wonderful stories and songs. She liked to hear us laugh, and she would puzzle us with problems, such as how old was the wife that Billy Boy was seeking. She would say, "Now, Children get your slates and work the problem, and the first one that gets it right will get an apple." Then she would sing "Billy Boy."

BILLY BOY

"O where have you been, Billy Boy, Billy Boy,
O where have you been, charming Billy?"
"O I've been to seek a wife, she's the joy of my live,
But she's a young thing and can't leave her mammy."

"O did she ask you in, Billy Boy, Billy Boy,
O did she ask you in, charming Billy?"
"O yes, she asked me in, she has a dimple in her chin,
But she's a young thing and can't leave her mammy."

"Can she bake a cherry pie, Billy Boy, Billy Boy,
Can she bake a cherry pie, charming Billy?"
"She can bake a cherry pie quick as a cat can wink its eye,
But she's a young thing and can't leave her mammy."

"How tall is she, Billy Boy, Billy Boy,
How tall is she, charming Billy?"
"She's as tall as a pine and straight as a pumpkin vine,
But she's a young thing and can't leave her mammy."

"How old is she, Billy Boy, Billy Boy,
How old is she, charming Billy?"
"Twice six, twice seven, twice twenty and eleven,
But she's a young thing and can't leave her mammy."

Of course, the next time Granny sang the song for us she would change the problem so that we would have to work it again.

Another funny song she liked to sing for us was about the girl who wanted to marry the soldier.

SOLDIER, WILL YOU MARRY ME?

(Gainer MS.)

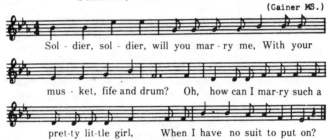

Sol - dier, sol - dier, will you mar - ry me, With your mus - ket, fife and drum? Oh, how can I mar-ry such a pret-ty lit-tle girl, When I have no suit to put on?

-2-

Away she ran to the tailor's shop
As fast as she could run,
She got a suit, a very fine suit,
And the soldier put it on.

-3-

Soldier, soldier, will you marry me,
With your musket, fife, and drum?
Oh, how can I marry such a pretty little girl,
When I have no shoes to put on?

-4-

Away she ran to the cobbler's shop,
As fast as she could run,
She got some shoes, some very fine shoes,
And the soldier put them on.

-5-

Soldier, soldier, will you marry me,
With your musket, fife, and drum?
Oh, how can I marry such a pretty little girl,
When I have no hat to put on?

-6-

Away she ran to the hatter's shop,
As fast as she could run,
She got a hat, a very fine hat,
And the soldier put it on.

150

Soldier, soldier, will you marry me,
With your musket, fife, and drum?
Oh, how can I marry such a pretty little girl,
When I have a sweet wife at home?

But I think the funniest song she ever sang was one about the farmer's wife and the devil. She would often preface this song by saying, "Maybe I oughtn't to sing this one to you, but I like to hear you laugh."

THE FARMER'S WIFE AND THE DEVIL
(Gainer MS., Child 278)

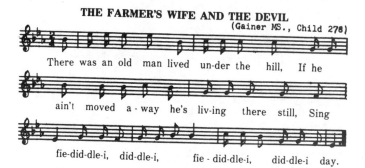

There was an old man lived un-der the hill, If he ain't moved a-way he's liv-ing there still, Sing fie-did-dle-i, did-dle-i, fie-did-dle-i, did-dle-i day.

-2-
Old Satan came to the man at the plow,
Said, "One of your family I'm goin' to have now."
Sing. . . . .

-3-
"O, it's not your son that I do crave,
But it's your old wife I'm goin' to have."
Sing . . . .

-4-
"O Satan, take her with all my heart,
I hope, by golly, you'll never part."
Sing. . . .

-5-
Old Satan took her upon his back,
He carried her away like an old miller's sack.
Sing. . . .

-6-
When he got her to the forks of the road,
Says he, "Old woman, You're an awful load."
Sing. . . .

-7-
When he got her to the gates of hell,
Says, "Stir up the fire, we'll scorch her well."
Sing. . . .

Ten little devils came rattling their chains,
She upped with her stick and knocked out their brains
Sing. . . .

And the little devils began to squall,
"Take her home, pappy, she'll kill us all."
Sing. . . .

Old Satan took her back to the old man,
Says, "Keep her at home now if you can."
Sing. . . .

When she got home the old man was in bed,
She upped with her stick and knocked him in the head.
Sing. . . .

Said he, "Old woman, did you fare well?"
Said she, "Old man, I flattened all hell."
Sing. . . .

Now you can see just what these women can do,
They can whip men and devils too.
Sing. . . .

Now there's one advantage women have over men.
They can go to hell and come back again.
Sing. . . .

What I have tried to give you in these pages is a sample from the vast treasury of traditional song which I have collected over a period of many years from the people of West Virginia. Some of it is a part of my own heritage from my home in Gilmer County, West Virginia. My grandfather was an excellent singer, and from him I learned not only many beautiful old songs but a great treasury of traditional literature and knowledge.

I can never forget those summer days, those evenings—

That time of day as soft as gray wool yarn,
When mother insects trilled their lullabies,
We sat together on the porch.
Farmwise, my grandparents knew that a child's heart,
Like a barn, has lofts and crannies waiting to be stored.
And from the green fields of their upbringing,
They filled my heart with lilting Irish singing.
Now, on days when I am feeling tired and bored,
My joy returns on some old ballad winging.

BIBLIOGRAPHY

Folk Songs from the West Virginia Hills, by Dr. Patrick W. Gainer, Seneca Books, Grantsville, W. Va. 1975

Folk Songs of the South, edited by John Harrington Cox, 1925, contains words to many folk songs from West Virginia. There are only a few tunes printed in the back of the book.

The West Virginia Centennial Book of 100 Songs, edited by Patrick W. Gainer, 1963, contains almost all of the songs, with words and tunes, which have been used in these pages. Available at WVU Bookstore. The record album, *Patrick Gainer Sings Folk Songs of the Allegheny Mountains,* contains sixteen numbers. All of the songs referred to in this paper are on this album. The album is available at the Book Exchange, Willey Street, Morgantown, West Virginia 26505.

Family and Home

HARRY B. HEFLIN, retired as vice president for administration and finance of West Virginia University in 1974. Prior to that his distinguished career as a teacher and educational administrator included two periods as acting president of West Virginia University, the presidency of Glenville State College, two deanships at Marshall University and positions at Appalachian State University in North Carolina and in the public schools of West Virginia. He also served as a member of the Central Examining Board of the Naval Air Training Command Staff during World War II.

Born and raised in Pennsboro, he received his AB degree from Glenville State College, his MA degree from George Peabody College in Tennessee and his PhD degree from the University of Pittsburgh. He has also been awarded an LLD degree by Concord College.

His retirement plans interrupted by the need for his services as vice chancellor of the West Virginia Board of Regents, Dr. Heflin is finally able to make himself at home on his farm in Pleasants County.

With a deft touch reflecting the characteristic mountain brand of humor, and mediated through the warmth of his memorable personal experiences, Dr. Heflin provides appreciative understanding and genuine insight into the mountaineer's home life. Here comes alive the devoted role of the mother who made the home the hub and strength of the mountain way of life.

CONTENTS

THE HAND THAT ROCKED THE CRADLE

IT TAKES A HEAP O' LIVIN'

In this day of liberated women and of liberated men, there should be no surprise that we also have liberated children. In a recent poll to determine whether parents knew where their children were, pollsters were surprised to learn that the children were quite often found at home but did not know where their parents were. What has happened to the home that was built on mutual respect, affection for each other, love for their children, and dependence on each other?

It is obvious that a firm hand no longer rules many homes but many of our younger generation are not so aware that the firm hand they are missing is the one Mother used to wield when we were young. Her hand shone in planning almost everything but the outside work, and included meals, clothes, visits, parties, orders from the catalogue, and the million details required to keep a home going. It was the hand that soothed the hot brow of the small child or adult in time of illness, that eased every bump and bruise; or that paddled the small behind when it was necessary to do so. For every trip to the woodshed with father, there were fifty smaller events with Mother.

In the home of 75 years ago, and especially the one with a rural setting, you can remember Mother in a thousand different ways. She was seldom either the first one up of a morning or the last one to bed of an evening, but she was always busy and for children, husband or visitor, she was always home. Her interests were not confined to the house, but involved the entire family enterprise. The days were long, much of the work heavy, the decisions were many, the routines pretty well established and Mother carried her full share of the partnership.

The home that Mother ruled was filled with children and each one was received with joy and love because in those days a large family was an asset. A new mouth to feed soon meant two hands to work and two feet to run errands. As strange as it may seem to us in a day when it is illegal to allow a husky fifteen-year-old to work where anything is moving, and one who is being educated for the professions has no time to seek employment until he is 25 or 30 years old, there were plenty of chores that a six or eight year old could perform that might range from filling the woodbox or getting the cows, to watching the baby. Under those circumstances, maturity came early along with dependability and a feeling of pride in being needed.

A family of eight or ten children was not uncommon and a mother and husband seldom had to worry about being left alone while they were still in their 40's. During the present period, such a family is a cause for panic and expressions of pity by the neighbors. And with our changed order of values and a different way of life, this is understandable. A recent report indicated that it now costs approximately $40,000 to care for a child until after college graduation. With our own goals being so strongly motivated by cash and the possession of things, a large family may be a cause for horror, but when the worth was measured by the number of healthy children, an entirely different attitude prevailed. $40,000 would have represented the lifetime earnings of many a family 75 years ago if anyone had cared to count cash income, but so many things, including children, were unrelated to cash there was seldom such an accounting.

A search of literature found in the turn-of-the-century home gives no evidence that discussions on sex occupied a great deal of time, and sex education wasn't found even once in the school books of the day. On the contrary, if references to sex had been removed from an issue of a recent popular magazine there would have been very little left but the back cover. In that day, reference to the "pill" meant a dose of medicine for something that already "ailed" you and had no reference at all to liberation.

With all of our modern technology, we have never been able to invent a machine as versatile or efficient as Mother. There were so many different things to do and so often more than one thing must be done at the same time that she had to develop ways to get them done and as a result her equipment was designed to meet the need. It was no accident that the cradle had rockers rather than legs because as Mother moved the up-and-down churn with one hand and held a book with the other, she rocked the cradle with her foot. Babies never developed crossed eyes by watching TV all day, but they developed a good ear for harmony as they fell asleep while Mother sang, rocked, and worked. "What Mother sings to the cradle goes all the way to the grave." said Henry Ward Beecher. If we now have a generation of twitching babies, who could prove it isn't caused by listening to the average radio program or rock and roll records?

The eight-hour day and the 40-hour week are recent inventions. Anything less than a 14-hour day and an 84-hour week would have been considered a vacation by Mother and an example of laziness by the neighbors. Father might light the light at 5:00 a.m. and stir up the fire, but he only did it so Mother could get breakfast started. From 5:30 a.m. until 8:30 p.m. Mother was free to pursue her duties.

THE WAY TO A MAN'S HEART

Breakfast for a working family was no hurried affair and there were no vacant chairs at the table. Most of the raw food was produced at home but only Mother's educated hands could make it look as it did on the table. A plate of steaming biscuits, large as the top of a can that once held Rumford baking powder, baked from Larabee's Best Flour, so flakey and tender that they parted at a touch; a large plate of fried eggs and another of cured ham; a dish of red-eye gravy that was appropriate company for the biscuits; a dish of fried potatoes; and a pot of coffee made from Arbuckles coffee with a touch of coffee essence, and boiled to get out all the strength, was enough to make an entire family appreciate the one who produced it. She did not use ground coffee as we get it today, but ground it in a coffee grinder. The aroma was just wonderful and the coffee too.

At some time during the winter, every kitchen would have a crock on the back of the stove that contained starter for buckwheat cakes, and a stack of these with maple syrup, and country sausage could substitute for almost any menu. One Mother was asked how she ever got enough cakes baked for a large family of boys. Her response was that she started baking as soon as she got up and when she could no longer see over them, it was time for the meal to be served.

Few families worried about being hungry-- Mother saw to that. The bright sunny days of summer were used to fill a cellar and a pantry with food for the long dreary days of winter. By fall, the shelves were filled with jars of beans, beets, corn, apples, pumpkins, jellies, jams, kraut, relish, fruits, and assorted goodies. There were always a few family delicacies that were hunted diligently and prepared lovingly in small quantities. Most of these came from wild fruits that would make a horticulturist turn up his nose--until he had a chance to taste and smell the product. They were usually hard to find, hard to gather, and difficult to prepare. The little dewberry that crawled on the ground on thin and shaly soil had a flavor all its own when made into jelly; wild strawberries as large as the end of your little finger for jam; wild grapes hanging high in the top of a tree where the sun hit at just the right angle, for jelly, spice or butter; quince for a honey unlike anything else; little cling peaches as large as an english walnut to spice or make into peach honey; huckleberries as large as a drop of water that grew on vines that put you near the ground to pick and also near any visiting copperheads or rattlesnakes; all yielded to Mother's magic and made an impression on taste buds in gaping mouths that fifty years cannot erase. Some things were made in greater volume and with greater ease such as pickled beans, pickled corn, sauerkraut, and stuffed mangoes. Vinegar was made and also homemade soap. Many people had cows and had their milk, butter, and buttermilk. The buttermilk with the specks of butter floating on top was delicious. The butter was a picture - made that way by using the old molds of all kinds. It was a beautiful yellow color especially when the green grass came in the springtime. It was always a delight when wild onions didn't come with the green grass. In "early America" the family produced their own soap from large rendering kettles over the backyard fires. Herbs and spices were added to give the soap it's fragrance. Sometimes it was molded by hand and sometimes put in a pan and cut.

In our day of high cholesterol, allergies, concern for overweight, fast action, and prepared foods, we have added twenty years to our life span and subtracted thirty years of pleasure in being able to enjoy good food and the time and labor it took to prepare it. How would your friends react to a menu for an ordinary day that consisted of:

Breakfast

Oatmeal	Fried Mush
Hot Biscuits	Strawberry Jam
Cured Ham	Butter
Fried Eggs	Coffee
Red-Eye Gravy	Cream

Dinner (Lunch to you)

Home Made Bread	Gravy
Country Fried Steak	Mashed Potatoes
Green Beans or Fodder Beans	Roasting Ears
or Pickle Beans	New Beets
Apple Sauce	

Jelly and Butter
Apple Dumplings or Cobbler
Coffee or tea
Cream

Supper (Dinner to you)

Hot Biscuits	Honey
Liver and Onions	Butter
or Country Sausage	Cream
Pan Fried Potatoes	Mince Pie or Dried Apple Pie
Green Beans	
or Home Made Sauerkraut	

Coffee or Tea
or
Milk

Or for dessert it might be old fashioned custard with nutmeg on top, or pound cake baked in an old tin pan. Cookie jars were filled with sugar cookies, ginger molasses cookies or lemon amonia crackers, which have a very delicate flavor and improve in taste if left in a stone jar in the cellar.

I remember Grandma's kitchen. She used to concoct such delicious dishes-- no short cuts -- the aromas that came from that kitchen are too difficult to describe.

On holidays or special days, the women cooked everything they could think of and the results were usually worth the efforts. Each fall the threshing machine and it's crew would visit the small farms to separate oats and wheat from straw and chaff. A crew of ten or twelve men who worked from daylight until dark as fast as they could, could make more food disappear than you can imagine. The big pans of apple cobbler or dumplings would melt in your mouth. The women from two or three families would prepare these meals and the work took on almost a festive air as the day progressed.

ALL WORK AND NO PLAY

Forms of recreation for women of the day tended to be simple and in company with others rather than alone. In face, from the modern point of view, much of it was just an extension of their usual work. However, visitors came infrequently enough to make considerable work acceptable just to have them. Seldom did they spend more than an afternoon or an evening, especially in rural areas. Occasionally they would come for the entire week end.

After the Christmas season was past and the cold and snow kept everyone inside, the old quilt frames were usually brought out and set up in the living room where they could be found until March or April. Once a quilt was put in the frame each spare moment was usually spent with the needle and there was always an extra needle and thimble for from one to five visitors. Six women could sit around a quilt cozily and it was an ideal arrangement for spreading all the neighborhood gossip. Most of the women would have a sore thumb and finger before the winter was over from the push and pull of the needle. Usually a little sheep tallow could be found on the top shelf of the cupboard to grease the sore spot.

There was a quality of quilting for every woman ranging from a knotted comforter which required very little quilting, to the feather or compass which required the most intricate designs and smallest stitches. Every woman in the area was rated as to the kind of stitches she made and if a prized design was being used, certain people were not invited to quilt.

At intervals, an invitation was extended to selected guests to spend the day for a quilting. At Quilting Bees more than one quilt was worked on at a time. Progress was often measured by the number of times the side of the frame could be rolled but more often the type of design and size of stitch made it impossible to anticipate a finishing date. It was not unusual for one who was really particular, to pick out some of the stitches when company was gone if their work was not up to desired standards. There was, however, a real pride in having the other quilters admire the handiwork. Quilts were seldom sold as they were needed to keep the family warm, or for the better ones, used as bedspreads. Even in recent years, these could be bought for $10.00 or $12.00, but the present price is more likely to be $125 or $150.

162

Many were the designs, some carried down in each family, but others developed by some quilter with artistic ability and a desire to create. A few common designs were *Star, Lone Star, Nine Patch, Feather, Wedding Ring, Tree of Paradise,* and *Flower Garden,* and *Grandmothers* wonderful *Patch Work* with it's bright colors and varied squares -- it is sometimes called *Crazy Quilt.*

After the quilt was pieced by hand, the squares were sewed together, a batting of cotton or wool was placed between a lining and a top that had often been pieced of left-over scraps of cloth--a way of saving materials. Today, with the development of so many allergies, a dacron filler is often used. If there were allergies at that time, they were seldom recognized.

When girls in the family showed great interest in quilting, it was a pretty good sign that a hope chest was being filled and a marriage was soon to come.

Men usually found it advantageous to get out of the house when a quilting was in progress, especially when the weather was suitable for other work. Not many men considered themselves a conversational match for five or six women who could concentrate on quilting and talking without any interference in either act.

Cooking was also a form of recreation for women as well as a necessity and a new recipe had to be tried at once. As the summer progressed, basket dinners at church or at family reunions were a common event. If you have never attended one of these affairs, it is hard to describe the amount and variety of food to be found.

Huge tables were set up in a grove of oak or maple trees and each family brought baskets full of food to be placed with that of other families on the tables. Every woman had a favorite recipe which was known to many friends and if it were as good as she thought, her cake, pie, or fried chicken were soon gone. It was cause for real unhappiness when the demand for your dish was so light that most of it must be carried home. As people passed around the tables filling their plates to overflowing, it was not uncommon for a lady or two to either advocate a dish or protect one until some favored individual came by. Many a sour look was given by other women who observed this side play.

It would be difficult to be surrounded by the beauties of nature and not enjoy walks along shaded trails or flowing streams. The fall season was especially enticing and rural families could often be seen on a Sunday afternoon walking through the fields. As they walked, it was only natural to pick herbs to dry for winter use or pick nuts to crack during the long winter evenings.

There was as much difference in the product of selected nut trees as with fruits and each family knew where the best hickory, walnut or chestnut trees were located. It is hard to realize that the West Virginia hills were once dotted by thousands of chestnut trees where now only an

163

occasional rotting stump can be found. The women and children could be relied upon to gather a supply of chestnuts, walnuts, hickory nuts, butternuts, and hazelnuts to appear later in cakes, candies, dressing or just to crack and eat.

CURE OR ---

A home full of children had all the usual accidents and diseases and a competent hand in Mother's to care for them. While Father wrung his hands, Mother was wringing hot cloths to relieve the pain. Her medicine chest had never recognized an antibiotic but it did get results. Almost any ache or pain could be relieved by a dose of castor oil, salts, or linament and it is a proven fact that any of these brought changes in the patient. A bad cough might call for chestnut leaves to be boiled in water until it reached the proper consistency and with some brown sugar melted in it, a cough syrup was ready; or mullen leaves were boiled, and with brown sugar added, a better tasting product was available. For chest congestion, you would probably find yourself flat on your back while Mother prepared on onion poultice. A recipe for such a poultice was:

> 1 tablespoon lard and 6 large onions
> Add about 1/8 cake of camphor gum and
> 3 or 4 drops of turpentine
> Cook together until tender.
> Cut a piece of material and make
> a sack about 6 inches square.
> Cut out a little to fit up around the neck
> When onions are tender, put in sack and
> baste back and forth through to hold in place.
> Put on chest as warm as possible being care-
> ful not to burn. If very sick, it is best to
> make two and have one warm by the time the
> other is cool. When removed, cover chest
> with heavy greased cloth.

Regardless of the medical results, you were guaranteed to be a slippery article until all the grease could be removed and this could not be done until you were well on your way to recovery.

Another remedy for chest problems was a mustard plaster. The formula for this was:

> White of one egg
> 2 tablespoonfuls of flour
> 1 heaping teaspoonful of ground mustard
> Stir well.

This should make a medium stiff batter.
If needed, add a little warm water. Spread
on a thin cloth to a thickness of ¼ inch.
Have cloth large enough to fold back over
plaster. Keep it between two thin cloths.
Fold over edges.
Leave on until the skin becomes pink,
being careful not to blister.

You should be warned that the time lapse between turning pink and blistering was a very fine one and many a patient was thoroughly blistered.

There were occasional diptheria scares and cures were inadequate. One common preventative measure was to place a small piece of asafetida in a bag and hang it around the neck. Its medical powers may have been uncertain, but most of those who wore it never had a disease. If you have had an opportunity to smell it, you can readily understand why it was so effective--you went no nearer than was absolutely necessary.

Lucky indeed was the youngster that got through the winter without taking some sulpher to purify his blood or Sassafras tea to thin it. Summer was a time to be concerned with worm medicine, and if you didn't have them, a little medicine wouldn't hurt anyway.

Mother was a doctor, nurse, mid-wife, paramedic or whatever was needed, and the effectiveness of her remedies is proven by the fact that so many of our friends are in their 70's, 80's, or 90's.

Abraham Lincoln said: "all that I am or hope to be I owe to my Angel Mother." Mary Ellen Chase said: "I can still smell the warm spicy smells of ginger snaps baking in the oven, of apple pies rich with cinnamon, and of the countless doughnuts bobbing about on the surface boiling fat." My Mother sang hymns as she went about her work and often encouraged us to sing with her. One of her favorites was "Shall we gather at the River?" and all of us, joining in the chorus, loved to assure her that we would most certainly gather there. "Yes, We'll gather at the river, the beautiful, the beautiful river," we would all sing together, each, I feel sure, thinking of that river only as some pleasant family picknicking ground on some happy undefined day in the future.

A little house well fill'd
A little land well till'd
And a little wife well will'd
Are great riches

-English Proverb

Religion

Camp Meeting

B. B. MAURER typifies a characteristic Appalachian Trait: Engineer, Pastor, Rural Sociologist, Musician, Educator. He is Extension Specialist for Cultural and Clergy Education at West Virginia University, a newly created position in the Center for Extension and Continuing Education. Under Dr. Maurer's leadership, the Mountain Heritage cultural education program in national competition received the National University Extension Association's 1974 top Creative Programming Award in its Arts and Humanities Division.

Dr. Maurer was born and raised in Morgantown and received his BS degree in engineering from West Virginia University. He served as an engineer with the Army Air Force during World War II. After receiving a BD degree from the Lutheran Theological Seminary, Gettysburg, Pennsylvania, he was ordained by the Synod of West Virginia in 1949 and served as parish pastor in Doddridge County. He earned his MS degree from the University of Tennessee and his PhD degree from Pennsylvania State University, both in rural sociology, serving on the faculties of both universities during this time. Dr. Maurer held Synod and denominational staff positions with the Lutheran Church in America, being secretary successively of the Divisions of Town and Country and of Church Planning of the Board of American Missions.

The Program of Continuing Education for Clergymen of the Appalachian Center is another of Dr. Maurer's special efforts. He has written widely for professional, church and lay periodicals, and has published several studies, the most recent of which is *Religion in an Appalachian State* which he coauthored with Dr. John Photiadis, of West Virginia University.

168

CONTENTS

RELIGIOUS HERITAGE PROGRAMS

Successful educational experiences in our religious heritage require adequate understanding and preparation. The following basics of religious heritage programming have been prepared to aid all who desire to incorporate the religious dimension into Mountain Heritage programs.

Purpose

The purpose of religious heritage programming is educational. It is designed to:

1. *Create a religious experience.*

Our desire is to recreate and relive a religious experience comparable to that of our mountain ancestors and seek to understand its meaning for them and us today. It is not the purpose of these programs to convert, save, or in any way propagate a particular faith. Our purpose is to achieve authenticity in religious program and experience for all participants.

The heart of our religious heritage is love, and thus it carries a strong, positive, emotional feeling. This is buttressed by the related (contagious) feelings of joy, happiness, wonder, and enthusiasm. Participation is not only with the mind, but involves the whole self: hands, voice, feet, eyes, as all together overflow, outpouring the wonderful experience within. Every mode of expression, non-verbal as well as verbal, combines to communicate and share the amazing Love of God.

It is through experiences of this type that participants become aware of and deepen understanding of the eternal verities and the fathomless depth of life which gives meaning and purpose to living.

2. *Using the medium of music.*

The medium of music is one of the most effective ways of giving expression to (communicating) life's deepest feelings. Music facilitates creativity and enables more fuller expression by utilizing both verbal and non-verbal means. The oral tradition is utilized to reduce the handicaps of linearity and the written word which tend to get in the way of full, free flowing expression.

3. *By sharing.*

It is absolutely essential for all leaders of religious heritage programs to put themselves into it and share their faith, hope, love, and joy. Since it is impossible to share what one does not have, and the media will not carry what has not been put into it, programs of this nature often turn out to be disappointing ''going through the motions.'' Leaders must be prepared to give of themselves and their faith if participants are to share an authentic religious experience.

170

Method

The *medium of music* is the primary means utilized to recreate meaningful religious heritage experiences. It is augmented by scripture reading, prayer, the spoken word, dress, atmosphere, and "live" leaders. The authenticity and meaningfulness of the experience is dependent upon the degree to which the "mix" of these resources is able to recreate, communicate, and involve participants in the experience. Religious heritage programs are designed to meaningfully involve participants; they are not performances for spectator viewing. The receptivity or openness of participants, their previous religious conditioning and attitudes, all influence the effectiveness of the program.

The guitar is the musical instrument most widely available and associated with the folk tradition today. It combines the past and the present. It has had rather widespread use throughout the hills for more than a half-century and has been readopted by youth today. In addition to availability, it provides a flexibility of use and expression that make it well suited for religious heritage programs.

Emphasis on the guitar does not mean it is the only instrument to be used. The dulcimer, both hammered and plucked, violin, pump organ, and piano all have their place and can be used effectively under appropriate conditions.

While the instrument provides the medium, it alone is insufficient. Its primary role is a supportive one to the voice, for it is the soul that breaks forth in song in religious heritage music. Depending upon the size of the group and setting, amplification may be needed. In religious heritage programming, it is important that the music fully reach out, surround, and embrace all participants.

The *oral tradition* as of old is followed in vocal music. Only as the music, the words, and their meaning are internalized by the individual do they become his own and serve as personal means for expressing his faith. The participant is thus united with the group and the past in the shared experiences of the occasion. The printed page and book get in the way and become barriers to full expression and participation. They are to be used only to learn where there isn't opportunity to learn by rote in an ongoing group. As they are sung over and over again until internalized and made part of the person, they develop into a natural way of spontaneously expressing and sharing the wonderful feelings of religious faith. Preparation and practice thus are keys to the successful use of music for communicating religious heritage experiences.

Expressiveness through the medium of music is achieved by variations in tempo and volume as well as voice. Changes in tempo and volume along with vocal emphasis and bodily expression combine to give greater accuracy in the communication of feeling and understanding between persons and within

171

groups. When this is achieved, an entire group can function as one. The individual becomes a part of the whole, and wonderful and memorable experiences are shared. Communication is facilitated when a group is used to lead the singing. The lead group usually has a more powerful, cumulative effect in communicating and sharing through the medium of music than does a single individual.

The *Message* is eternal. The heart of the Gospel is Love! The great songs of faith are love songs. To love is to live, and to live is to love and be human in the fullest sense of the word. Music is the medium which makes possible a fuller expression and understanding of the Message. Its timelessness bridges the gap between then and now. It transcends the centuries and enables us to join hands with our forebearers and share the reality of their experience.

Setting

The setting for religious heritage programming is of prime importance. Although appropriate for most any occasion, group or place, it is highly desirable to fit the program to the situation. The selection of songs and length will of necessity vary with the composition of the group. There are times of the day and sites more conducive to religious heritage experience than others.

The resource paper, "Our Religious Heritage," is designed to provide for flexibility of use. It can be used as a study guide, for vespers, or a music piece. Songs, scripture, prayer, and format as well as the length, can be varied to fit the occasion. It can be adapted for use with small and large groups, formal and informal occasions. With careful preparation, religious heritage programs can deepen appreciation and understanding and enrich the lives of West Virginians of all ages throughout the State.

OUR RELIGIOUS HERITAGE

"Prelude"

God's Not Dead	Key: E
He's Got the Whole World	Key: C

Introduction

The heart of our mountain heritage lies in its religious faith. Without an understanding of our religious heritage we cannot fully understand our background, for it was religion that gave meaning to the mountain way of life.

Our purpose is educational—to recapture the essence of our religious heritage as a living, real life experience, and seek to understand its relevancy for today. Therefore, our program will not be a religious service in the usual sense, but an attempt to reconstruct and relive to the extent possible, that which was a meaningful part of the life of our forebearers.

To this end, we'll use the media of music, prayer, scripture, and the spoken word. Our music is soul music (mountain brand), with a beat, overflowing with joy—happy soul music straight from the warm mountain heart in the finest, folk tradition. We don't use books, for they get in the way. We favor the oral tradition where it flows plumb out of the heart, unhampered by the written page. Sing, if you don't know the words hum or listen, clap your hands and stomp your feet—leave yourself open to the music and its message, step out and cut 'er loose as the Spirit takes hold of your soul. Put yourself into it and when you feel it welling up inside to overflowin'—let 'er go!

Prayer: As befits the occasion
(following is an example for a gathering in an outdoor setting)

Oh Lord, how wonderful are Thy ways. When we pause and consider How Great Thou Art, this place of forest and mountain, of flowing streams and pure air, of wild life—creatures of the woods, fields, air, and water, of ourselves—male and female, the array of talents gathered here, the wonderful heritage that is ours, of these hours together, the depth and richness of human relationships—truly we are most blessed. What is man that Thou art so mindful of him—created in Thine own image to inherit Thy Kingdom. Help us to drink deeply of the abundance of Thy great love and joy, and find the overflowing fullness, richness, and meaning of life.   Amen

Scripture: St. Matthew 25:31-40 (or other appropriate passage)
"Anthem": L-O-V-E (or similar fitting selection)

Meditation:

Edwin Markam tells the story of Conrad a humble cobbler who in his little shop received a vision that Christ would visit him on a certain day. As the day

173

approached, Conrad's heart overflowed with joy in the expectation of his Lord's coming. His shop was set in order and made tidy from top to bottom. The day finally arrived and in the course of his daily routine Conrad befriended three of his needy fellowmen.

A beggar wandered into his shop seeking alms. Conrad warmed and fed him and noticing his feet wrapped in blood-stained rags, provided him a pair of shoes he had made and sent him on his way.

An elderly lady hobbled into his shop, cold and hungry. He warmed her with food and kindness and sent her on her way.

Finally, a young child, bursting with tears, lost and searching for its parents, found its way into his shop. Again Conrad responded, laid down his tools, calmed its fears, took it by the hand, and searched up and down the street until he found and restored it to its home.

The day had nearly come to a close and Markam pens these words:

> And Conrad sighed as the day turned gray,
> "Why is it Lord that your feet delay,
> Did you forget this was the day?"
> Then soft in the silence a voice was heard—
> "Lift up your heart for I kept my word,
> Three times I came to your friendly door,
> Three times my shadow was on your floor.
> I was the beggar with the bruised feet,
> I was the woman you gave to eat,
> I was the child on the homeless street."

A man's life consisteth not in the abundance of things he possesseth, but in the measure of his love and devotion to God and his fellowman!

If you really want to know a man's religion, observe how he lives –

Our forefathers first came into these mountains as a frontier wild and untamed —in many ways a hostile environment. At best it was a rough and primitive existence filled with hardships and privation—a rough hewn way of life. The question we pose is, How do you find meaning to life under wilderness conditions like these?

Their answer is—religious faith! Religion was the way in which they searched and found meaning. Many strains combine to make up our rich religious heritage, but undoubtedly the dominant one is the great American-born

174

revival tradition of frontier days which continues unabated in its primitive form in many of the back hollows of Appalachia. Its songs are rooted deep in the mountain folk tradition.

Our mountain ancestors saw their world and their lives in a religious framework, and they expressed its meaning in powerful, vivid, religious terms—a vocabulary which is almost lost today, and its words seldom heard in most homes. They were powerful, life-shaking, soul-stirring words like sin, evil, hell, lust, lost, hate, wickedness, damnation, judgment, perdition, and wonderful words of eternal promise— love, joy, hope, peace, glory, redemption, conversion, salvation, born again, eternal life, the kingdom, and they filled their hearts with hope and strength.

These were the religious tools (concepts) with which they hammered out meaning on the anvil of life and they did it with powerful effect on the lives of men.

Historian W. W. Sweet in *The Story of Religion in America* gives us a bit of the picture of the early camp meetings and the power of their religious experience:

"In one of their visits, they baptized seventy-five at one time, and in the course of one of these journeys, which generally lasted several weeks, they baptized upwards of two hundred. It was not uncommon at one of these great meetings, for many hundreds to camp on the ground in order to be present the next day — — —. There were instances of persons travelling more than one hundred miles to come to one of these meetings; to go forty or fifty was not uncommon."

"I attended with eighteen Presbyterian ministers, and Baptist and Methodist preachers, I do not know how many, all being either preaching or exhorting with more harmony than could be expected. The Governor of the State was with us and encouraging the work. The number of people estimated from 10,000 to 21,000 — —. The whole people were serious, all the conversation was of a religious nature — —. Great numbers were on the grounds from Friday until the Thursday following, night and day without intermission, engaging in some act of worship. They are commonly collected in small circles of ten to twelve, close adjoining another circle and all engaged in singing Watt's and Hart's hymns, and then a minister steps upon a stump or log and begins an exhortation or sermon, when, as many as can hear collect around him. On the Sabbath I saw a hundred candles burning at once and I saw 100 persons at once on the ground crying for mercy, of all ages from eight to sixty years — —. When a person is struck down he is carried by others out of the congregation where some minister converses with and prays for him; afterwards a few gather around and sing a hymn suitable to the case. The whole number brought to the ground, under convictions, were about 1000, not less. The sensible, the weak, the learned, the unlearned, the rich and poor, are the subjects of it."

The change in behavior wrought by their religious experience was no less remarkable. "A considerable number of persons appear to me to be greatly reformed in their morals. This is the case within the sphere of my particular acquaintance. Yes, some neighborhoods, noted for their vicious and profligate manners are now as much noted for their piety and good order. Drunkards, profane swearers, liars, and quarrelsome persons are remarkably reformed."

In Kentucky the effect of the religious revival was thus described:

"On my way I was informed by settlers on the road that the character of Kentucky travellers was entirely changed, and that they were as remarkable for sobriety as they had formerly been for dissoluteness and immorality. And indeed I found Kentucky to appearances the most moral place I had ever been. A profane expression was hardly ever heard. A religious awe seemed to prevade the country. Upon the whole, I think the revival in Kentucky the most extraordinary that has ever visited the Church of Christ; and all things considered, it was peculiarly adapted to the circumstances of the country into which it came."

The influence of their religious faith took deep hold in the lives of mountain folk and manifested itself in many ways. The names of their offspring bore the unmistakable imprint of the heroes of scripture: Abe, Si, Lem, Amos, Nate, Jake, Seth, Levi, Ben, Josh, Luke, Matt, and Zeke, and Ruth, Naomi, Sarah, Rachel, Mary, Elizabeth, Hannah, Rebekah, and Miriam grace family Bibles, scrapbooks and headstones across the State.

Likewise their living identification with mountaintop experiences and divine acts of Holy Writ are manifest in their home communities. Along with the Possum Bottom's, Bear Meadows, Polecat Hollows, Gobblers Knobs, Brushy Forks, Fishing Creeks, and Pine Groves, are Annamoriah, Berea, Bethany, Bethlehem, Beulah, Canaan, Dothan, Eglon, Etam, Gilboa, Hebron, Jordan Run, Mathias, Mt. Hope, Mt. Moriah, Mt. Nebo, Mt. Olivet, and Mt. Zion, Nabob, Pisgah, Philippi, Salem, Sardis, Seth, and the St. Albans, St. Marys, St. Georges, and St. Josephs, Paradise, Heaven, New Haven, Churchville, and White Chapel and hundreds of other communities throughout Appalachia beaming ongoing testimony of the influence of their faith.

Our interest, however, is not in veneration of the past but in determining what our religious heritage, forged in this mountain fastness, has to say to us now. We look back to learn from the experiences of the past only to view the present in perspective and look ahead to the future. In so doing we begin to understand the richness of the religious heritage that is ours.

Of the many characteristics our religious heritage has to pass on to us today, there are five that I believe are of enduring value and just as practical now as then.

1. The first is the living awareness of an *intensely personal relationship with God.*

They knew Him, talked with Him, walked with Him, and looked forward to spending eternity with Him. He was theirs and they were His. Many had come to know Him through a vivid personal experience. They sought and found answers to life in living and talking with the Lord and the words of His Book. The Bible carried authority and was used as the standard of faith and practice. Theirs was a living, face-to-face relationship with the Lord and they fiercely resisted all attempts to formalize it through an organization, or to interject any intermediary between them. Likewise they fought any attempt to dehumanize their relationships with one another and reduce them to chattels or cogs on a machine.

Their best loved songs of faith embody the spirit of this intensely personal relationship with the Lord, and their hymn books are full of them. Two of the best known hymns well illustrate the intensity of their feeling and love and devotion.

In the Garden catches and conveys the believer's wonder and joy of walking and talking with the living Lord—"And the *joy* we share as we tarry there, none other has ever known."

(*In the Garden,* verses 1 and 2) Key: G

Another of the old favorites which has been dusted off and repopularized via recording and radio is one that carries the believer's fervent plea for the most important part of his life—*Just a Closer Walk With Thee.* "Grant it Jesus this my plea; Daily may it ever be, just a closer walk with Thee."

(*Just a Closer Walk With Thee,* verses 1, 2 and 3) Key: G

2. The second characteristic of our religious heritage grows out of the first—a sense *of independence* (maturity) built upon the security of God's love.

Because of the intensely personal relationship with God, they were able to develop a sense of self-importance and worth as individuals and great personal strength. They were children of God, sons and daughters of the Almighty. Because they had value in His eyes, they had value with one another. They did not have an identity problem for they knew unmistakably who they were.

The mountain fortress was their home, and they were rooted in it. It was His creation and the evidence of His handiwork was ever about them. They were never alone, isolated, or without a friend. Independence, self-reliance, and resourcefulness grew out of their trust and reliance on Him.

3. The third characteristic of our religious heritage is related to the previous two—*the ability to withstand hardship and privation.*

The primitive way of frontier life in the mountains was rigorous to say the least. To survive, they soon developed the same rugged characteristics of the hills that sustained them. Like a knotty and gnarled, weatherbeaten oak they weathered the hardships and privation which were their daily fare. Material possessions and comforts were few, but their faith was a tower of strength in sustaining them. They had a mission which gave reason and purpose to existence—which made it all add up. They were pilgrims wandering through the wilderness on their way to the Promised Land. Here testing and hardship was their expected lot. Their eyes were firmly fixed on the Kingdom and their Lord led the way.

Many of the songs are filled with the message of hope and expectation of the Kingdom — the promised glory of the new life.

One which has had popular revival in recent years and carries the full scent of joy and expectation is *When the Saints Go Marching in*—"O Lord I want to be in that number, when the saints go marching in."

(*When the Saints Go Marching In,* verses 1, 2, and 4) Key: A

Another which pictures in joyous tones the coming of that great day, and welcomes it with buoyant confidence and enthusiasm is *When the Roll is Called Up Yonder, I'll Be There*—"When His chosen ones shall gather to their home beyond the skies, and the roll is called up yonder, I'll be there."

(*When the Roll is Called Up Yonder, I'll Be There*, verses 1 and 2)
Key: G

4. The fourth characteristic of our religious heritage is the *ability to accept people as they are.*

A person as a child of God was valued for himself as a human being. He had been created by God and that was endorsement enough. The color of his blood, achievement, pedigree, shades of his past, or economic status, notwithstanding, he was accepted on the basis of their experienced personal relationship now.

Opinions were formed on the basis of personal relationship—as they personally came to know him, and other information was tested in this light. The family and kin ties were strong. Generally once a person was accepted by a member of a group, he was accepted by the group. Friendships were strong and enduring and highly valued. A man's word was sufficient. The world outside might treat a person hostilely, but home was always a haven.

5. The fifth characteristic of our religious heritage sets forth the tone of the Gospel in song—*Joy!* How great and unspeakable the joy that bubbles up within and overflows the spirit-possessed soul. It's got to come out—the face beams the radiance of happiness in the Lord, and the buoyant heart rejoices. The feet, hands, and voice all join in a pean of praise. Happy in the Lord, cleansed and forgiven, new life, Hallelujah! Foot stompin', hand clappin', and whooping it up are all part of the liturgy of joy in our religious heritage.

Perhaps no other of the songs coming out of the folk tradition so well expresses this happy note as *I've Got the Joy*, "I've got the joy, joy, joy, joy — — down in my heart to stay!"

(*I've Got the Joy*, verses 1-5) Key: A

As music is the language of love and faith, so poetry more than prose captures the happiness of the reborn soul. Out of the hills of Wayne County from one of its native sons comes:

Farmer Brown's Testimony

Archie Conway

One night I went down to the church
Just to sort uv listen in
Hadn't even been a thinkin'
Uv gettin' rid uv sin.
I wasn't feelin' guilty none
About this life I lead,
Until I got to listenin'
To the things the preacher said.

I didn't know that preacher man,
But he seemed to know of me,
Because he told me how I lived
As purty as could be.
He said that I wuz headin' for
A burnin' lake of fire,
And then he said, "God sees ye
A-settin' there where you are."

I thought I'd just get up and leave,
But somehow I couldn't make it,
So I just slid down in my seat
And decided I could take it;
But land sakes I couldn't, folks,
Such a load wuz on my chest;
Then the preacher made an altar call
And I plumb forgot the rest.

I guess I fainted in my seat
A-settin' there twixt them men;
How long I stayed unconscious
I had no idea then.
But when I came to myself agin
I wuz feelin' purty swell
With somethin' a-tuggin' at my heart
And a-tellin' me to yell.

I allus could call hogs at home,
And so I let'er fly,
A winder-bustin' beller

That sounded to the sky.
All the sisters started shoutin'
And the brothers said amen,
Then while I hugged the preacher man
I let'er go agin.

T'aint nothin' but salvation
This stuff I'm tellin' uv
The kind that comes from heaven
Plumb full of joy and love;
The sort the old apostles had
In the days of long ago,
Which made their dear old hearts
Just up and overflow.

There ain't no tongue can tell it,
The joy that sinners know
When they've been fergiven
And washed as white as snow.
To know the Saviour loved 'em
And saved 'em from their sin,
And left His Holy Spirit
Abidin' away down in.

You folks can see I'm ignorant,
Never went to school no how,
And allus had to stay at home
And hoe and grub and plow.
I aint't got no education.
But I'm minded to let it be,
Fer I'm shore a-feelin' happy
Over what God done fer me.

Now the baby sees the difference,
Cause I heard her tellin' ma,
Somethin' mighty funny
Has done come over pa.
The old brindle cow has found out
And the old gray mule to boot
Well religion that no one knows about
It just ain't worth a hoot.

Out of our rich religious heritage of the past comes light for today:

An intensely personal relationship with God.

A sense of independence and maturity.

The strength to face and withstand hardship and privation.

The ability to accept people as they are.

Joy—in the Lord!

> And Conrad sighed as the day turned gray,
> "Why is it Lord that your feet delay,
> Did you forget this was the day?"
> Then soft in the silence a voice was heard -
> "Lift up your heart for I kept my word,
> Three times I came to your friendly door,
> Three times my shadow was on your floor,
> I was the beggar with the bruised feet,
> I was the woman you gave to eat,
> I was the child on the homeless street."

"Verily, verily I say unto you, inasmuch as ye have done it unto one of the least of these my brethren, ye have done it unto me." Matt. 25:40.

Closing: (*Amen*) Key: E

Black Culture

P. AHMED WILLIAMS, Professor Emeritus in Residence at West Virginia State College, is one of West Virginia's most distinguished educators in the field of music, with a long, productive and influential career.

Moving with his family from Danville, Virginia to West Virginia in his early years, Dr. Williams lived in Kimball and completed his public schooling in McDowell County. He received his Bachelor of Music degree *magna cum laude* from West Virginia Collegiate Institute (now West Virginia State College) and his MA and EdD degrees from the School of Education of New York University.

First as a teacher and supervisor of music in McDowell County, and later as a member of the faculty of West Virginia State College, Dr. Williams worked in both traditional and innovative ways to encourage the development of his students and to provide performance opportunities for them. He organized and directed the first McDowell County music festival, and later the West Virginia State College Men's ROTC Glee Club, which toured extensively in concert for 25 years. Dr. Williams continued his assistance to students as planner and director of the cultural education opportunities program for Upward Bound at West Virginia State College. He has been cited for outstanding achievement by West Virginia State College and its alumni, and was given both the Recognition of Outstanding Service Award and the Civilian Service Award by the Department of Army.

At the present time Dr. Williams is a member of the board of directors of the Intercollegiate Musical Council as well as Professor Emeritus in Residence at West Virginia State College. He is much in demand as a consultant and lecture performer on topics dealing with Black experience in music, literature and history, and devotes a major part of his time to filling these engagements.

184

CONTENTS

I REMEMBER
"THE FREE STATE OF McDOWELL"

HISTORY RECORDS

History records the earliest settlers came into southern West Virginia in the wake of the closing of the Civil War. These settlers carved their way into a virtual wilderness of undeveloped mountain terrain unbelievable in its beauty and richness of vast mineral deposits. The foremost of these was King Coal. At first a few settlers wandered in from Old Virginia, sometimes referred to by early citizens as East Virginia. They established themselves in their crude homes in a land plentiful in wild game, great forests, and clear unpolluted streams. This was a veritable paradise for those who were desirous of a new life. One recalls how even as late as the early twenties, descendants of these early families were referred to as "old mountain hootchies." Little did we realize then we were ridiculing the real cultured gentry, nor that the correct reference should have been Hoosier which defined meant earliest settler and carried with it none of the indignity or condescension of the term "hootchie" as ascribed.

The peace and serenity of this area (538 square miles) was short lived, for soon industrial prospectors and speculators came finding large coal deposits, often facetiously spoken of as "Black Diamond." With this discovery came an era of industrialization requiring an altogether new approach to living.

Sensing the beginning of a great mining empire, the Norfolk and Western Railroad pushed out from Roanoke to Bluefield with the idea of eventually terminating at Columbus, Ohio. Because of rough mountain terrain, building of the railroad through the area was a tremendous undertaking. Sometimes railroad beds had to be laid high upon the mountainsides with trestles spanning deep chasms from mountain to mountain. When it was too arduous to go around mountainous obstacles, tunnels had to be cut. The longest tunnel on the Norfolk and Western was opened at Coaldale around 1887 making possible completion of transit facility to Maybeury where the first mine was opened.

On all of the road projects, Negro labor was responsible for hewing the wood, laying the cross-ties, and doing any other jobs considered menial for whites. The men who worked on these road crews were referred to as "section hands" or "section gangs." Many who came to work on these gangs, later stayed in the vicinity to work in the coal mines. These men were later joined by other ethnic groups such as Poles, Hungarians, Greeks, Italians, and many other nationalities.

No one is definitely certain as to when Negroes began to refer to McDowell County as the "Free State of McDowell." As a young man growing up in the coalfields, it is easy to recollect time and again hearing

186

M. T. Whittico (always spoken of intimately as Tom Whittico) use the Free State reference in his political speeches around the county. Tom Whittico was founder and editor of the McDowell Times, the first Black newspaper in the state of West Virginia. His influence in the free State of McDowell connotation was (1) that Negroes had more freedom to fight for equal rights than in many other parts of the country, (2) that Negroes had the power of the ballot, as well as (3) freedom from segregation in public transportation.

The Negro philosophy was "share and share alike." In sum and substance, this meant that what political administration provided for white citizens must also be provided for Negro citizens. As an outgrowth of this ideal, the Free State of McDowell had the first Black World War Memorial Building, and high schools in every district; one each at Gary, Kimball, Northfork, Elkhorn, and Excelsior. In many instances, precedence for establishing and maintaining public institutions was brought about through political pressure.

ELECTED OFFICIALS

Certain early elected public offices were almost always filled by Negroes. This practice began in 1896 with the offices of Justice of the Peace, Constable, and one member of the Board of Edueation in each district. Six justices served at various times in the Elkhorn District alone. As a young man, it pleases me to speak of two public elected officials whom I knew intimately in the persons of Justice Samuel Crider and Constable Henry Richards. Both men were elected in the Browns Creek District, Mr. Crider serving as justice for 36 years, and Mr. Richards serving as Constable for 32 years. Both of these gentlemen worked ardently for equal rights and justice during the entire period of their careers in office. Adkins District and Big Creek District also had elected constables and justices.

It is also easy to recall five Board of Education members in districts and later under the county unit system, three Negro county assistant superintendents in the persons of E. L. Watkins, J. B. Carrol, and Clyde Johnson.

BLACK MIGRATION

When King Coal was at its most productive period, money was plentiful in the area. The question of cultured Blacks swarming to McDowell County was purely economic. The same is evidently true of those who came for some of the more desirable labor occupations, as well as those who came for less desirable purposes. In putting these facts

187

together, many strange sequences come to mind.

In early days for some strange reason, (possibly because of its central location) the little town of Keystone sported one of the biggest red light districts in existence.

CINDER BOTTOM AND "THE LADIES"

On payday Saturday nights, men, young and old, came from far and near to pay their respect to the "ladies", and for other sports such as drinking and gambling.

Big open top automobiles were in style during the early twenties. The Chalmers, Pierce Arrows, Peerless, Packard, and Cadillac were possibly the more expensive and elaborate machines. Anyone who could afford one or two of these machines, usually used them for public conveyance as taxis. One gentleman is reputed to have owned at least three of these expensive machines, each driven at various times or the other by one of his sons, for the purpose of hauling passengers mainly from town to town and most assuredly to and from the Bottom.

It was common in the early days to speak of "going to catch some air." This meant going for an automobile ride purely for pleasure. In the back of my mind there is a pleasurable memory of seeing carloads of the "ladies" dressed in their finest garb, being driven through various communities in the county waving to those they knew as friends and vice versa. Suffice to say the young bucks gaped in awe, while some of the older clientele wishing not to be recognized on their home territory, shied away shamelessly. There is one truism which must be mentioned. To my knowledge, which of course on this subject may be limited, "the ladies" whenever in public, always conducted themselves in a most ladylike manner. This is even more remarkable in face of the fact that public dances were attended by all segments of society. Dances were the main source of diversion and were always invitational social events. Those who wanted more exclusive social life attended private home parties or affairs (sociables) sponsored in homes by small private clubs or individuals. Believe it or not, all social events, public and private, were definitely chaperoned.

Music for dancing at home parties was usually furnished by individual guests who accepted it as correct and proper to take their turn at the piano. Anyone who played a fairly good jazz piano was always assured of an invitation. Music for the better public dances was almost always furnished by the Edward Watkins Saxaphone Orchestra from Bluefield. This organization was reorganized in the early twenties and became known as Edward's Collegians, employing exclusively young musicians who were students at leading Negro colleges. The group remained intact for a long period playing dance engagements in many of the large cities throughout the South, East, and Middlewest. However, dancing and partying were not the only public gatherings. The church was a more vital factor of public affluence.

CHURCHES, MINISTERS, AND SERMONS

The first Black church in the Free State of McDowell was organized and built at (Elkhorn, Crosier) by Rev. T. J. Brandon of Danville, Va. Lately, as interviews were being held with younger living persons now in the area, there seems to be a matter of conjecture here as some contend that Rev. L. Dabney should receive this honor. The writer has no way of knowing for in the year of 1896 a great flash flood came down the Elkhorn Valley washing away everything in its path, including some churches. Going through McDowell recently it was quite obvious that practically all of the old churches (especially Baptist) were constructed on elevated plots on the mountainside in order seemingly to forever avoid the reoccurence of such a tragedy. Because of these high locations some churches are almost inaccessible in time of bad weather.

It is highly impractical to mention all of the ministers who served the area; however, as early arrivals, the following readily come to mind: Reverends T. J. Brandon, L. Dabney, J. W. Coger, R. H. McCoy, J. V. Whittico, W. H. Pittard, Alexander Gregory, J. E. Woody, John Pryor, and J. W. Robinson. Of these, J. V. Whittico is attributed with the founding of the first Negro Presbyterian church.

Books could be written about the services of these men alone, but one must consign himself to incidents of the more closely related. For example, one particular minister was always the suave, gentlemanly scholar whether in the classroom, in the street, or in the pulpit. As far as is known, all of those mentioned above possessed charm, intellectual wisdom, wit, and leadership ability, which was freely exerted for the betterment of all concerned.

Several stories come to mind like the one told to me by a son of one of the ministers in a community where I was teaching. It was (the occasion is well remembered) as follows: a member of the community died after having lived a life of all possible vices. Among other things, the person in question had seemingly never set foot inside of church, plus dying from what was believed to be an overload of bad drinking whiskey. The family requested a Christian burial with church services and a sermon by the minister. People flocked from far and near to hear and see how the minister would handle such a delicate situation. Following is the sermon to the letter:

"Christ was born and lived 31 years and he died.
Methusaleh was born and lived 999 years and he died.
Sister Jessie was born and lived 29 years and she died."
(End of sermon)
"Let us have the Doxology."

189

For several years while a student at Browns Creek District High School, the writer was organist for a small Baptist church spoken of as "up Bottom Creek hollow." Though most everything else in the hollow is in disreputable ruin, Lovely Zion still stands sacred, staunch, and influential. During my years of service as organist, we had a minister who believed in preaching to "the letter." With proper biblical reference he could condemn or justify any action or situation. He was probably the most outspoken and also one of the most popular ministers in the section. Fire and Damnation reigned on many occasions. We often suspicioned many persons flocked to church to see just who was in for it on that particular day. Woe unto him who sinned and let it get to the Reverend. Regardless of however unsavory, whatever went into his ears during the week came out of his mouth right from the pulpit on Sunday. Despite this fact, he was one of the most scholarly men imaginable. Many of the things learned from him from a biblical, literary, and musical background still serve as guiding posts for the writer after 50 years. Speaking of God's Trombones, (James Weldon Johnson applies this name to early Negro ministers) if there ever was one in the Free State of McDowell, it was the pastor of our little church.

The reader has probably observed by this time that this thesis is not intended as a factual presentation, but rather as past life situations which in large, are everyday recollected living experiences. These experiences may or may not make history, but it is certainly hoped that they give a clearer insight into life style situations which contributed to the making of history.

"THE DEFENSE RESTS"

For example, one particular lawyer looked anything but a professional man, but in court he was unsurpassable. Around our high school in Kimball the students from a little town nearby had it as quite a joke that when all else failed to sway the court this particular jurist as a last resort cried through his one eye. He had to be a good lawyer because he won so many cases in court he became known as "jail robber." On the other hand, another highly respected attorney was known everywhere as a jurist supreme. He was suave, polished, and scholarly, truly the "Barrister's Barrister."

One of my acquaintances relates as to how he killed a neighbor and was jailed. First degree was evident. The client, Cicero, jailed in Lynch, Kentucky, sent for the above mentioned barrister to come and plead his defense. The Lawyer arrived and was allowed to see his client. "All right Cicero, how did it happen?" Incidentally, Cicero had only one arm, the other lost in a mine mishap. Cicero began a long diatribe on how the accused had come to his house, beat up his wife, broken up the furniture and general raised hell. Cicero demonstrated that having only one arm he coundn't defend himself adequately, so he ran to the dresser drawer, took out his pistol and shot the intruder. Seems fairly logical but not to the defending lawyer. According to Cicero, the lawyer said, "Cicero, you're telling a damn lie and I'm going back home and let them hang you." Whereupon Cicero says he fell to his knees crying, "Lord, Lord don't let them hang me. I'll tell the truth." Cicero then proceeded to tell how he came home and found that the intruder had beat his wife. Cicero being highly incensed got a gun and went looking for the assailant, finally finding him at home sitting on the porch reading quietly his evening paper. Cicero stated that in his rage at the assailant's complacency, he shot him right between the eyes. "Why didn't you tell the truth in the first place, Cicero?" replied the lawyer. "This is a case of self-defense, he intimidated you." Cicero was not convicted.

In 1918, I. W. Harper from Keystone was the first Negro ever elected to the West Virginia Legislature. Harry J. Capehart was second, taking office in 1920, whereupon he proceeded in introducing, and steering through to its final passage what is commonly known as the "Capehart Anti-Lynch Law." This is still the most important and progressive piece of legislation ever enacted on the important question of lynching.

THE MEDICAL PROFESSION

It's startling to read in the Charleston Gazette (March 21, 1975) that out of 1,887 physicians in the state of West Virginia, only four are Negroes. The writer does not take it upon himself to condemn or justify this situation. It does give a chance to recall from memory a partial list of the men in medical professions practicing in McDowell County in early days. Dr. G. N. Marshall of Keystone was the first to come (1899) followed by (not necessarily in a chronological order) Doctors H. D. Hereford--Northfork, Joe E. Brown--Keystone, Roscoe C. Harrison--Kimball, H. D. Dismukes--Kimball, E. L. Youngue--Welch, Matthew Craighead--Kimball. Dr Wright of Welch, Dr. Drew of War, Dr. Craighead of Kimball, and Dr. J. E. Brown of Keystone (all deceased) were the last remaining Black physicians of the early era in the county in 1940. Dr. J. P. Wade of Northfork and Dr. Matthew Craighead of Kimball were the first two native local men in the area to matriculate in the field of medicine in the early thirties, both graduating from Meharry Medical College in Nashville, Tennessee.

Early recollection brings to mind the fact there was a time one could afford the luxury of staying in sick with a degree of certainty of a house call from a physician. No more. You drag to the office, sit for hours, get

191

medication, crawl back home and depending on your luck, either recuperate or die in peace. This is no criticism of the medical profession. It is a mere statement of fact that will probably get worse before it gets better.

Two more interesting facts come to mind. Dr. R. C. Harrison and Dr. H. D. Dismukes were both excellent surgeons and both founded private hospitals in Kimball, saving with their skill, lives of many Blacks and foreigners.

The county also supported several dentists and pharmacists. Of the dentists one recalls Doctors Stewart Adams (Northfork), Clinton Yancey (Northfork), D. T. Murray (Keystone), and J. S. Cardwell (Gary).

Pharmaceutical wise Dr. P. G. Howard of Keystone owned and operated the last Black drug store in the area up until his death seven or eight years ago. Dr. Vernon Bridgeford of Keystone was the pioneer in this line. (1912) In the twenties and thirties the small town of Kimball boasted two drug stores; one Valentine's and the other Webb's. James Webb was a licensed pharmacist while Valentine a layman, hired the service of pharmacist Robert Black who later became co-owner.

Many persons prominent in professional and educational circles today received their early education in Free State of McDowell schools.

PUBLIC SCHOOLS AND TEACHERS

In reading this treatise, the reader is cautioned to please understand that the writer is not trying to say that physical inequities did not exist in buildings and equipment. Where there is separation, one side always suffers. One of the infamous generosities of these times was the practice of building a new school for Whites while turning over the old school to Negroes. Many times this caused great consternation among Negro leaders and was never a completely acceptable solution. Black Free Staters seemingly always fought doggedly for their rights, many times assuredly coming out profitably.

There was a wide and varied selection of teachers for the schools, especially at the high school level. This was due to the fact that many Black degree-holding college graduates sought coalfield employment as the quickest and surest way to earn money for later study in higher professional fields. Because of this, high school facilities profited from the services of Ohio University, Harvard, Ohio State University, Fisk, Howard, Lincoln, Oberlin, Yale, Radcliffe, and other leading institutions. Partly because of its superior faculty rating, Browns Creek District High School of Kimball was one of the first schools in the state acredited by the North Central Association. This faculty status was not enjoyed by the elementary schools. Most of the teachers on the lower level were local persons holding Short Course or Standard Normal Certificates from Bluefield Institute, or West Virginia Collegiate Institute.

It is a most pleasant experience to recall the seeming religious and intellectual fanaticism with which most of the early teachers approached their assignments. One little story will do much to show the philosophy so inherent in much of the teaching. The related incident happened during my first teaching experience when I sought advice from one of my most loved and respected former high school English teachers.

"Mama Clara, what do you do when one of your pupils just seems to not want to learn? Every now and then I run across one who just won't try." Her answer was classic. "First," she replied," exhaust every means possible to try to find out whether he has the natural ability to do the task. If he doesn't have the ability, there is little you can do; if he has the ability and won't do the job, get a stick and make him do it." This method worked wonders for a lot of us.

WOMEN OF RENOWN

The greater portion of this article has extolled the achievements of males. Women, however, from a seemingly obscure background have always been the prime guiding influence for Black Appalachian youth. The writer remembers many, but five were ideally symbolical.

As I reminisce on trying to grow up culturally in the early days in the Free State of McDowell, it seems most strange that women always predominate. They are legend, they are history, and they are characters.

For present purposes four hang in the recesses of my mind definitely as My Women. Capitalized if you please. A fifth one is being added because she was a dynamic member of the crew for years. Vivacious, snappy, witty, clever, with a torso about the size of a shoe string. This was No. 5. More later.

My five women in their order were Sarah, Memphis, Maggie, Ida, and Arleyne. Everyone of them migrated into McDowell to teach and probably to find husbands. They all did. Suffice to say if I had a hand in the choices there would have been some changes or omissions. Anyway they all came to the coalfield at a time in the teens, 1909-1919, when your humble servant had no training, experience, or inclination to be a marriage counselor. Truthfully, survival was my prime concern, what with dodging stray bullets being a fruitful and necessary pastime. But let me get back to My Women.

In this day and age, four of My Women could have been referred to as Black. One never. She was one shade whiter than most whites but she made her choice when instead of passing, she married the blackest, most vocal, oratorical, brilliant man she could find. He was Tom Whittico, editor of The McDowell Times, a militant Black publication through which she carried the fight for equal rights for years following his death.

193

Not long ago when attending Ida's last rites in Point Pleasant, it was noticeable to me that all active participants were "other folks" (undertaker, preacher, etc.). One couldn't help thinking of what a heck of a lifetime she spent putting up a fight for "us" when she could have deserted and probably "easy-streeted" along with "them."

Arleyne, No. 5 on my list, was the most physically active woman of the group. She went to all of the dances, public and otherwise; danced every dance with the youngest man in the house, as well as the oldest. She could talk incessantly on any subject. All you had to do was select the topic and listen. Many's the time I heard her say, "If you don't want it told, don't tell it to me because my mother fed me 'tellit' berries when I was young and I'm still getting the reaction."

At one time four of my women taught at Keystone-Eckman Elementary and Junior High. The other taught at Gary. In 1926 all hell broke loose. The Democrats came into power and their first act was to scatter this gang of 'filthy' Republican women. Sarah and Maggie were sent to the hinterlands at the opposite, most inaccessible locations in the county. Memphis and Ida were fired outright and it seems to me that Arleyne got the ax also. Fortunately, she was without encumbrances at the time and took off for the Nation's Capitol where she spent her remaining days working, as they used to say, in the Government.

Upon dissolution of the gang Maggie was transferred to Bishop, West Virginia where her one room school sat right on the Virginia State Line. Guess this was meant to be quite an insult because if you made a misstep on your way to the outhouse you stepped on old Virginia soil. Maybe the assumption of the powers-that-be was to remind her of what a privilege it was to be in West Virginia.

Maggie was the first Black woman in McDowell County to really own and operate a car to any extent. She drove to every Bluefield home game for forty years and took many other long trips, driving until she was well into her eighties. In the old days I used to love to take that dangerous drive from Kimball to Bluefield with her. The roads, laid over trails suitable for mountain goats only, were something else. Providence rode with us on every trip since I am still here as living proof of survival.

Maggie was the heaviest member of the group from the weight angle. She would have made two of any of the rest of the group and on a given day you could have thrown in Arleyne without unbalancing the scales. Ida used to jokingly say, "Abraham's bosom will really be full when Maggie passes along."

One last thing about Maggie has to do with her generosity. She was generous to a fault. When a quarter was considered fair shakes for a youngster, she would whip out a dollar bill on you in a minute. Her sharing with others was a virtue.

Sarah was the only one of the gang to make it to Maggie's funeral. She was past ninety at the time, so my fears were that it would be an emotional trauma. It was for everyone else possibly, but when we arrived at Bottom Creek Baptist where the last rights were held, everybody and everything was moved aside to give Sarah a place of honor right up front near the casket. This would not have been so bad but her seat was directly in the path of everyone either going up to view the body, or returning therefrom. When I realized that old friends, former pupils, were jammed around shaking hands with Sarah. I was flabbergasted. Oh well, a receiving line at her funeral, I am sure Maggie would have loved that. At least it's what she would have expected knowing Sarah's flare for center staging. I can hear Maggie now, "God, yes, leave her alone. You know Sarah Page."

If there ever was a name which creates a sensation it's the name of my friend Memphis Tennessee Garrison, a brilliant, dynamic speaker, writer, and foremost champion for human rights and dignity. People often ask, how did she get that name? My answer is, "Her mama gave it to her." But why Memphis Tennessee? I guess because her mother never heard of Biloxi, Mississippi. Could have been worse you know.

Memphis is my No 2 woman. Not long ago we spoke jointly in a community and came near starting a slight revolution. We marched on Washington together and also collaborated on several race pride productions in the good old days in McDowell County.

Memphis can still turn more thought into action than almost any other woman I know. Positive action that is. You name it--Memphis has done it. If there ever should be national N. A. A. C. P. monuments to any persons, my nominations go unqualifiedly to male, Walter White; and female, Memphis Tennessee Garrison.

In 1971 Marshall University conferred on Mrs. Garrison the honorary degree of Doctor of Humanities. A part of her citation reads as follows:

Memphis Tennessee Garrison, civic leader,
teacher, humanitarian, you are held in
admiration, respect, and affection for
your outstanding achievements of more than
fifty years in the fields of education,
civil rights, and christian service.

And now we come to my No. 1 character, by far the most difficult to write about because of our very personal and intimate relationships for near onto seventy years. Unfortunately, the stories cannot be divulged at this writing. She would probably bring suit against me and knowing her as I do, she just might.

One of my early recollections of Sarah Page was of her singing The Battle Hymn of the Republic at Emancipation Day Ceremonies in High Street Baptist Church in Danville, Virginia. Her singing was a pure revelation of black pride. Freedom became a continuing reality of attainment from the first note. This is probably why I became a musician instead of a bricklayer.

When Sarah moved to West Virginia in 1920 to teach, everybody in Danville just knew that in such wild country she would be shot while getting off the train. Not Sarah Page; she is still on West Virginia soil at the chipper age of 95 and still never misses an opportunity to register a complaint or to issue an order which she expects to be expedited *now*. When you deal with Sarah Page you learn that valor may not be one of the greatest virtues.

Each of my women could do some one thing in a more superior manner than anyone else. Nobody, but nobody, including Paul Lawrence Dunbar, could make Dunbar live like Sarah. Dunbar's characters came alive and paraded across the stage at every reading. One of my fond early recollections is to being snatched from hamlet to hamlet assisting her in concerts.

It was also customary to have May Queens each Spring and my job was to play the piano while Madame directed. Good times, these were good times! Nobody could ever tell us we weren't the best.

One last item. Sarah was a great church worker and organizer, her chief organizations being the Baptist Church and the St. Luke Fraternal Order. Unlike the rest of my women, Sarah used her prerogative to turn any place out singing and shouting whenever she felt the urge. She stopped only in old age when she no longer had the strength. I was always suspicious that she felt all religious services needed a little warming up. Lots of the ministers appreciated Sister Page for this little lift.

When Sarah came into McDowell County, she was already a long standing member of the Independent Order of Saint Luke's, a leading fraternal order for ladies and gentlemen of color and quality.

Sarah took it as a personal challenge to organize the juveniles of the county. Needless to say she proceeded to indoctrinate indiscriminately. Page's Pride Juvenile Order is even to this day made up of people who were solicited for the order before they could walk.

I used to accuse her of going when she heard of a pregnancy, asking the mother to give her the child for a St. Luke member. She denies this, but I still believe it was true.

There are so many things I could tell, but after all one has to be careful as to what he says about his mother.

The Women--Sarah H. Page, Memphis T. Garrison, Maggie Bailey (Pugh), Ida Whittico (Brown) and Arleyne Parsons--contributed constructively to the lives of thousands of Black students. They were not the only ones by any means; there were hundreds of others who did equally as well or better. I simply knew this crew more intimately because

196

they banded together and for me were accessible. They are my favorites, "My Women."

I wonder if the fact that they all fed me, petted me, and gave me money occasionally, prejudiced me.

This little treatise is a tribute to all of the fine Negro women of early West Virginia who gave their all for "mere peanuts" just to teach others. If you "younger generationers" want to know who laid the ground work for you to be so Black and Beautiful, they did.

AFTER THOUGHT

Many questions have arisen about Growing up Black in Appalachia. Like most other places life was at times frustrating and beset with many deprivations. On the other hand, there was inspiration with occasional moments of glory beckoning one to higher achievements. The will to fight, survive, and to succeed were inherent factors of Black Mountain Heritage in The Free State of McDowell.

Appreciation to Dr. Memphis T. Garrison for patience and guidance, and especially for the privilege of her personal recollections and the use of her files and news clippings.

The Author

The Mountain State

BETTY P. CRICKARD, brings to the subject of mountain heritage a wealth of personal knowledge and experience as a native West Virginian and staff member of the West Virginia University Extension Service. She has worked successfully throughout the State with people of all ages and from all walks of life.

After public school education in Elkins, Dr. Crickard received a BS degree from Berea College, and ME degree from the University of Maryland and a PhD degree from Walden University, with additional studies at West Virginia, Marshall and Colorado State Universities and the U. S. Department of Agriculture Graduate School. She was honored by selection as a National 4-H Fellow and National Association of Extension Home Economists Fellow, each for one year, and was the recipient of the Distinguished Serrvice Award of the National Association of Extension Home Economists.

After more than 18 years' experience as 4-H agent and home demonstration agent in Upshur, Randolph and Cabell Counties, Dr. Crickard joined the Charleston Area staff of the West Virginia University Extension Service in 1968 where she has been Program Coordinator and Acting Area Director and now serves as Leadership Development Specialist.

Dr. Crickard is one of those who have directed the Mountain Heritage program of the West Virginia Extension Service. It has become a State wide educational resource both for schools and for informal adult education, and was recognized nationally in 1974 as the most excellent Cultural education program of any university extension service in the United States.

CONTENTS

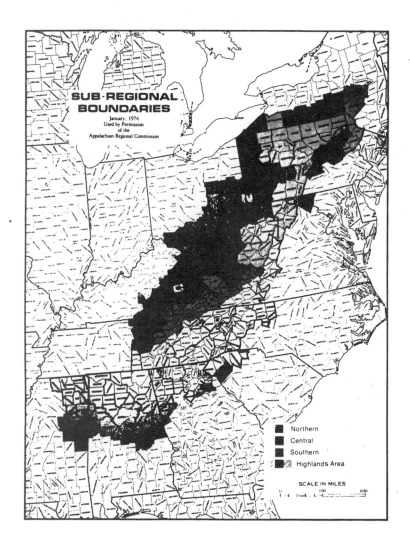

SUB-REGIONAL BOUNDARIES

January, 1974
Used by Permission
of the
Appalachian Regional Commission

■ Northern
■ Central
■ Southern
▨ Highlands Area

SCALE IN MILES

202

THE MOUNTAIN STATE
A Bicentennial Cultural View

IN THE EYE OF THE BEHOLDER

West Virginia, The Mountain State, is the only state falling completely within the region known as Appalachia. Appalachia is the section of the eastern United States dominated by the Appalachian Mountains stretching through parts of thirteen states from New York to Alabama. To understand the culture of the people of the West Virginia hills, it is necessary to look at it in the larger context of the Appalachian subculture. Likewise, understanding the culture of the Mountain State provides insight into the culture of the Appalachian region. They are part of the same whole.

From the perspective of the Nation's Bicentennial and the passage of 200 years of history we raise the question, "What is Appalachia today?" and the answers we receive, even as in times past, are quite varied. The broad stereotyped images of Appalachia seem to conceal as much as they reveal.

1. *The Popular National Image* is generally one of a backward, shiftless people who talk "quare" and practice strange religious customs - a land of poor people living in the midst of rich natural resources. This image has been propagated by the mass media: television documentaries and caricature programs, comic strips, and feature writers, together with political candidates, the war on poverty, and commercial tourism. Appalachia across the nation has become synonomous with coal mining, welfare, moonshine, and barefoot hillbillies.

2. *The . Official Government Image* seems to be one of an underdeveloped, lagging region -- lagging behind rural, urban, and metropolitan America. As such, it has been the target of many development type programs designed to provide jobs, improve health and education, build roads and waste disposal systems, reclaim stripped lands, and generally bring the area up to the level of the rest of the nation. In this respect Appalachia has proven to be a hardy perennial, continuing to provide almost unlimited opportunity for developmental type government programs.

3. *Industry's Image* of Appalachia appears to be one of a land of rich natural resources awaiting development to serve the needs of the nation. Coal, oil, gas, timber, water, and other natural resources abound in substantial amounts. The importance of these in West Virginia is dramatically attested to in the absentee corporate ownership of over two-thirds of the non-public land and its natural resources.[1]

4. *The Self-Image of West Virginians* likewise is a varied one. Educated, middle-class West Virginians generally see themselves as no different from other middle-class Americans, with little or no acknowledged identifications with Appalachia. These West Virginians have acquired the amenities and identified with main stream society.

On the other hand, many West Virginians of heightened cultural sensitivity, identify with, and take justifiable pride in their hill country heritage.

The academic proponents of Appalachian Studies identify a distinctive Appalachian subculture characterized by a wide degree of heterogeneity and undergoing the throes of change.

The cultural practitioners - artists, craftsmen, writers, and musicians see the Appalachian way as a good life worth preserving, practicing, and passing on to future generations.

These broad stereotyped image responses to the question, "What is Appalachia?" tend to incorporate the common failing of overemphasizing one characteristic of Appalachia to the exclusion of others thereby continuing the distortion of the real nature of the region and its people.

The history of mankind records the influence of environment on the ways of life of the people of the world. Distinctive cultures have been found related to the deserts, tropics, seas, artics, mountains, and fertile river bottoms. Even with the control over the environment afforded by science and technology, its unmistakable influence continues.

At the outset, when the first settlers made their way into the mountain fastness, and the wilderness was the dominant environmental influence, life in Appalachia was quite similar to life elsewhere on the American frontier. With the passing of time however, and the interaction of the environment with the culture of the early settlers, economic development, and technological advancement, a distinctive subculture began to emerge.

Much has been written in the initial two centuries of the Nation on the way of life in the mountains. That which is pertinent to our understanding of the culture of the Mountain State and Appalachia will be examined simultaneously from 1) the overall perspective of the Appalachian region, and 2) the specific situation as it prevails in West Virginia.

A REGION IN TRANSITION

Appalachia has been characterized as a region of contrasts. Within the mountains are found variations in life style all the way from the frontier past of deep isolation to the middle class product of the fringe areas of urban society. Within this spectrum are found rural and urban families, poverty and affluence, subsistence and commercial farming, coal miners and coal mine owners, alienation and hope. The region has been described as "... an interplay between stability and change; isolation and contrast; the primitive and progressive. Where else can one find such contrasts as Elizabethan folklore and atomic reactors; planting by the moon and scientific agriculture; medieval demonology and modern medicine; beliefs that God sends floods to wipe out the sinful as in Noah's time and TVA; the primitive Protestant emphasis on individualism and the overloaded welfare roles?"[2]

Every culture has its distinctive attributes and emphasis. The distinctive themes of Appalachian culture in earlier days were not difficult to identify, since they attracted the attention of practically all who visited and wrote about the region. In examining the web of mountain life, the themes of individualism, traditionalism, familism, and religion are found intertwined. At the same time most so-called "mountain traits" are to be found in one form or another throughout the nation.[3] To a considerable extent, the popular but erroneous impression of a homogenous mountain culture stems from the fact that most contemporary studies have been of isolated communities, often selected because they reflected a way of life rapidly disappearing from the region. Not only has this bias created a false impression of homogeneity, but it has also tended to obscure the nature of the tremendous cultural changes that have been taking place over the years.[4]

Sociologists and anthropologists have long recognized that all parts of a culture do not change at an equal rate. As a general rule, the technological aspects are the first to change, followed more slowly by adaptations of social organizations to new technologies. Most resistant to change are sentiments, beliefs, and values.

Values are basic components of personality developed primarily during the early years of life. They are deeply embedded and tend to endure, providing stability and helping to decide what is good or bad, right or wrong, important or unimportant, desirable or undesirable. As basic determinents of behavior they constitute the basis for the nature and integration of the social systems of Appalachia.[5]

A BICULTURAL PEOPLE

Writers have observed that Appalachian people have developed the ability to function biculturally. This is to say, exposure to the values of the greater society in addition to those of their own heritage, provides opportunity to utilize whichever values give most meaning to the immediate situation.[6]

Studies of the region on the one hand, provide substantial evidence the major factors which contributed to the development and maintenance of Appalachian culture have all but disappeared under the levelling impact of mainstream society over the past fifty years. On the other hand, they indicate Appalachian culture has demonstrated a remarkable persistence - continuing as a kind of cultural underlay permeating life throughout the region with varying degrees of intensity.

Hence, seemingly contradictory conclusions may be drawn from studies of Appalachia. While it is still possible to find isolated communities where residents fully reflect the culture of the past, it is equally possible for other natives of the region to move with the greatest ease and freedom in mainstream society without showing or professing any personal identity with their cultural heritage. Many thus are found who no longer identify with the region yet still carry much of the Appalachian value pattern.

It is precisely this heterogenity and fluidity of the state of cultural change that lies at the heart of the problem for those who would live and work with Appalachians. The challenge confronting all who would understand and be involved in the development of the region is to be sensitive to the extent to which the cultural heritage is operative among those individuals where it is least evident or expected, and at the same time function effectively among those where the culture is more clearly in evidence.

Of even greater significance is the task of helping Appalachians who are seeking to participate more fully in mainstream society, to retain those cultural values and life patterns which give life meaning today. In the face of the growing depersonalization accompanying the urbanization of American society, it is increasingly important to retain the person-orientation, family and kin relationships, and basic religious beliefs which give meaning to life. Herein, Appalachian culture has much to contribute to the urbanized culture of mainstream America.

PATTERN OF VALUES

Culture, broadly defined, is a way of life. The Appalachian subculture thus embraces those distinctive patterns of living found in the region which give it an identity and set it apart from mainstream American society. Cultural values represent the goals of social behavior which give life meaning and purpose. Values are deep seated and resistant to cultural change. It is through values that Appalachian culture is most readily identified.

The Appalachian value pattern was the subject of a 1973 comparative study of West Virginia Extension agents[7] The research focused on a pattern of nine selected values identified as being characteristic of Appalachian culture. Individually each of the values are not unique to Appalachia. The

Cultural distinctiveness exists in the specific pattern of the values, their interrelationships, and the intensity with which they are held. Under the broad umbrella of traditionalism, the values fall into three clusters: (1) the Familism Cluster: familism, neighborliness, and love of home place; (2) The Individualism Cluster: individualism, personalism, modesty, and sense of humor; and (3) Religion.

Appalachian Value Pattern
Traditionalism

Familism	Individualism	Religion
Neighborliness	Personalism	
Love of Home Place	Modesty and Being One's Self	
	Sense of Humor	

The sensitivity of West Virginia Extension agents to the nine cultural values and the extent to which they entered into and influenced their work was determined. West Virginia Extension Agents showed greater sensitivity to the Appalachian value pattern than did New Jersey or North Dakota Extension Agents. Older, more experienced, and more effective Extension Agents in West Virginia showed greater sensitivity to the pattern of values than did younger, less experienced West Virginia Extension agents. The findings of the study indicated that awareness, sensitivity, and utilization of the Appalachian Value Pattern, and success of work with West Virginia Extension education program, were related.

Traditionalism [8]

As long ago as 1899, William G. Frost characterized the people of Appalachia as "contemporary ancestors" and several years later Horace Kephart described the mountaineer as being bound to the past in an amazing way: "... their adherence to old ways is stubborn, sullen and perverse to a degree that others cannot comprehend."

As recently as 1970, Jack Weller characterized them as "yesterday's people". He observed that while much of American culture has faced so many changes within the last hundred years as to leave many people virtually rootless, mountain life has preserved the old traditions and ideas.

Brown, Schwarzweller, and Mangalam found in their Beech Creek, Kentucky, study in 1970 that "... traditionalism, in short served as the standard of standards, the legitimating principle integrating the various elements of culture and social structure and thereby tending to protect the integrity of this system, maintaining stability, and warding off the system-disturbing influences of modernization." Most of the beliefs and practices were handed down relatively intact from one generation to another, and because they were the beliefs and practices of forefathers, they were deemed right; they were prescriptions to be followed.

While writers have generally agreed that traditionalism is a dominant value in Appalachian culture, they have not always recoginzed its interdependence with other values.

However strong this value may have been a generation ago, under the pressure of progress, it has been substantially weakened in recent years. In the Extension study, West Virginia agents were found to be much more sensitive to traditionalism than were Extension agents in New Jersey, indicating the continuing persistence of this Appalachian cultural value when compared to an urbanized state.

Familism [9]

The strength of the mountain society lay in the family and kin group relationships. Here are found, preserved and passed on attitudes, patterns of behavior, outlook on life, and ways of dealing with everyday problems. Personal ties, identity, loyalty, and well being were within a given family and tended to remain very similar generation after generation.

The extended family provides additional outlets for fulfillment of children's emotional needs and affection. Children are reared by parents but often close relatives share affectional roles with them. In early times, life in Appalachia made it necessary for kin group members to rely on each other in times of need. As a result, there is a deep respect and abiding loyalty to kinfolk; "this alone may be the key distinguishing feature of the Appalachian family."

In Appalachia there is a place for everyone from the newborn to the elderly. There is respect for the aged and they are usually spared the feeling of uselessness and abandonment so common in American society.

Through the years the family has served as a means of transition to city life. The migrant family not only performs the function of informing relatives of job opportunities but also helps them in the socialization and adjustment process in the new environment.

The extended family provides the individual with a haven of safety in time of economic crises and a social psychological cushion in time of personal stress. Recent evidence suggests that traditional patterns of family behavior are being disturbed and the stability of the rural Appalachian family is under pressure from the forces of change.

In the Extension study, West Virginia Extension agents of greater experience and effectiveness reflected more sensitivity to familism as a cultural value in their work than did younger, less effective agents.

208

Neighborliness[10]

Closely related to the value of familism and the extended family is the basic quality of neighborliness and hospitality. Frontier conditions created an interdependence among families as they built houses, raised barns, exchanged farm implements and fought Indians.

A high value was placed on having good neighbors. It was important to have someone to lend a hand, someone to turn to when needed and someone to trust. Food and shelter was always provided for travelers. No greater compliment could be paid a mountain family than referring to them as being "clever." This did not refer to cunningness or intelligence, but rather indicated hospitality and generosity with food and lodging.

Again the extension study indicates that older, more effective agents gave greater consideration to the value of neighborliness in their work than did their younger, less experienced counterparts.

Love of Home Place[11]

Mountain people never really cut their ties to their place of native origin, and though forced to live elsewhere, try to return as often as possible to the old homeplace.

The homeplace is symbolic of the family and reinforces the strong family loyalty felt by the mountaineer. There weems to be a lifelong tie with the people and experiences associated with the homeplace. Identification with the land, people, buildings, and the community persist. This is reflected in the numbers of West Virginians who return for family reunions, holidays, church and community homecomings, to retire, or to be buried in the family cemetery.

Once again our study shows older more effective extension agents display greater sensitivity than did younger, less experienced agents.

Individualism[12]

Individualism, independence and self-reliance are recognized as characteristics of Appalachian people by most writers. Heredity and environment have conspired to make the Appalachian an extreme individualist. While railroads and highways joined the life of the urban Appalachian more closely to that of the rest of the country over a century of time, the rural Appalachian remained isolated and the existence of the pioneer ways persisted.

Appalachian people are more tuned to timing of the seasons and the personal relations they enjoy with others. The artificiality of the time clock is tolerated but not always respected. Discipline has not always been a part of the behavior pattern and individuals were often reticent to make definite assertions... Sometimes, they just got out of the notion!

Initially isolation was a given for the mountain people, they accepted it as inevitable. But in time they came to love the solitude for its own sake and to find compensation for lack of society.

The independent and self-reliant spirit remains a valuable asset of Appalachian people. It is a source of great strength and stamina. Brown, in the Beech Creek studies, concluded that individualism was an obvious characteristic of the personality and ''... appeared to have been derived from the basic tenets of puritanism coupled with a firm belief in the ultimate rightness of democracy. It provided the Beech Creeker with an unsettling, but driving strength.''

The study of West Virginia Extension agents indicates that individualism, long recognized as a distinctive Appalachian Cultural value, may be increasing in importance throughout American society almost as though in reaction to the dehumanizing effects of mass society.

Personalism[13]

A person is of primary importance in Appalachia! The major goal of Appalachian people is to have meaningful relationships with other persons as total individuals. Time is secondary; it becomes meaningful only in the context of relationships.

Applachian people tend to accept others on face value as human beings rather than on credentials, looks, or accomplishments. A high value is placed on personal standing and reputation with other people.

The Appalachian tends to see others as whole individuals -- good and bad included. Unlike the urban oriented individual who often sees other people only in specific roles, the Appalachian sees the whole person unencumbered by role definition.

It is in sensitivity to the cultural value of personalism that work performance of older, more effective West Virginia Extension agents tends to show the most difference from their younger, less experienced counterparts.

Modesty[14]

Most mountain people tend to be modest about their abilities. The mountaineer believes he is as good as anyone else but no better. He is looked upon as ''one of the most egalitarian persons alive. This belief in equality coupled with his place in the family and his tendency to be satisfied with whatever fate deals him, has almost completely eliminated any competitiveness from his makeup. Mountaineers tend to have a pretty realistic view of themselves. They never believed that man could be perfect'' and will go to great lengths to avoid becoming embroiled in situations where a difference of opinion exists.

Once again the greater sensitivity of older more effective agents to the cultural value of modesty is clearly indicated over that of younger, less effective agents.

Sense of Humor [15]

"Humor has sustained people in hard times in Appalachia. The mountain man's humor can be tied to his concept of man and the human condition. He sees humor in man's pretensions to power and perfection and in his inevitable failures.'' A practical joking kind of humor still exists in the region, particularly in the rural areas.

The humor of Appalachian people is often reflected in their song, story, and speech, for it is here that they have mastered the simile and metaphor. Dial stated that ''... speakers of Southern Mountain dialect are past masters of the art of coining vivid descriptions. Their everyday conversation is liberally sprinkled with such gems as: 'That man is so contrary, if you throwed him in a river he'd float upstream!' or 'She walks so slow they have to set stakes to see if she's movin!''

It was in sensitivity to the cultural value of modesty that older, more effective agents showed the greatest difference over their younger, less experienced counterparts.

Religion [16]

Religious values so thoroughly permeate the culture of the Appalachian region that it is impossible to treat meaningfully any aspect of life without taking them into consideration. Because religious values underlie so many attitudes and beliefs, they exert complex and frequently subtle influences on behavior which are not always apparent to outside observers or even to the people themselves.

Writers are generally agreed that the culture of the people is intertwined with their religious faith. Hill, in discussing southern Protestantism wrote ''... formal cultural experience... the religious factor is not official creeds but what people perceive the church's truth-claims to be, in line with the complex of assumptions and pictures with which cultural participation has equipped them.'' Maurer observed, ''it was religion that gave meaning to the mountain way of life.'' Salvation was seen as pivotal for the fundamentalist Christian belief-system and it enabled the individual to ''... make some kind of sense out of the world in which he finds himself." Brown and Schwarzweller found in their Beech Creek studies that while puritanism of the people was not exactly the same as that of early settlers, it was nevertheless a form of puritanism, and that it was woven into one of the fundamental value complexes in the culture. A belief prevailed that every man should be economically independent and that poverty was due to individual failings. Thus, the "belief system not only legitimized but sanctioned the individual's drive toward economic success, his concern for the future and repression of immediate desires, his hard work and his conviction that he had within himself the power to 'become'."

Kaplan, in his description of the religious life in Blue Ridge, most insightfully showed the direct relationship of the religious faith to the behavior of the residents. "Much of their religious service is concerned with open talk about low social and economic status, but they believe that the mansion of heaven will compensate them for their low positions. Indeed, many believe that suffering makes them holier in this life."

Jones points out that: "One has to understand the religion of the mountaineers before he can begin to understand mountaineers. In the beginning there were Presbyterians, Episcopalians, and other formally organized denominations, but these churches required an educated clergy and centralized organization, impractical requirements in the wilderness, and so locally autonomous sects grew up. These individualistic churches stressed the fundamentals of the faith and depended on local resources and leadership.

"Many social reformers . . . view the local sect churches as a hindrance to social progress. What they fail to see is that it was the church which helped sustain us and made life worth living in grim situations. Religion shaped our lives, but at the same time we shaped our religion. Culture and religion are intertwined. The life on the frontier did not allow for an optimistic social gospel. One was lucky if he endured. Hard work did not bring a sure reward. Therefore the religion stressed rewards in another life. The important thing was to get religion—get saved—which meant accepting Jesus as one's personal savior. It was and is a realistic religion which fitted a realistic people. It is based on belief in the Original Sin, that man is fallible, that he will fail, does fail. Mountaineers readily see that the human tragedy is this, man sees so clearly what he should do and what he should not do and yet he fails so consistently . . . There is strong belief in the Golden Rule. These beliefs, and variations on them, have sustained us, have given our lives meaning and have helped us to rationalize our lack of material success. Every group of people must have meaning in their lives, must believe in themselves. There are few Appalachians atheists . . . Many of the values and beliefs have religious origins."

212

Once again in the extension study, older more effective agents evidenced greater sensitivity in their work to the cultural value of religion than did their younger, less experienced counterparts.

THE PROUD PEOPLE

What is Appalachia from the perspective of the Bicentennial? Appalachia is first and foremost people. People with a long standing, rich tradition deeply rooted in the American birthright. People whose mountain environment interacting with their ancestral cultural background, exploitive development of natural and human resources, and technological advancement over the years, has produced a distinctly American subculture—a way of life which persists as a broad cultural underlay of the region, influencing life on every level in varying degrees of intensity.

Appalachia is a region of cultural transition caught in the grip of change under the pressure of mainstream American society. Its people, of necessity are bicultural, encompassing both the old and the new from the extremes of frontier folk practice to orbital communications with every gradation in between. They are engrossed in a struggle to reconcile the longstanding, trusted, though archaic ways of the past with the untried, unsure, somewhat questionable promise of the future. Many are not sure the cost they pay in what they give up for a more developed, mass media lifestyle is worth it. It is precisely the fluidity of the state of cultural change, and heterogeneity of the pattern of life in the mountain region, masked by a stereotyped popular image of Appalachia, that gives the greatest difficulty for those who would understand and work with its people.

Throughout the region and across the Mountain State, a new sense of understanding, appreciation, and pride is emerging in a pattern of values and a way of life—an Appalachian Renaissance—which bodes well and has much to contribute to national welfare on the occasion of the Bicentennial.

FOOTNOTES

[1] Miller, Tom D., *Who Owns West Virginia*, Huntington Advertiser and Herald Dispatch reprint booklet, Huntington, West Virginia, December, 1974.

[2] Ernst, Harry and Drake, Charles H., "The Lost Appalachians," *Appalachia in the Sixties*, edited by David S. Walls and John B. Stephenson (Lexington: University of Kentucky Press, 1972), p. 5; see also Campbell, John, *The Southern Highlander and His Homeland*, p. XIV.

[3] Ford, Thomas, "The Passing of Provincialism," in *The Southern Appalachian Region : A Survey* (Lexington: University of Kentucky, 1962), pp. 11-12.

[4] Ford, "The Passing of Provincialism," p. 10.

[5] Photiadis, John D. and Maurer, B. B., *Community Size and Social Attributes in West Virginia*, Research Report 5 (Morgantown: West Virginia University, Appalachian Center, 1972), pp. 7-8.

[6] For discussion see: Lewis, H., "Fatalism or the Coal Industry," *Mountain Life and Work*, December, 1970, pp. 5-15; also, Ford, "Passing of Provincialism," p. 16.

[7] Crickard, Betty P., "A Study of Cultural Values Influencing Educational Programming in West Virginia," Unpublished Ph.D. dissertation, (Walden University, 1974).

[8] For a discussion of Traditionalism, see: Schwarzweller, Harry K., Brown, James S., and Mangalam, J. J., *Mountain Families in Transition*, (University Park and London: The Pennsylvania State University Press, 1971), p. 67; Ford, "The Passing of Provincialism," pp. 15-16; Frost, William G., "Our Contemporary Ancestors in the Southern Mountains," *Atlantic Monthly*, LXXXIII (March, 1899), pp. 311-19; Kephart, Horace, *Our Southern Highlanders*, (New York: Outing Publishing Company, 1913), p. 23; Weller, Jack E., *Yesterday's People* (Lexington: The University Press of Kentucky, 1971), p. 33.

[9] For a discussion of Familism, see: Brown, James and Schwarzweller, Harry K., "The Appalachian Family," *Change in Rural Appalachia*, eds. John D. Photiadis and Harry K. Schwarzweller (Philadelphia: University of Pennsylvania Press, 1970), pp. 85-97; Weller, *Yesterday's People*, p. 49; Brown, *Appalachia in the Sixties*, p. 154.

214

[10] For a discussion of Neighborliness, see: Jones, "Appalachian Values," p. 113; Simpkins, O. Norman, "Culture" in *Mountain Heritage*, edited by B. B. Maurer, (Ripley: Mountain State Art and Craft Fair, 1974), pp. 37-40; Dial, Wylene P., "Language" *Mountain Heritage*, p. 56.

[11] For a discussion of Love of Home Place, see: Simpkins, "Culture," *Mountain Heritage*, p. 44; Jones, "Appalachian Values."

[12] For a discussion of Individualism, see: Turner, Frederick, "The Significance of the Frontier in American History" in Report of the Historical Association, 1893, pp. 199-227; Kephart, *Our Southern Highlanders*, p. 306; Weller, *Yesterday's People*, p. 30; and Schwarzweller, Brown, and Mangalam, *Mountain Families in Transition*, p. 214.

[13] For a discussion of Personalism, see: Weller, *Yesterday's People*, pp. 53-57; Jones, "Appalachian Values," pp. 114-115; Simpkins, "Culture," *Mountain Heritage*, p. 40.

[14] For a discussion of Modesty, see: Jones, "Appalachian Values," pp. 116-117; Jones, "The Impact of Appalachian Culture on Aspiration"; Weller, *Yesterday's People*, p. 47.

[15] For a discussion of Sense of Humor, see: Jones, "Appalachian Values," p. 12; Simpkins, "Culture," *Mountain Heritage*, p. 44; Dial, "Language" *Mountain Heritage*, p. 60.

[16] For a discussion of Religion, see: Ford, "The Passing of Provincialism," p. 21-22; Hill, Samuel S., "The South's Two Cultures," in Samuel J. Hill, Jr., *et al.*, *Religion and the Solid South*, (Nashville, Tennessee: Abingdon Press, 1972), p. 32; Maurer, "Religion" in *Mountain Heritage*, p. 105; Photiadis, John and Maurer, B. B., *Religion in an Appalachian State*, Research Publication No 6 (Morgantown: West Virginia University, 1974), p. 1; Schwarzweller, Brown, and Mangalam, *Mountain Families in Transition*, pp. 61-63; Kaplan, Berton H., *Blue Ridge, An Appalachian Community in Transition*, Office of Research and Development (Morgantown: West Virginia University, 1971), p. 121; Jones, "Appalachian Values" pp. 110-111, and Coles, Robert, *Migrants, Sharecroppers, Mountaineers*, Boston, Little Brown, and Company, 1971, pp. 473-477, 578-617.

Songs

CONTENTS

FOLKSONGS

Patrick W. Gainer

In this year of 1974, there is much confusion resulting from the vague and incorrect use of the term "folksong." The term is often incorrectly applied to any type of popular song that is sung in a certain informal style, especially if accompanied by a guitar, banjo, auto-harp, or other stringed instrument.

This conception of folksong really began with the advent of radio and the public juke-box, when a new kind of music called "hillbilly" was first heard by the American public. It was supposed to have come from the hills, but no real hill-dweller had ever before heard it. Actually, much of it came from the pens of those who sang it, with a good part of it coming from the confines of Tin Pan Alley.

It was not until the late 50's that the term "hillbilly music" was almost entirely dropped in favor of "country music," but it was the same music except for the addition of some new vocal and instrumental "gimmicks" which had been gradually acquired through the years by the performers of this twentieth century musical phenomenon. The term "hillbilly" was dropped probably because the term had always been used contemptuously by real hill-dwellers, and applied only to those among them who are considered ignorant and degenerate.

Now, in 1963, the term "folksong" was being applied to this same "hillbilly" or country music, as well as to many songs that truly deserved the name of folksong. True folksong is song that has been preserved in the minds of the people for a reasonable length of time -- certainly for more than a generation -- so that it has become the property of all of the people. Since it is not written but preserved in oral tradition, a folksong will change just as language changes through the years. Some of you will say, "My mother used to sing "Barbara Allen" but her tune was different." This may be true of many of the songs we will sing.

Folksongs were generally sung as a part of the everyday life of the people in the home. There was no stopping in the daily work for folksong, but it was sung as Mother sat at the spinning wheel or the loom, or as she went about her work of taking care of the house and the children. She sang for her own satisfaction, often because the song helped her to live in her imagination in a land of love and adventure, or helped her to express her sorrow or joy or sometimes her love to God. And so she sang "Lord Batemen," "Barbara Allen," "Lord

Thomas," "The Orphan Girl," or "The Pilgrim of Sorrow." These songs were not sung to any kind of instrumental accompaniment.

There were also times in the home, especially on long winter evenings, when children were entertained by parents or grandparents, who sang such songs as "Billy Boy," "Soldier, Will You Marry Me?," "Old Joe Clark," or "The Soldier's Poor Little Boy."

Some of the religious songs were printed in shape-notes. This method of writing music in notes of varied shapes to indicate their position in the scale is an American invention which became popular in rural America, especially in the South, during the nineteenth century and the early twentieth century. It was a system of singing taught in the singing schools by the itinerant "singing master," who went from one community to another teaching the "subscription school." Each family in the community would subscribe a small amount of money to keep the school in session. Both young and old learned to read music in this manner, always without accompaniment, so that after the singing master had gone on his way, the people met each week in the church or schoolhouse to have song. This gathering to sing became an important social institution in the rural communities of West Virginia.

AIKEN DRUM

Leprechauns were the good but mischievous little elves of the isles. This is a song about one such elf whose name was Aiken Drum.

G7 C   F   C   G7
There came a man to our town, to our town, to our town,
      C   F   C   G7 C
There came a man to our town, and his name was Aiken Drum.
       C   F   C   G7
And he played upon a ladle, a ladle, a ladle,
       C   F   C   G7 C
And he played upon a ladle, and they called him Aiken Drum.

His *hat was made of * *good roast beef, of good roast beef, of good roast beef,
His hat was made of good roast beef, and his name was Aiken Drum.
And he played upon a ladle, a ladle, a ladle,
And he played upon a ladle, and his name was Aiken Drum.

There came a man to our town, to our town, to our town,
There came a man to our town, and his name was Aiken Drum.
And he played upon a razor, a razor, a razor,
And he played upon a razor, and his name was Aiken Drum.

221

And he ate up all the good roast beef, the good roast beef, the good roast beef,
And he ate up all the good roast beef, and his name was Aiken Drum.
And he played upon a razor, a razor, a razor,
And he played upon a razor, and his name was Aiken Drum.

*Fill in with name of article of clothing or part of body.
**Fill in with name of different things to eat.

THE ASH GROVE

While the Welsh version, "Llwyn On," has words too difficult for most of us
(for example, Ym Mhalas Llwyn On gynt, fe drigal pende fig), this beautiful
old Welsh melody has gained much popularity.

```
      G          Em           Am      D
The ash grove, how graceful, how plainly 'tis speaking,
      Em        C         G       D7  G
The wind thro' it playing has language for me;
G          Em           Am       D
Whenever the light thro' its branches is breaking,
    Em          C     G    D7  G
A host of kind faces is gazing on me;
    G          Em        C        D7
The friends of my childhood again are before me,
      G        Em        D    A7  D
Fond memories waken as freely I roam.
      G          Em        Am       D
With soft whispers laden, its leaves rustle o'er me,
      Em      C              G      D7   G
The ash grove, the ash grove that sheltered my home.
```

My laughter is over, my step loses lightness,
Old country side measures steal soft on my ear;
I only remember the past and its brightness,
The dear ones I mourn for again gather here.
From out of the shadows their loving looks greet me,
And wistfully searching the leafy green dome,
I find other faces fond bending to greet me,
The ash grove, the ash grove alone is my home.

The tunes of the Welsh and Irish songs derive from the ancient harp and pipe
tunes of the Celtic people. In nearly every case the tunes are many hundreds of
years old while the words are only a few hundred years old. "The Ash
Grove" is such a song.

222

AUNT RHODY

This lyric is a popular nursery song. Appalachian Mountain tune.

F
Go tell Aunt Rhody,

C7   F
Go tell Aunt Rhody,

F
Go tell Aunt Rhody,

  C7   F
Her old gray goose is dead.

The one she's been savin',
The one she's been savin',
The one she's been savin',
To made a feather bed.

The goslins are weeping,
The goslins are weeping,
The goslins are weeping,
Because their mother's dead.

She died in the mill pond,
She died in the mill pond,
She died in the mill pond,
A-standing on her head.

She was buried last Tuesday,
She was buried last Tuesday,
She was buried last Tuesday,
So the preacher said.

BARBARA ALLEN

This folk song originated in Scotland and dates back at least to the beginning of the seventeenth century, at which time there were both Scottish and English versions. Today, there are literally hundreds of versions of "Barbara Allen," but the central theme is always the same -- that of a young girl whose true love dies of a broken heart. His death brings her such misery that she soon joins him in the grave. They are at last united when the rose bush and the briar tie in a true-love knot.

Dm Am Dm
In Scarlet Town where I was born,

    Am   Dm
There was a fair maid dwelling,

    Dm Am   Em Am
Made ev'ry youth cry, "Well, a way,"

Dm   Am   Dm
And her name was Barbry Allen.

'Twas early in the month of May,
When the green buds were a-swellin',
Young Johnny Green on his death-bed lay,
For the love of Barbry Allen.

He sent his servant to the town,
Where his love was a-dwellin'
Saying, "Follow me to my master dear,
If you name be Barbry Allen."

So slowly, slowly she got up,
And slowly she went nigh him,
But all she said when she got there,
"Young man, I think you're dyin' ".

"O don't you remember the other night,
When you were at the tavern?
You drank a health to the ladies round,
But slighted Barbry Allen."

"O yes, I remember the other night,
When I was at the tavern,
I drank a health to the ladies round,
But gave my love to Barbry Allen."

As she was walking through the town,
She heard the death bell tollin'
And ev'ry toll is seemed to say,
"Hard-hearted Barbry Allen."

"O Mother, O Mother, go make my bed,
Go make it soft and narrow,
Young Johnny Green died for me today,
And I'll die for him tomorrow."

O she was buried in the old churchyard,
And he was buried a-nigh her,
And out of her grave grew a red, red rose,
And out of his a green briar.

And they grew till they reached to the top of the church,
And they couldn't grow any higher;
And there they met in a true-lover's knot,
The red rose and the green briar.

BILLY BOY

While the melody probably originated somewhere in the British Isles centuries ago, the lyric idea seems based on the old English ballad "Lord
Randall." As the Irish, Scots and English began moving south and westward
from New England, many migrants decided not to go beyond the
Appalachians, so this is the area where the song became firmly established.

G
Oh, where have you been, Billy Boy, Billy Boy?
                     D7
Oh, where have you been, charming Billy?
                           G
Oh, I've been to seek a wife, she's the joy of my life,
            D7   G
But she's a young thing and can't leave her mammy.

Did she ask you in Billy Boy, Billy Boy?
Did she ask you in, charming Billy?
Oh, yes, she asked me in, she has a dimple in her chin,
But she's a young thing and can't leave her mammy.

Did she set for you a chair, Billy Boy, Billy Boy?
Did she set for you a chair, charming Billy?
Yes, she set for me a chair, she has ringlets in her hair,
But she's a young thing and can't leave her mammy.

Can she bake a cherry pie, Billy Boy, Billy Boy?
Can she bake a cherry pie, charming Billy?
She can bake a cherry pie, quick as a cat can wink its eye,
But she's a young thing and can't leave her mammy.

Can she bake a sweetened pone, Billy Boy, Billy Boy?
Can she bake a sweetened pone, charming Billy?
She can bake a sweetened pone, you can eat it or let it alone,
But she's a young thing and can't leave her mammy.

Can she make a feather bed, Billy Boy, Billy Boy?
Can she make a feather bed, charming Billy?
She can make a feather bed, put the pillows at the head.
But she's a young thing and can't leave her mammy.

How tall is she, Billy Boy, Billy Boy?
How tall is she, charming Billy?
She's as tall as a pine and straight as a punkin vine,
But she's a young thing and can't leave her mammy.

How old is she, Billy Boy, Billy Boy?
How old is she, charming Billy?
Twice six, twice seven, twice twenty and eleven,
But she's a young thing and can't leave her mammy.

BASHFUL NEIGHBOR BOY

G   D7   G
When are you gonna come courtin, courtin, courtin,

When are you gonna come courtin,
   D7   G
My bashful neighbor boy?

I reckon it'll be next Sunday, Sunday, Sunday,
I reckon it'll be next Sunday,
If the weather be good.

What are ya gonna bring courtin, courtin, courtin,
What are ya gonna bring courtin,
My bashful neighbor boy?

I reckon I'll bring my hog sled, hog sled, hog sled,
I reckon I'll bring my hog sled,
If the weather be good.

When are we gonna get married, married, married,
When are we gonna get married,
My bashful neighbor boy?

I reckon it'll be any day now, day now, day now,
I reckon it'll be any day now,
If the weather be good.

How're you gonna come to the weddin, weddin, weddin,
How're you gonna come to the weddin,
My bashful neighbor boy?

I guess I'll drive my ox cart, ox cart, ox cart,
I guess I'll drive my ox cart,
If the weather be good.

What ya gonna wear to the weddin, weddin, weddin,
What ya gonna wear to the weddin,
My bashful neighbor boy?

I reckon I'll wear my buck skins, buck skins, buck skins,
I reckon I'll wear my buck skins,
If the weather be good.

Who ya gonna bring to the weddin, weddin, weddin,
Who ya gonna bring to the weddin,
My bashful neighbor boy?

I reckon I'll bring my children, children, children,
I reckon I'll bring my children,
If the weather be good.

I didn't know you had any children, children, children,
I didn't know you had any children,
My bashful neighbor boy.

227

Yes, I have six children, children, children
Yes, I have six children,
Seven, if the weather be good.

There ain't gonna be no weddin, weddin, weddin,
There ain't gonna be no weddin,
Not even if the weather be good!

CINDY

This is a typical folk song, born of American pioneers, when we were a nation of only seventeen states. It is still a favorite with mountaineer fiddlers and banjo pickers, and groups often enjoy singing it as well.

    G
You ought-ter see my Cindy,
          D7
She lives away down South,
  G   CF
Now she's so sweet the honey bees,
    G   D7   G
They swarm around her mouth.

The first I seen my Cindy,
          D7
A standin' in the door,
  G   C
Her shoes and stockin's in 'er hand,
  G   D7
Her feet all over the floor.

Chorus
  G   C
Git along home, Cindy, Cindy,
     G
Git along home Cindy, Cindy,
    C
Git along home Cindy, Cindy,
    G D7   G
I'll marry you some day.

I wish I was an apple,
A-hangin' on a tree,
An' ev'ry time my Cindy passed,
She'd take a bite of me.
If I were made of sugar,
A-standin' in the town,
Then ev'ry time my Cindy passed,
I'd shake some sugar down.

My Cindy got religion.
She had it once before.
But when she heard my ol' banjo,
She leaped upon the floor.
She took me to her parlor,
She cooled me with her fan,
She said I was the purtiest thing,
The shape of mortal man.

Now Cindy is a sweet girl,
My Cindy is a peach,
She threw her arms around me tight,
An' hung on like a leech.
She kissed me an' she hugged me,
She called me sugar plum,
She hugged so tight I hardly breathed,
I thought my time had come.

If I had thread an' needle,
If I knew how to sew,
I'd sew that gal to my coat tail,
An' down the road I'd go.
I want my Cindy, Cindy
Her lips an' arms an' feet,
I never seen another gal,
That Cindy couldn't beat.

COCKLES AND MUSSELS

"Cockles and Mussels" or "Molly Malone" apparently dates from the 19th century and unlike the usual folk songs has had little or no variation in form or text.

```
     G                      D7
In Dublin's fair city, where girls are so pretty,
  G                        C   D7
I first set my eyes on sweet Molly Malone,
        G                        D7
As she rushed her wheel-barrow thru streets broad and narrow,
         G                   D7 G
Crying, "Cockles and mussels alive, alive oh!
  G            D7
Alive, alive oh! Alive, alive oh!"
            G                   D7 G
Crying, "Cockles and mussels alive, alive oh!"
```

She was a fish monger, but sure 'twas no wonder,
For so were her father and mother before,
And they each wheel'd their barrow thru streets broad and narrow,
Crying, "Cockles and mussels alive, alive oh!
Alive, alive oh! Alive, alive oh!"
Crying, "Cockles and mussels alive, alive oh!"

She died of a fever, and no one could save her,
And that was the end of sweet Molly Malone;
Now her ghost wheels her barrow thru street broad and narrow,
Crying, "Cockles and mussels alive, alive oh!
Alive, alive oh! Alive, alive oh!"
Crying, "Cockles and mussels alive, alive oh!"

COMIN' THRO THE RYE

```
G       D7           G   D7    G
If a body meet a body, comin' thro the rye;
        C            G   D7 G
If a body kiss a body, need a body cry?
            D7          G
Ev'ry lassie has her laddie, nane they say ha'e I;
  G     D7      G     D7      G   D7      G
Yet a' the lads they smile on me, when comin' thro' the rye.
```

If a body meet a body, comin' frae the town,
If a body greet a body, need a body frown?
Ev'ry laddie has her lassie, nane they say ha'e I;
Yet a' the lads they smile on me, when comin' thro' the rye.

Amang the train there is a swain I dearly love mysel';
But what's his name, or where's his hame, I dinna choose to tell.
Ev'ry lassie has her laddie, nane they say ha'e I;
Yet a' the lads they smile on me, when comin' thro' the rye.

DANNY BOY

This is the famous "Londonderry Air" which is known and loved by people all over the world. These first lyrics in Ireland were known as "Morning in Barra."

```
G7        C   G7  C          C7      F
Oh, Danny Boy, the pipes, the pipes are calling.
 G7        C                         G7
From glen to glen, and down the mountain side,
             C         C7       F  Fm
The summer's gone, and all the roses falling,
          C     F  C     Dm G7 C
It's you, it's you must go, and I must bide.
G7        C           F              C
But come ye back when summer's in the meadow,
G7        Am      F                   G7
Or when the valley's hushed and white with snow,
         C      F         C    Am
It's I'll be here in sunshine or in shadow,
G7        C   C7      F   G7   C
Oh, Danny Boy, oh, Danny Boy, I love you so!
```

But when ye come, and all the flow'ers are dying,
If I am dead, as dead I well may be,
Ye'll come and find the place where I am lying,
And kneel and say an Ave there for me;
And I shall hear, though soft you tread above me,
And all my grave will warmer, sweeter be,
For you will bend and tell me that you love me,
And I shall sleep in peace until you come to me!

DUMBARTON'S DRUMS

A text for this song was first printed in 1724, but the music has been traced a century earlier, where it was entitled "I serve a worthie lady." In 1726 it was printed as "Dumbarton's Drums" in a book called *Musick for the Scots Songs in the Tea-Table Miscellany.* Only recently has the song been sung again, and the song we now sing has been collected from oral tradition in America. It is a wistful, yearning romance about a young Scot who is the bell-keeper in Dumbarton, as sung by his lassie. (Chorus and verses have the same tune.)

Chorus

```
C                                    G7
Dumbarton's drums, they sound so bonnie,
                                C
When they remind me of my Johnny,
            F              C
What fond delight can steal upon me,
            G7               C
When Johnny kneels and kisses me.
```

Across the fields of bounding heather
Dumbarton tolls the hour of pleasure,
A song of love that has no measure,
When Johnny kneels and sings to me.

Repeat Chorus

Tis he alone that can delight me,
His graceful eye, it doth invite me,
And when his tender arms enfold me,
The blackest night doth turn and dee.

Repeat Chorus

My love is a handsome laddie
And though he is Dumbarton's caddie
Some day I'll be the captain's lady,
When Johnny tends his vow to me.

THE FARMER'S WIFE AND THE DEVIL

The legend of a violent, repulsive old hag who can outdevil the devil himself is widely known, and it is one that never fails to be funny. Wherever the ballad appears in the English, Scottish, or American tradition, the story line is about the same. The devil appears to an ancient henpecked farmer and demands the farmer's wife. The farmer graciously grants the devil's request, but after various outrages, his satanic majesty can take no more, and the old wife is carried back to earth and her unfortunate farmer-husband.

    G
There was an old man lived under the hill.
 C   G
If he ain't moved away he's living there still.
    G   C   G
Sing fie-did-dle-i, did-dle-i, fie-did-dle-i, did-dle-i day.

Old satan came to the man at the plow,
Said, "one of your family I'm goin' to have now."
Sing. . . .

"O, it's not your son that I do crave,
But it's your old wife I'm goin' to have."
Sing. . . .

"O Satan, take her with all my heart,
I hope, by golly, you'll never part."
Sing. . . .

Old Satan took her upon his back,
He carried her away like an old miller's sack.
Sing. . . .

When he got her to the forks of the road,
Says he, "Old woman, You're an awful load."
Sing. . . .

When he got her to the gates of hell,
Says, "Stir up the fire, we'll scorch her well.
Sing. . . .

Ten little devils came rattling their chains,
She upped with her stick and knocked out their brains
Sing. . . .

233

And the little devils began to squall,
"Take her home, pappy, she'll kill us all."
Sing. . . .

Old Satan took her back to the old man,
Says, "Keep her at home now if you can."
Sing. . . .

When she got home the old man was in bed,
She upped with her stick and knocked him in the head.
Sing. . . .

Said he, "Old woman, did you fare well?"
Said she, "Old man, I flattened all hell."
Sing . . . .

Now you can see just what these women can do,
They can whip men and devils too.
Sing . . . .

Now there's one advantage women have over men.
They can go to hell and come back again.
Sing . . . .

FROGGY WENT A-COURTIN'

First printed in England in 1611 under the title ''A Moste Strange Weddinge of the Ffroge and the Mouse,'' this favorite song was listed long before that in Scotland (1549) and ''The Frog Cam (came) to the Myl Dur (mill door.)'' It seems that Queen Elizabeth (1533-1603) gave her various suitors the amusing nicknames of animals, so the song actually has its roots in political satire. It refers to her romance with Duc d'Alencon (her frog), which was so unpopular with her subjects.

```
C                        F        C
Froggy went a-courtin' and he did ride, um-hum! um-hum!
                                 G7
Froggy went a-courtin' and he did ride, um-hum!
C                        C7
Froggy went a-courtin' and he did ride,
F            E7          C       G7      C
Sword and a pistol by his side, um-hum! um-hum! um-hum!
```

He rode down to Miss Mousie's door,
Where he'd often been before.

Little Miss Mousie came tripping down,
In her velvet satin gown.

Then Miss Mousie asked him in,
Where she sat to card and spin.

He took Miss Mousie on his knee,
Said: ''Miss Mousie, will you marry me?''

''Without my Uncle Rat's consent
I would not marry the pres-i-dent.''

Soon Uncle Rat came home:--
''Who's been here since I been gone?''

''Nice young man with a moustache on,
Askin' me to marry him.''

Uncle Rat gave his consent,
So they were married and a-way they went.

O where will the wedding supper be?
Away down younder in a holler tree.

O what will the wedding supper be?
Two butterbeans and a blackeyed pea.

O the first to come in was a little white moth,
Spreading down the table cloth.

O the next to come in was a garter-snake
Passin' around the wedding cake.

O the next to come in was the betsy-bug,
Passin' round the cider jug.

O the next to come in was the bumble bee,
Turned his banjo on his knee.

O the next to come in was the nimble flea,
Took a jig with the bumble bee.

O the next to come in was two little ants,
Fixin' around to have a dance.

O the next to come in was the old grey goose,
She picked up her fiddle and she cut loose.

O the next to come in was the old red cow,
She tried to dance but she didn't know how.

O the next to come in was the little old tick,
A-walkin' around with his walkin' stick.

O the next to come in was the little old gnat,
With his high-top shoes and a derby hat.

O the next to come was the old grey cat,
Said she'd put an end to that.

The bride went a-scrambling up the wall,
Her foot slipped and she got a fall.

Froggy went a-swimmin' across the lake,
He got gobbled by a big black snake.

The song book's settin' on the shelf, um-hum! um-hum!
Song book's settin' on the shelf, um-hum!
Song book's settin' on the shelf,
If you want any more you can sing it yourself, um-hum! um-hum! um-hum!

(Follow pattern of first and last verses. Verses may be omitted as desired.)

GET UP AND BAR THE DOOR

This is an ancient Scottish tale—one of a group which may or may not have had a single archetype. It is a tale about a man and his wife who are lying in bed arguing over the simple matter of who will bar the door. Finally, they make a pact that the one who speaks first shall shut the door.

   Em
The wind blew high, the wind blew cold,
 G
It blew across the moor,
   Em   Bm Em   Am
When John Jones said to Jane, his wife,
   Em   Am Em
"Get up and bar the door."

"Oh, I have worked all day," said she,
"I've washed and scrubbed the floor,
So come on now you lazy man,
Get up and bar the door."

"Oh, I have worked so hard," said he,
"I know I can't do more;
So come, my own, my dearest wife,
Get up and bar the door."

Then they agreed between the two,
A solemn oath they swore,
That the one who spoke the very first word,
Would have to bar the door.

The wind blew east, the wind blew west,
It blew through the open door,
But neither one would say a word,
For barrin' of the door.

Three robbers came along that way,
They came across the moor;
They saw a light and walked right in,
Right in through the open door.

"Oh, is the owner of this house,
A rich man or a poor?"
But neither one would say a word,
For barrin' of the door.

They ate the bread, they drank the ale,
Then said, "Come, give us more."
But neither one would say a word,
For barrin' of the door.

"Let's pull the old man's beard," said one,
"Let's beat him till he's sore."
But still the old man wouldn't speak,
For barrin' of the door.

"I'll kiss his pretty wife," said one,
"Oh, her I could adore."
And then the old man shook his fist,
And gave a mighty roar.

"Oh, you'll not kiss my wife," said he,
"I'll throw you on the floor."
Said she, "Now, John, you've spoken first,
So get up and bar the door."

GOIN' DOWN CRIPPLE CREEK

Old American Fiddle Tune

```
C              F       C
I got a gal and she loves me,
              G7        C
She's as sweet as sweet can be.
              F
She's got eyes of baby blue,
              G7    C
And my love for her is true.
```

Refrain:
```
  C
Goin' down Cripple Creek, goin' in a whirl,
                          G7    C
Goin' down Cripple Creek, to see my girl.
  C
Goin' down Cripple Creek, goin' in a run,
                          G7    C    G7     C
Goin' down Cripple Creek, have some fun, have some fun.
```

Horses come and horses go;
Some are fast and some are slow.
In that saddle I sit tight,
Squeeze my knees with all my might.

Crossed the creek and went to the fair,
Found my partner then and there.
He swung me round and round,
Till we both fell on the ground.

GROUNDHOG

```
  C                F         C
Shoulder up my axe, whistle up my dog,
  C                F         C
Shoulder up my axe, whistle up my dog,
    C              F
Goin' up the holler to ketch a groun'hog,
  G7   C
Groun'hog!
```

One in the rocks, and two in the log,
One in the rocks, and two in the log,
I heard one whistle and knowed it was a hog,
Groun'hog!

Run here, Tom, with a ten-foot pole,
Run here, Tom, with a ten-foot pole,
Twist that groun'hog outen his hole.
Groun'hog!

Took that pole and twisted him out,
Took that pole and twisted him out,
Good Lord-a-mighty, ain't a groun'hog stout!
Groun'hog!

Took him home and tanned his hide,
Took him home and tanned his hide,
Made the best shoestrings I ever tried!
Groun'hog!

Yander comes Bill with a snigger and a grin,
Yander comes Bill with a snigger and a grin,
Groun'hog grease all over his chin.
Groun'hog!

Old Aunt Sal hoppin' with her cane,
Old Aunt Sal hoppin' with her cane,
Swore she's have that whistlepig's brain.
Groun'hog!

Old Aunt Sal skippin' through the hall,
Old Aunt Sal skippin' through the hall,
She had enough whistlepig to grease them all.
Groun'hog!

The meat's in the kibberd, the hide's in the churn,
The meat's in the kibberd, the hide's in the churn,
If that ain't groun'hog, I'll be durned!
Groun'hog!

HOME CAME THE OLD MAN

This comic ballad is also quite old, coming again to this country from Scotland.

```
C                              F        C
Home came the old man, drunk as he could be
  F                    C                        G7     C
He saw a strange horse in the stall where his horse ought to be
    F            C              F            C
My dear wife, my darling wife, my lovin' wife, says he
  F                    C                    G7     C
Whose horse is that in the stall where my horse ought to be?
  F          C                F                C
You old fool, you blind, fool, you daughterin' fool, says she
              F        C         D7          G
Why it's nothin' but a milk cow my mammy sent to me
  C                              F              C
A thousand miles I've traveled, a thousand miles or more
              F       C      G7  C
But a saddle on a milk cow I never did see before.
```

(Continue same pattern. Lines 1, 3, 5, and 7 remain same for all verses.)

He saw a strange coat on the hook where his coat ought to be
Whose coat is that on the hook where my coat ought to be
Why it's nothin' but a bed quilt my mammy sent to me
But pockets on a bed quilt I never did see before.

He saw a strange hat on the rack where his hat ought to be
Whose hat's that on the rack where my hat ought to be?
Why it's nothin' but a dinner pot my mammy sent to me
But a hat band on a dinner pot I never did see before.

He saw strange boots beneath the bed where his boots ought to be
Whose boots are those beneath the bed where my boots ought to be?
That's nothin' but some milk jugs my mammy sent to me
But spurs on a milk jug I never did see before.

He saw a strange pair of pants where his pants ought to be
Whose pants are on the table where my pants ought to be?
Why it's nothin' but a petticoat my mammy sent to me
But suspenders on a petticoat I never did see before.

241

He saw a strange head on the pillow where his head ought to be
Whose head's that on the pillow where my head ought to be?
Why it's nothin' but a cabbage head my mammy sent to me
But a mustache on a cabbage head I never did see before.

I KNOW WHERE I'M GOING

This song is of Irish origin. The first line of the fourth verse refers to the black Irish who had dark hair and eyes as opposed to fairer Irish who had light hair and eyes.

```
G       D        G                           D7
I know where I'm goin' And I know who's goin' with me;
   G          EM              Am               D7
And I know who my love is, But the dear knows who I'll marry.
```


I have stockings of silk, Shoes of bright green leather,
And combs to buckle my hair, And a ring for every finger.

Featherbeds are soft, Painted rooms are bonny,
But I would trade them all, For my handsome, winsome Johnny.

Some say he's black, But I say he's bonny;
The fairest of them all, Is my handsome, winsome Johnny.

I know where I'm goin', And I know who's goin' with me,
And I know who my love is, But the dear knows who I'll marry.

JOHN HENRY

Originally a hero of the rock-tunnel gangs on the Chesapeake and Ohio Railroad in West Virginia in 1870, the steel-driver John Henry has become a legendary and mythical figure throughout the United States. To John Henry's countless admirers, he will always be a hero, idol, and symbol of "natural" man.

D   D
John Henry was a little baby,
                    A7
Sittin' on his daddy's knee,
  G   D
Said, "The Big Bend Tunnel on the C. and O. Road,
                    G   D
Is bound to be the death of me, Lord, Lord,
                    G   D
Is bound to be the death of me.

John Henry said to his Captain,
"I ain't nothing but a man,
But before I'll let your steam drill beat me down,
I'll die with my hammer in my hand, Lord, Lord,
I'll die with my hammer in my hand."

John Henry said to his shaker,
"Shaker, why don't you sing?
I'm throwin' twelve pounds from my hips on down,
Jes' listen to the cold steel ring, Lawd, Lawd,
Jes' lissen to the cold steel ring.

John Henry got a thirty pound hammer,
Beside the steam drill he did stand.
He beat that steam drill three inches down,
And he died with his hammer in his hand, Lord, Lord,
He died with his hammer in his hand.

John Henry had a little woman,
Her name was Julie Ann,
She went down the track never lookin' back,
Says, "John Henry, you have always been a man, Lord, Lord,
John Henry, you have always been a man."

John Henry was hammerin' on the mountain,
An' his hammer was strikin' fire,
He drove so hard till he broke his pore heart,
An' he laid down his hammer and he died, Lawd, Lawd,
He laid down his hammer an' he died.

They took John Henry to the graveyard,
And they buried him in the sand,
And ev'ry time that train comes roaring by,
Says, "There lays a steel-drivin' man, Lord, Lord,
There lays a steel-drivin' man."

JOHNNY I HARDLY KNEW YOU

This is a traditional Irish anti-war ballad. It first appeared at the time of the
Napoleonic Wars. It tells of the effect of war on an individual's life. The tune
became, in America, "When Johnny Comes Marching Home."

   Em
Where are your legs that used to run
  G
Hurroo, hurroo
   Em
Where are your legs that used to run
  G
Hurroo, hurroo
      Em   D
Where are your legs that used to run
     Em   D
When first you went to carry a gun
  Em   D   Em   D
I fear your dancing days are done.
Em   D   Em
Johnny, I hardly knew you.

You haven't an arm you haven't a leg
Hurroo, hurroo
You haven't an arm you haven't a leg
Hurroo, hurroo
You haven't an arm, you haven't a leg
You're an eyeless, boneless, chickenless egg
You'll have to be put with a bowl to beg
Johnny, I hardly knew you.

They're rolling out the guns again
Hurroo, hurroo
They're rolling out the guns again
Hurroo, hurroo

They're rolling out the guns again
But they'll never take our sons again
No they'll never take our sons again
Johnny, I'm swearing to you.

MY BONNIE

In the late 1870's, a great number of people began requesting at the music stores a song bearing the title "My Bonnie." The story has it that a certain music publisher, wanting to capitalize on this ready-made demand, persuaded composer Charles E. Pratt to produce this song. Perhaps Pratt had access to the missing Scottish folk song, or perhaps he really created a new tune. In any case, he did produce "My Bonnie Lies Over the Ocean" under the names J. T. Wood (words) and H.J. Fulmer (music).

```
  G          C        G
My Bonnie lies over the ocean,
                    A7     D7
My Bonnie lies over the sea;
  G          C        G
My Bonnie lies over the ocean,
    C              D7       G
Oh, bring back my Bonnie to me.
```

Chorus:

```
           C     A
Bring back, bring back,
  D7                      G  D7 G
Bring back my Bonnie to me, to me;
             C     A7
Bring back, bring back,
    D7                     G
Oh bring back my Bonnie to me.
```

Last night as I lay on my pillow,
Last night as I lay on my bed;
Last night as I lay on my pillow,
I dreamt that my Bonnie was dead.

Oh, blow, ye winds, over the ocean,
And blow, ye winds, over the sea;
Oh, blow, ye winds, over the ocean,
And bring back my Bonnie to me.

The winds have blown over the ocean,
The winds have blown over the sea;
The winds have blown over the ocean,
And bro't back my Bonnie to me.

MY BOY WILLIE

Just as "Billy Boy" is said to have been derived from the famous ballad "Lord Randal," this song too is thought to have derived as a comic version of "Lord Randal." Most folk song collectors place the development of "My Boy Willie" in an earlier period than "Billy Boy." Whatever the case may be, both the derived versions and the original were brought to America with the early colonists.

```
     G                    D7        G  D7  G
O, where have you been all the day, my boy Willie?
                          D7          G
O, where have you been all the day, Willie, won't you tell me now?
  D       G              Am        ·D7
I have been all the day courtin' of a lady gay,
   G          Am         D7          G
But she is too young to be taken from her mammy.
```

O, can she bake and can she brew, my boy Willie?
O, can she bake and can she brew, Willie, won't you tell me now?
She can brew, she can bake, she can make a weddin' cake,
But she is too young to be taken from her mammy.

O, can she make up a bed, etc.
She can make up a bed fifty feet above her head, etc.

O, can she cook a plate of fish, etc.
She can cook a plate of fish with her fingers in the dish, etc.

O, can she sew and can she spin, etc.
She can sew and she can spin, she can do most anythin', etc.

O, how old can she be, etc.
She is two, she is seven, she is twenty-and-eleven, etc.

O, did you ask her to wed, etc.
Yes, I asked her to wed, and these are the words she said:
"I am much too young to be taken from my mammy."

OLD JOE CLARK

```
      C7     C
I never did like old Joe Clark,
            G7
I never think I shall.
C     C7    C
I never did like old Joe Clark,
  C       G7     C
But I really like his gal.
```

Chorus

```
  C
Fare thee well, old Joe Clark,
              G7
Fare thee well I say.
 C
Fare thee well, old Joe Clark,
  C       G7    C
I ain't got long to stay.
```

I never did like old Joe Clark,
And I'll tell you the reason why,
He caught his heel in my rail fence,
And tore down all my rye.

The purtiest girl I ever saw,
Came runnin' round the house.
A yellow dog skin around her neck,
The tail stuck in her mouth.

Old Joe Clark is a mean old man,
And old Joe Clark will steal.
Old Joe Clark can go the road,
But he can't come through my field.

O WALY, WALY

This is an old Scottish tune which can be placed roughly in the early seven-teenth century. There are many variations of the song, and lines and phrases from it appear in many other songs in England and America.

G   C   G
The water is wide, I cannot cross o'er
          Em   D
And neither have I wings to fly
        G C   G
Build me a boat that can carry two
C   G   D7   G
And both shall row, my love and I

Down in the meadows the other day,
A'gath'ring flowr's both fine and gay,
A'gath'ring flowr's both red and blue,
I little thought what love could do.

I put my hand into one soft bush,
Thinking the sweetest flow'r to find.
I prick'd my finger to the bone,
And left the sweetest flow'r alone.

I lean'd my back up against some oak,
Thinking it was a trusty tree.
But first he bended and then he broke,
So did my love prove false to me.

Where love is planted, O there it grows,
It buds and blossoms like some rose;
It has a sweet and pleasant smell,
No flow'r on earth can it excel.

Must I be found, O, and he go free,
Must I love one that don't love me!
Why should I act such a childish part,
And love a man that will break my heart.

There is a ship sailing on the sea,
She's loaded deep as deep can be,

But not so deep as in love I am;
I care not if I sink or swim.

O love is handsome and love is fine,
And love is charming when it is true;
As it grows older it groweth colder,
And fades away like the morning dew.

A PAPER OF PINS

Courtship songs are teasing, singing games and are among the oldest and most widespread of all traditional songs.

  D
I'll give to you a paper of pins,
     A7
And that's the way our love begins,
  D
If you will marry, marry me,
  A7   D
If you will marry me.

I'll not accept your paper of pins,
If that's the way our love begins,
And I'll not marry, marry you,
And I'll not marry you.

I'll give to you a dress of red,
Stitched all around with golden thread,
If you will marry, marry me,
If you will marry me.

I'll not accept your dress of red,
If that's the way our love begins,
And I'll not marry, marry you,
And I'll not marry you.

I'll give to you a dress of green,
That you may look just like a queen,
If you will marry, marry me,
If you will marry me.

I'll not accept your dress of green,
If that's the way our love begins,
And I'll not marry, marry you,
And I'll not marry you.

I'll give to you a little tray dog,
To go with you when you walk abroad,
If you will marry, marry me,
If you will marry me.

I'll not accept your little tray dog,
If that's the way our love begins,
And I'll not marry, marry you.
And I'll not marry you.

I'll give to you a coach and six,
Six black horses black as pitch,
If you will marry, marry me,
If you will marry me.

I'll not accept your coach and six,
If that's the way our love begins,
And I'll not marry, marry you,
And I'll not marry you.

I'll give to you the key to my heart,
That we may marry and never part,
If you will marry, marry me,
If you will marry me.

I'll not accept the key to your heart,
If that's the way our love begins,
And I'll not marry, marry you,
And I'll not marry you.

I'll give to you the key to my chest,
That you may have money at your request
If you will marry, marry me,
If you will marry me.

I will accept the key to your chest,
If that's the way our love begins,
And I will marry, marry you,
And I will marry you.

O miss, I see that money is all,
And woman's love means nothing at all,
So I'll not marry, marry you,
And I'll not marry you.

PRETTY SARO

(This version from collection of Mrs. Patrick (Ann) Williams.)

Down in some lone valley,

In a lonesome place,

Where the wild birds do whistle,

There notes do increase.

Farewell pretty Saro,

I'll bid you adieu,

And I'll think of my darling,

Wherever I go.

My love she won't have me,
This I understand,
For she wants a free holder,
And I own no land.
I cannot maintain her,
With silver or gold,
Or buy all the pretty fine things.
That my love's house can hold.

Oh, if I were a merchant,
And could write a fine hand,
I would write my love a letter,
That she'd understand.
I'd write it by the water,
Where the river overflows,
And I'd think of my darling,
Wherever I go.

At the foot of yon mountain,
There lies a deep snow,
Oh, it's not this long journey,
I'm dreading to go.
It's not this long journey,
Or leaving friends that I know,
But it's leaving my darling,
My pretty Saro.

THE RIDDLE SONG

This very old ballad seems to have originated in the rural areas of Britain. The lyrics are based on four of the riddles in the ancient ballad "Captain Wedderburn's Courtship." Riddles in courtship situations have been used frequently as a basis for folk songs. While pioneer children enjoyed all kinds of games and riddles to pass the time, this was a riddle they could sing, and thus, it became one of their favorites.

```
  G              C                 G
I gave my love a cherry that has no stone;
  D            G            D
I gave my love a chicken that has no bone;
  D7          G            D
I told my love a story that has no end;
  Em                         G
I gave my love a baby, there's no cryin'.
```

How can there be a cherry that has no stone?
How can there be a chicken that has no bone?
How can there be a story that has no end?
How can there be a baby, there's no cryin?

A cherry when it's blooming, it has no stone;
A chicken when it's pipping, it has no bone;
The story of our love, it has no end;
A baby when it's sleeping, there's no cryin'.

SHADY GROVE

"Shady Grove" is a song which unquestionably grew out of the Appalachian Mountains. As with most folk songs, there are several versions still sung today.

Chorus:
  Em   D   Em
Shady Grove my little love,
  G   D   Em
Shady Grove my darlin',
  G   D
Shady Grove my little love,
  Em   D   Em
I'm goin' back to Harlan.

Cheeks as red as a rose in spring,
Eyes of the deepest brown,
You're the darlin' of my life,
Stay till the sun goes down.

First time I saw Shady Grove,
She was standin' in the door.
Shoes and stockings in her hand,
And her little bare feet on the floor.

Wish I were an apple,
A hangin' on a tree,
And every time my Shady'd pass,
She'd take a bite of me.

Wish I had a little gold box,
To put my true love in,
I'd take her out and kiss her twice,
And put her back again.

Peaches in the summer time,
Apples in the fall,
If I can't have my Shady Grove,
I'll have no love at all.

Snow in the winter time,
Rain in the spring,
If I can't have my Shady Grove,
I'll take just any ole thing.

Wish I had a needle and thread,
As fine as I could sew,
I'd sew the girls to my coat tail,
And down the road I'd go.

Wish I had a big white horse,
Corn to feed him on,
All I'd need is a pretty little miss,
To feed him while I'm gone.

If I had my Shady Grove,
I'd put her on a shelf,
And if she winked her eye at me,
I'd climb up there myself.

Shady Grove, my little love,
Shady Grove, I say,
Shady Grove, my little love,
I'll marry you someday.

Shady Grove, my little love,
Shady Grove, I say,
Shady Grove, my little love,
Don't wait till the judgment day.

SOURWOOD MOUNTAIN

G   C   G
I've got a girl in the Sourwood Mountain,
        D7   G
Ho de um de iddle de day.
                C   G
She won't come and I won't call her,
        D7   G
Ho de um de iddle de day.

Roosters crowin' in the Sourwood Mountain,
G   D7
Ho de um de iddle de day.

So many pretty girls I can't count them,
G   D7   G
Ho de um de iddle de day,

254

Big dogs bite and little ones bite you,
Ho de um de iddle de day.
Big girls court and little ones fight you,
Ho de um de iddle de day.
My true-love lives up in Letcher,
Ho de um de iddle de day.
She won't come and I won't fetch her,
Ho de um de iddle de day,

I've got a girl at the head of the holler,
He de um de iddle de day.
She won't come and I won't foller.
Ho de um de iddle de day.
Old man, old man, can I have your daughter,
Ho de um de iddle de day.
To bake me bread and carry me water,
Ho de um de iddle de day.

THE APPENZELLER

Many German and Swiss people came to this country during the Civil War.
They sought a section of the country where they might be free to live and
labor as they desired. Some of the German-speaking Swiss settled in Helvetia,
Alpena, and Adolph in Randolph County. The industrious and frugal
attitudes of the original settlers remain with those who now reside in these
communities, and they still maintain great pride in their rich heritage. These
three Swiss folk songs are among those still heard in Helvetia. Notice that
each song rings with love for the homeland.

Min Vater ischt en Appenzeller

Dee ah lah oo dee ah lah oo doo lee ho

Het weder wi no Moscht im Cheller

Dee ah lah oo dee ah lah oo ho.

(Repeat second and fourth lines with all verses)

Min Vater ischt en brave Ma,
Het d'Sonntighosen am Werchtig a

Min Vater ischt en Appenzeller;
Er isst de Chas mit samt em Teller.

Mini Meuter ischt e Schwizeri,
Het d'Schtube volle Gitzeli.

Mini Mueter ischt e Chuechlifrau,
Ond wenn si het, so get s'mer au.

Ond wenn i sag, das sei nod vil
So get s'mer met em Besestil

Di schonschte Matli vo-n-i wass
Die wohnid z'Appezoll ona z'Gass

My father is an Appenzeller
He has no wine down in his cellar

My father, he is honest, too,
Wears Sunday trousers all week thru

My father comes from Appenzell;
With cheese he eats the plate as well.

My mother was a Swiss girl fair;
Young goats our living-room may share,

My mother makes the finest cakes;
She gives me some each time she bakes.

Then if I say "That's not enough,"
She beats me with the broom-stick rough.

The nicest girls, as I can tell,
They live in Gais and Appenzell.

256

VO MINE BERGE
(Far From Home)

Vo mine Berge muss i scheide wo's gar so lieblich ist und schon, kann numme i der Heimat bleive, muss in die weite Ferne gehn.

O mountain heights I loved in childhood,

O well-worn paths my feet have known.

In distant lands I now must wander,

How sad and homesick and alone.

Chorus:

Hol de ho le ho, hol du le a ho, hol de ho le ho, hol du le a ho.

Hol de ho le ho, hol du le a ho, hol de ho le ho, hol du le a ho.

Behut di Gott, mi liebi Senn'rin und gib mir noch einmal d die Hand. Gar lang wirst mich ja numme sehen, denn i reis' in e fremdes Land.

I think of thee, my own beloved one,
And then my heart is full of pain,
The day will come when backward turning,
At last I see my home again.

Repeat Chorus

MEITELI
[Vreneli]

Sag Meiteli, sag Meiteli, wo hesch du de dys Hei?
I has amen Ort im Schwyzerland, es isch vo Holz and Stei.
I has amen Ort im Schwyzerland, es isch vo Holz und Stei.

Chorus:
       C   G
Yo, ho, ho, Tra la, la, la; Yo, ho, Tra la, la, la;
       D   G
Yo, ho, ho, Tra la, la, la; Yo, ho, Tra la, la la;
       C   G
Yo, ho, ho, Tra la, la, la; Yo, ho, ho, Tra la, la, la;
       D   G
Yo, ho, ho, Tra, la, la, la; Yo, ho, ho.

      G
"O Vreneli, my pretty one, Pray tell me where's your home."
    C   G   D   G
"My home it is in Switzerland, It's made of wood and stone;"
    C   G   D   G
"My home, it is in Switzerland, It's made of wood and stone."

"O Vreneli, my pretty one, Pray tell me where's your heart?"
"O that," she said, "I gave away, But still I feel it smart."
"O that," she said, "I gave away, But still I feel it smart."

"O Vreneli, my pretty one, Pray tell me where's your head?"
"O, that I also gave away, It's with my heart," she said.
"O, that I also gave away, It's with my heart," she said

THE WIFE WRAPT IN WETHER'S SKIN

The story of the ballad was in all likelihood traditionally derived from the good old tale of the Wife Lapped in Morrel's Skin. Here a husband, who has put up with a great deal from an excessively restive wife, slays his old horse Morrell and salts the hide, takes the shrew down to the cellar, and after a sharp contest for master, beats her with birchen rods till she swoons. Then he wraps her in the salted hide: by which process the woman is perfectly reformed! (Scottish)

There was an old man who came from the west,

Dandoo, dandoo,

Who married the woman that he loved best,

Declare the kitchen and the clingo,

Who married the woman that he loved best,

Come a hance come bottom cleesh me ac and a clingo.

This old man came in from the plow,
Dandoo, dandoo.
Says, "Wife, is my breakfast ready now?"
Declare the kitchen and the clingo.
Says, "Wife, is my breakfast ready now?"
Come a hance come bottom cleesh me ac and a clingo.

"There are some dumplings in the pot,"
Dandoo, dandoo.
"You can eat them now while they are hot."
Declare the kitchen and the clingo.
"You can eat them now while they are hot."
Come a hance come bottom cleesh me ac and a clingo.

This old man went to his fold,
Dandoo, dandoo.
He skinned a wether fat and old.
Declare the kitchen and the clingo.
He skinned a wether fat and old.
Come a hance come bottom cleesh me ac and a clingo.

He put the skin on his wife's back,
Dandoo, dandoo.
And with a stick went whicketty whack.
Declare the kitchen and the clingo.
And with a stick went whicketty whack.
Come a hance come bottom cleesh me ac and a clingo.

"I'll tell my father and all my kin."
Dandoo, dandoo.
You whip me on my naked skin."
Declare the kitchen and the clingo.
"You whip me on my naked skin."
Come a hance come bottom cleesh me ac and a clingo.

"You can tell your father and all your kin,"
Dandoo, dandoo.
"That I'm only tanning my wether's skin."
Delcare the kitchen and the clingo.
"That I'm only tanning my wether's skin."
Come a hance come bottom cleesh me ac and a clingo.

Since then she's been a very good wife.
Dandoo, dandoo.
And I hope she'll be to the end of her life,
Declare the kitchen and the clingo.
And I hope she'll be to the end of her life.
Come a hance come bottom cleesh me ac and a clingo.

WEST VIRGINIA HILLS
(West Virginia State Song)

Oh, the West Virginia hills!
How majestic and how grand,
With their summits bathed in glory,
Like our Prince Immanuel's Land!
Is it any wonder then,
That my heart with rapture thrills,
As I stand once more with loved ones
On those West Virginia hills.
Chorus:
Oh, the hills, beautiful hills
How I love those West Virginia hills!
If o'er sea or land I roam,
Still I think of happy home,
And my friends among the West Virginia hills.

HOME TO WEST VIRGINIA
Billy Edd Wheeler
(with permission)

```
  G      C      G
Home is where the heart is,
          C             G
And my heart is heaven bound,
                 C
I hope heaven's gonna be,
  G      D      G
Just like West Virginia.

  G
I wanna go see my Mom and Dad,
          C             G
And my Uncle down in Bluefield,
                              D
Like to see Aunt Sally up in Wheelin',
      G
We'll have a big reunion.
      C                 G
I can smell that country cookin',
                  C
Home to West Virginia,
```

   D   G
Gives me a good time feelin'—
          C   G
Oh, the redbird is callin' in the rhododendron,
                                     D
Hear the squirrels squawkin' at the mornin' sun,
         G
You can move away but you can't leave 'em,
   C   G
Once you got 'em in ya,
                 G
Talkin' about the hills,
         D   G
And, the people of West Virginia.

                      C   G
Oh, there's no place like home,
     D
So wherever you roam come home,
   C   G
Home to West Virginia!

Goin' up the big Coal River,
See my Grandad in Sylvester,
Listen to him sing, COME HOME IT'S SUPPERTIME,
Take a ride on the old Cass Railroad,
See the Hall of Fame in Richwood,
Maybe I'll just go fishin',
Soak up some mountain sunshine.
Oh, the HATFIELDS and McCOYS is showin' in Beckley,
Sunday, I'll go hear some old time preachin',
A stranger's always welcome here,
And folks don't try to skin ya,
Talkin' about my homeland,
And the people of West Virginia.

Oh, there's no place like home,
So wherever you roam come home,
Home to West Virginia!

    G
Pocatalico, Institute, Pocahontas,

Parkersburg, Horse Pin, Pipestem, Tomahawk,
    C
Morgantown, Fairmont, Clendenin, Tuckahoe,

Williamson, Huntington, and Shanghai,
  D
Kenova, Confidence, Buffalo, Eskdale,

Zenith, Logan, Moundsville, Mohawk,
    G
Ronceverte, Panther, Pansy, Buckhannon,

Pickaway, and Brandywine.
    G
Bradshaw, Cane Brake, Red Jacket, Elkins,

Turtle Creek, Wolf Creek, French Creek, Peach Creek,
    C
Whitesville, High Coal, Martinsville, Clarksburg,

                                   D
Dry Creek, Rock Creek, Sleepy Creek, and Mullens.

                           D7   G
So many places that you can come home to in West Virginia,
  C   G
Good old West Virginia!

WEST VIRGINIA WALTZ
(As sung by Russell Fluharty)

     C
Under the bright blue moon above,
      F   D
We met one night and fell in love
    G   C
In West Virginia where the mountains touch the sky.

                    C
The Rhododendron were in bloom,
        F   D
As we strolled beneath the moon
                G   C
They played the West Virginia Waltz for you and I.

C   F   C
It seems I hear the hills of West Virginia calling,
                                        G

The ground is bare the autumn leaves will soon be falling.
C
Back to the land where skies are blue,
                F   D
Sweetheart I'm coming home to you
    G
So play the West Virginia Waltz again for me.

WILDWOOD FLOWER

Though known widely throughout the mountains, little is known about the origin of this piece. The degree of variation in known texts suggests that it existed in oral tradition for some time. The wildwood flower itself was probably the amaranthus in early versions.

C   F   C   G7   C
I will twine with my mingles of raven black hair,
        F   C   G7   C
With the roses so red and the lilies so fair,
                        F   C
The myrtle so bright with its emerald dew,
                        G7   C
And the pale and the leader and eyes look so blue.

I will dance, I will sing and my life shall be gay,
I will charm every heart, in its crown I will sway,
I woke from my dream and all idols was clay,
And all portions of lovin' had all flown away.

He taught me to love him and promised to love,
And cherish me over all over above,
My poor heart is wondering, no misery can tell,
He left me no warning, no words of farewell.

He taught me to love him and called me his flower,
That was blooming to cheer him through life's weary hour,
How I long to see him and regret the dark hour,
He's gone and neglected his frail wildwood flower.

ALL GOD'S CHILDREN GOT SHOES

G
I got a shoe, you got a shoe, all God's children got shoes.
                            D
When I get to Heab'n gonna put on my shoes,
      G   D7   G   D7   G
Gonna walk all ober God's Heab'n, Heab'n, Heab'n.
                         C
Ev'rybody talkin' 'bout Heab'n ain't agoin' there,
 G   D7
Heab'n, Heab'n
      G   D7   G
Gonna walk all ober God's Heab'n.

I got a song, you got a song, all God's children got a song,
When I get to Heab'n gonna sing a new song,
Gonna sing all ober God's Heab'n, Heab'n, Heab'n!
Ev'rybody talk about Heab'n ain't agoin' there,
Heab'n, Heab'n
Gonna sing all ober God's Heab'n.

I got a cross, you got a cross
When I get to Heab'n gonna lay down my cross,
Gonna shout all ober God's Heab'n.

I got a robe, you got a robe.
When I get to Heab'n gonna put on my robe,
Gonna shout all ober God's Heab'n.

I got a harp, you got a harp.
When I get to Heab'n gonna play on my harp,
Gonna play all ober God's Heab'n.

AMEN

Chorus:

```
 G
A-men, A-men,
         C   G   D  G
A-men, A-men, A-men.
```

Verse:
```
 G
See the little baby,
```

Wrapped in the manger,

```
On Christmas morning,
C  G   D  G
A-men, A-men.
```


See Him in the temple,
Talking with the Elders,
Who marvelled at his wisdom,

See Him by the Jordan,
Where John was baptizing,
And saving all sinners,

See Him by the seaside,
Talking with the fishermen,
And making them disciples,

Marching thru Jerusalem,
Over palm branches,
In pomp and splendor,

See Him in the garden,
Talking with His father,
In deepest sorrow,

Led before Pilate,
There they crucified Him,
But He rose on Easter,

Alleluia,
He died to save us,
He lives forever,

Alleluia, Alleluia,
Alleluia, Alleluia!

CHILDREN GO WHERE I SEND THEE

This spiritual was first heard when it was recorded by black children at
Breedings Creek Colored School in Kentucky late in the 19th Century.

C
Children go where I send thee!

How shall I send thee?
      F C
Well, I'm gonna send thee one by one;
      F C
One for the little bitty baby
   C F C G7 C
That was born, born,—born in Bethlehem

Children go where I send thee!

How shall I send thee?

Well, I'm gonna send thee two by two;

Two for Paul and Silas, one for the little bitty baby

That was born, born, born in Bethlehem

(Repeat this cycle after each new verse)

Three for the Hebrew children

Four for the four a-knocking at the door

Five for the Gospel preachers

Six for the six that couldn't get fixed

Seven for the seven went up to heaven

Eight for the eight that stood at the gate

Nine for the nine got left behind

Ten for the ten commandments.

EZEK'EL SAW THE WHEEL

Chorus:
```
  G                           D        G
Ezek'el saw the wheel, way in the middle o' the air
  G                           D        G
Ezek'el saw the wheel, way in the middle o' the air
  G
The big wheel moved by Faith
                          D      G
The little wheel moved by the Grace o' God
  G                           D        G
A wheel in a wheel, way in the middle o' the air.
```

Verse:
```
  G
Just let me tell you what a hypocrite 'll do
  G         D         G
Way in the middle o' the air
  G
He'll talk about me and he'll talk about you
  G         D         G
Way in the middle o' the air
```

Watch out my sister how you walk on the cross
Way in the middle o' the air
Yo' foot might slip and yo' soul get lost
Way in the middle o' the air

You say the Lord has set you free
Way in the middle o' the air
Why don't you let yo' neighbor be
Way in the middle o' the air

Repeat chorus between each verse

268

GO DOWN MOSES

"Go Down Moses," is one of the classics of our Black musical heritage. There have been two important phases in the song's development. The first phase involved Bishop Francis Asbury of the Methodist Episcopal Church (1784). Because his work brought him in close contact with the Blacks whom he taught, helped, and treated with respect, they lavished praise upon the Bishop. He was their personal Moses, and using Biblical phrases, they made up a song about Moses and deliverance.

The second important phase occurred when "underground railroads" were in operation. Harriet Tubman, a Black woman, made many trips into the South at great personal risk to rescue countless numbers of slaves. Fellow Blacks often referred to her as "Moses." "Go Down, Moses" became a musical tribute to their hero, Harriet Tubman.

```
       Em   B7   Em          Em   B7   Em
When Israel was in Egypt's land, let my people go,
         B7        Em            Em   B7   Em
Oppressed so hard they could not stand, let my people go.
        Am    B7          Em
Go down Moses, way down in Egypt land,
   C    Em       Em   B7   Em
Tell ole Pharaoh, let my people go.
```

Thus saith the Lord, bold Moses said, let my people go,
If not, I'll smite your first-born dead, let my people go.
Go down, Moses, way down in Egypt land,
Tell ole Pharaoh, let my people go.

O 'twas a dark and dismal night,
When Moses led the Israelites.

The Lord told Moses what to do,
To lead the children of Israel through.

O come along Moses, you'll not get lost,
Stretch out your rod and come across.

As Israel stood by the water side,
At the command of God it did divide.

When they had reached the other shore,
They sang the song of triumph o'er.

Pharaoh said he would go across,
But Pharaoh and his host were lost.

O Moses the cloud shall clear the way,
A fire by night, a shade by day.

You'll not get lost in the wilderness,
With a lighted candle in your breast.

Jordan shall stand up like a wall,
And the walls of Jerico shall fall.

Your foes shall not before you stand,
And you'll possess fair Canaan's land.

'Twas just about in harvest-time,
When Joshua led his host divine.

O let us all from bondage flee,
And let us all in Christ be free.

We need not always weep and moan,
And wear these slavery chains forlorn.

I WANT TO BE READY
(OR WALK IN JERUSALEM JUST LIKE JOHN)

Chorus:
```
C                   F           C
I want to be ready, I want to be ready,
C          F         C
I want to be ready, To walk in Jerusalem,
G7     C
Just like John.
```

Refrain: Walk in Jerusalem just like John.

Verse 1:
C   G7   C
Oh John, Oh John now didn't you say? Walk in Jerusalem just like John.
C   G7   C
That you'd be there on that great day. Walk in Jerusalem just like John.

Some came crippled, and some came lame,
Some came walkin' in Jesus' name,

Now, brother, better mind how you step on the cross,
Your foot might slip and your soul get lost,

If you get there before I do,
Tell all my friends I'm a-comin' too,

John said that city was just four square,
And he declared he'd meet me there,

When Peter was preaching at Pentecost
Oh he was filled with the Holy Ghost

Repeat refrain after each line of each verse.

Repeat chorus between verses.

OH MARY, DON'T YOU WEEP

Chorus:

                    D7
Oh. Mary, don't you weep, don't you mourn;
                    G
Oh, Mary, don't you weep, don't you mourn;
    C   G
Pharaoh's army got drownded,
          D7   G
Oh, Mary, don't you weep.

Verse 1:

G   D7
If I could I surely would,
                              G
Stand on the rock where Moses stood
    C   G
Pharaoh's army got drownded,
            D7
Oh, Mary, don't you weep.

Wonder what Satan's grumblin' 'bout,
Chained in Hell an' he can't git out.
Pharaoh's army got drownded,
Oh, Mary, don't you weep.

(Conclude each verse with last two lines as above.)

Ol' Satan's mad an' I am glad,
He missed a soul he thought he had.

Brother, better mind how you walk on the cross,
Foot might slip and your soul get lost.

One of these nights about twelve o'clock,
This old world's goin' to reel and rock.

I went down in the valley to pray,
My soul got joy and I stayed all day.

Now don't you believe the Bible ain't true,
Cause you'll be sorry if you do.

That primrose path is wide and fair,
Many a soul's done perished there.

One of these mornings bright and fair,
I'll take my wings and cleave the air.

When I get to Heaven goin' to sing and shout;
Nobody there for to turn me out.

When I get to Heaven goin' to put on my shoes,
Run about glory and tell all the news.

See that sister dressed so fine,
She ain't got religion on her mind.

STEAL AWAY

Chorus:

```
D                               A7   D
```
Steal away, steal away, steal away to Jesus!
```
                                A7   D
```
Steal away, steal away home, I ain't got long to stay here.

Verse 1:
```
Bm        D
```
My Lord calls me, He calls me by the thunder;

```
                                         A7  D
```
The trumpet sounds within my soul, I ain't got long to stay here.

Green trees are bending, poor sinner stan's a-trembling;
The trumpet sounds within my soul, I ain't got long to stay here.

Tombstones are bursting, poor sinner stan's a-trembling;
The trumpet sounds within mv soul, I ain't got long to stay here.

My Lord calls me, He calls me by the lightning;
The trumpet sounds within my soul, I ain't got long to stay here.

SWING LOW, SWEET CHARIOT

"Swing Low, Sweet Chariot" was born in the heart of Sarah Hannah Sheppard in 1847. To escape slavery she was about to throw herself and her baby daughter in the river when a prophetic old Negress said tenderly, "Wait! Let the chariot of the Lord swing low." Mrs. Sheppard returned home and "Swing Low, Sweet Chariot," is her expression of an inner eagerness for the chariot of the Lord.

```
      D        G   D                   A7
Swing low, sweet chariot comin' for to carry me home,
      D          G   D          A7      D
Swing low, sweet chariot comin' for to carry me home.
      D                                              A7
I looked over Jordan and what did I see comin' for to carry me home?
      D          G        D          A7      D
A band of angels comin' after me comin' for to carry me home.
      D                          A7
Swing low, sweet chariot comin' for to carry me home.
      D        G   D          A7      D
Swing low, sweet chariot comin' for to carry me home.
```

Swing low, sweet chariot comin' for to carry me home,
Swing low, sweet chariot comin' for to carry me home.
And if you get up there before I do, comin' for to carry me home,
Tell all my friends that I'm a-comin' too, comin for to carry me home.
Swing low, sweet chariot comin' for to carry me home.
Swing low, sweet chariot comin' for to carry me home.

Swing low, sweet chariot comin' for to carry me home,
Swing low, sweet chariot comin' for to carry me home.
The brightest of bright days that ever I saw, comin' for to carry me home,
When Jesus washed my mortal sins away, comin' for to carry me home.
Swing low, sweet chariot comin' for to carry me home,
Swing low, sweet chariot comin' for to carry me home.

Swing low, sweet chariot comin' for to carry me home,
Swing low, sweet chariot comin' for to carry me home.
I'm sometimes up and I'm sometimes down, comin' for to carry me home,
But still my soul feels heavenly bound, comin' for to carry me home.
Swing low, sweet chariot comin' for to carry me home,
Swing low, sweet chariot comin' for to carry me home.

WHEN WAS JESUS BORN

Chorus:

Oh tell me
  C   F   C   F   C
When was Jesus born, in the last month of the year
       F   C   F   C
When was Jesus born, in the last month of the year

            F   C
Was it January? "No" "No"
                F   C
    February? "No" "No"
    F   C
March, April, May
        F   C
Was it June, July, or August
        F   C
September, October, November?
              F   C
But on the 25th day of December
      F   C
In the last month of the year

Well they laid him in a manger, In the last month of the year
Well they laid him in a manger, In the last month of the year
And all the cattle gathered round him
With Joseph, Mary his Mother
In the litttle old town of Bethlehem
In the last month of the year.

Repeat chorus

Well, the wise men came to visit him, In the last month of the year
Well, the wise men came to visit him, In the last month of the year
And with them they brought gold, frankincense and myrrh
Gifts for the baby Jesus, who was lying in a manger
In the little ole town of Bethlehem
In the last month of the year.

Repeat chorus

AMAZING GRACE

E   A   E
Amazing Grace, how sweet the sound,
                  B7
That saved a wretch like me!
  E   A   E
I once was lost, but now am found;
        B7
Was blind but now I see.

Through many dangers, toils, and snares,
I have already come;
'Tis grace that bro't me safe this far,
And grace will lead me home.

When we've been there ten thousand years,
Bright shining as the sun.
We've no less days to sing God's praise,
Than when we first begun.

CHURCH IN THE WILDWOOD

             G   D
There's a church in the valley by the wildwood,
                G
No lovelier place in the dale.
    C   G
No spot is so dear to my childhood,
     D   G
As the little brown church in the vale.

  D

Oh come, come, come, come, to the church in the wildwood,
                                     G

Oh come to the church in the dale.
      C   G

No spot is so dear to my childhood,
        D   G

As the little brown church in the vale.

How sweet on a bright Sabbath morning,
To list to the clear ringing bell.
Its tones so sweetly are calling,
Oh come to the church in the vale.

DO LORD

G
I've got a home in glory land that outshines the sun,
C   G
I've got a home in glory land that outshines the sun,

I've got a home in glory land that outshines the sun,
 G   D   G
Look a way beyond the blue.

Refrain:

 G
Do Lord, O do Lord, O do remember me!
  C   G
Do Lord, O do Lord, O do remember me!
 G
Do Lord, O do Lord, O do remember me!
 G   D
Look a way beyond the blue.

I've got a heavenly Father who hears and answers prayer,
(Repeat this line 2 more times.)
Look a way beyond the blue.

I took Jesus as my Saviour, you take Him too,
(Repeat this line 2 more times.)
Look a way beyond the blue.

FARTHER ALONG

D   G   D
Tempted and tried we're oft made to wonder,
                                A7
Why it should be so all the day long,
D   G   D
While there are others living about us,
              A7   D
Never molested tho in the wrong.

Refrain:

D   G   D
Farther along we'll know all about it,
D   A7
Farther along we'll understand why;
D   G   D
Cheer up, my brother, live in the sunshine,
D   A7   D
We'll understand it all by and by.

When we see Jesus coming in glory,
When He comes from His home in the sky;
Then we shall meet Him in that bright mansion,
And we'll understand it all by and by.

GOD'S NOT DEAD

```
  E
God's not dead, He's still livin'!
  A                   E
God's not dead, He's still livin'!

God's not dead, He's still livin'!
                  A
I can feel Him in my hands,
             B7
Feel Him in my feet,
  E        A   E
Feel Him all over me!
```

HEAVENLY SUNSHINE

```
  C      F              C
Heavenly sunshine, heavenly sunshine,
         G7         C
Flooding my soul with joy divine,
      F                C
Heavenly sunshine, heavenly sunshine,
   G7          C
Hallelujah, Jesus is mine!
```

HE'S GOT THE WHOLE WORLD

Refrain:

```
  C
He's got the whole world in His hand,
           G7
He's got the whole wide world in His hand,
           C
He's got the whole world in His hand,
           G7
He's got the whole world in His hand.
```

He's got you and me brother in His hand,
He's got you and me sister in His hand,
He's got you and me neighbor in His hand,
He's got the whole world in His hand.

He's got everybody here in His hand,
He's got everybody here in His hand,
He's got everybody here in His hand,
He's got the whole world in His hand.

HOW GREAT THOU ART

G   C
O Lord my God, when I in awesome wonder,
     G   D   G
Consider all the worlds Thy hands hath made,
                        C
I see the stars, I hear the rolling thunder,
                G   D   G
Thy power throughout the universe displayed.

Refrain:

                     C   G
Then sings my soul, my Saviour God to Thee;
              D   G
How great Thou art, how great Thou art!
                     C   G
Then sings my soul, my Saviour God to Thee,
              D   G
How great Thou art, how great Thou art!

When Christ shall come with shout of acclamation,
And take me home, what joy shall fill my heart!
Then I shall bow in humble adoration,
And there proclaim, my God, how great Thou art!

IN THE GARDEN

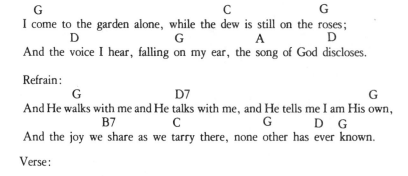

```
G                                    C              G
I come to the garden alone, while the dew is still on the roses;
       D            G           A           D
And the voice I hear, falling on my ear, the song of God discloses.
```

Refrain:
```
       G                 D7                          G
And He walks with me and He talks with me, and He tells me I am His own,
               B7        C          G      D  G
And the joy we share as we tarry there, none other has ever known.
```

Verse:

He speaks and the sound of His voice is so sweet the birds hush their singing,
And the melody that He gave to me, within my heart is ringing.

I'VE GOT THE JOY

```
            A
I've got the joy, joy, joy, down in my heart,
   E            A
Down in my heart, down in my heart,
```

```
I've got the joy, joy, joy, down in my heart,
   E                A
Down in my heart to stay!
```

I've got the love of Jesus, down in my heart,
Down in my heart, down in my heart!
I've got the love of Jesus down in my heart,
Down in my heart to stay!

I've got the peace that passeth understanding down in my heart,
Down in my heart, down in my heart,
I've got the peace that passeth understanding down in my heart,
Down in my heart to stay!

I know the devil doesn't like it, but it's down in my heart,
Down in my heart, down in my heart,
I know the devil doesn't like it, but it's down in my heart,
Down in my heart to stay!

Now there is therefore now no condemnation down in my heart,
Down in my heart, down in my heart,
Now there is therefore now no condemnation down in my heart,
Down in my heart to stay.

I've got a Hal-le-lu-jah down in my heart,
Down in my heart, down in my heart!
I've got a Hal-le-lu-jah down in my heart,
Down in my heart to stay.

JUST A CLOSER WALK WITH THEE

G   D
I am weak but Thou art strong,
　D7   G
Jesus keep me from all wrong;
　　　　　　C
I'll be satisfied as long,
　　G   D   G
As I walk dear Lord close to Thee.

Refrain:

Just a closer walk with Thee,
Grant it Jesus this my plea;
Daily may it ever be,
Just a closer walk with Thee.

Verses:

Thru this world of toil and snares,
If I falter, Lord who cares?
Who with me my burden shares?
Let me walk dear Lord close to Thee.

When my feeble life is o'er,
Time for me will be no more,
Guide me to that peaceful shore.
Let me walk dear Lord close to Thee.

LONESOME VALLEY

G   C
Jesus walk'd this lonesome valley
        G   D
He had to walk it by himself
            G   C
Oh, nobody else could walk it for Him
        G   D G
He had to walk it by himself

We must walk this lonesome valley
We have to walk it by ourselves
Oh, nobody else can walk it for us
We have to walk it by ourselves

You must go and stand your trial
You have to stand it by yourself
Oh, nobody else can stand it for you
You have to stand it by yourself.

L-O-V-E

  G   C G
There's a four lettered word L-O-V-E
                       A7   D
It's why Christ gave his life on Calvary
      G   C   G
Now this wonderful word means so much to me.
C   G   D G G7
It's the word L-O-V-E.

```
C                      G
```
L- is for the lost Christ died for on the tree
```
Am                      D
```
O- is for the offering He made for you and me.
```
G                      C
```
V- is for the victory, He rose from the grave.
```
G              D        G
```
E- is forever your life He can save.

Now this four lettered word L-O-V-E.
Is why He gave his son for you and for me.
For the world was bound in sin, but now can be free
Because of the word L-O-V-E.

OLD RUGGED CROSS

```
      G                  C
```
On a hill far away stood an old rugged cross,
```
        D                G
```
The emblem of suffering and shame;
```
                          C
```
And I love that old cross where the dearest and best,
```
        D                G
```
For a world of lost sinners was slain.

Refrain:

```
        D                  G
```
So I'll cherish the old rugged cross,
```
            C              G
```
'Till my trophies at last I lay down;
```
                          C
```
I will cling to the old rugged cross
```
        G          D      G
```
And exchange it some day for a crown.

To the old rugged cross I would ever be true,
Its shame and reproach gladly bear;
Then he'll call me some day to my home far away,
When His glory forever I'll share.

OLD TIME RELIGION

Refrain:

G
Gimme that old time religion
        D
Gimme that old time religion
        G   C
Gimme that old time religion
   G   D   G
It's good enough for me.

It was good for Paul and Silas
It was good for Paul and Silas
It was good for Paul and Silas
And it's good enough for me.

It was good for my o'l pappy
It was good for my o'l mammy
It was good for the whole durned family
And it's good enough for me.

Makes me love everybody
Makes me love everybody
Makes me love everybody
And it's good enough for me.

PRECIOUS MEMORIES

```
 E              A      E
Precious memories, unseen angels,
                         B7
Sent from somewhere to my soul!
  E              A   E
How they linger, ever near me,
      B7         E
And the sacred past unfold.
```

Refrain:
```
 E                                 A                   E
Precious memories, how they linger, how they ever flood my soul.
 E        A   E                 B7        E
In the stillness of the midnight, precious, sacred scenes unfold.
```

Verses:

```
In the stillness of the midnight
Echoes from the past I hear;
Old time singin', gladness bringin'
From that lovely land somewhere.

As I travel on life's pathway,
Know not what the years may hold.
As I ponder, hope grows fonder,
Precious memories flood my soul.
```

SOFTLY AND TENDERLY

```
C                F    C
Softly and tenderly Jesus is calling,
        F        G
Calling for you and for me,
C                    F          C
See on the portals He's waiting and watching,
F        G         C
Watching for you and for me.
```

Refrain:
```
   C    G        C   G C
Come home, come home!
G          A7        G  D7 G7
Ye who are weary, come home,
   C              F      C
Earnestly, tenderly, Jesus is calling,
  F      G         C
Calling, O sinner, come home!
```

Oh for the wonderful love he has promised!
Promised for you and for me;
Tho' we have sin'd, He has mercy and pardon.
Pardon for you and for me.

TAKE MY HAND

```
G                               C
When my way groweth drear, precious Lord linger near,
        G          D
When my life is almost o'er'
G                               C
Hear my cry, hear my call, hold my hand lest I fall;
        G          D          G
Take my hand, precious Lord, lead me home.
```

Refrain:

Precious Lord, take my hand, lead me on, let me stand,

I am tired, I am weak, I am worn;

Thru the storm, thru the night, lead me on to the light;

Take my hand, precious Lord, lead me home.

Verse:

When the shadows appear, and the night draweth near,
And the day is past and gone,
At the river I stand, guide me on to that Land,
Take my hand, precious Lord, lead me home.

WAYFARING STRANGER

Dm
I'm just a poor wayfaring stranger
        G   Dm
A trav'lin' through this world of woe

But there's no sickness, toil nor danger
            G Am   Dm
In that bright world to which I go.
      Dm   G
I'm goin' there to see my mother
      Dm
I'm goin' there, no more to roam
    Dm
I'm just agoin' over Jordan
      G   Am Dm
I'm just agoin' over home.

My father lived and died a farmer
A-reapin' less than he did sow
And now I follow in his footsteps
A-knownin' less than he did know.
I'm goin' there to see my father
He said he'd meet me when I come
I'm just a-goin' over Jordan
I'm just a-goin' over home

I know dark clouds will gather 'round me
My way is steep and rough, I know
But fertile fields lie just before me
In that fair land to which I go
I'm goin there to see my brother
I'm goin' there no more to roam
I'm just a-goin' over Jordan
I'm just a-goin' over home.

I want to sing salvation's story.
In concert with the blood-washed men.
I want to wear a crown of glory.
When I get home to that good land.
I'm goin' there to see my classmates,

Who passed before me one by one.
I'm just a-goin' over Jordan
I'm just a-goin' over home.

I'll soon be free from ev'ry trial,
My body'll rest in the old churchyard.
I'll drop the cross of self-denial,
And enter into my reward.
I'm going there to see my Saviour,
Who shed His precious blood for me,
I'm just a-goin' over Jordan
I'm just a-goin' over home.

WHEN THE ROLL IS CALLED UP YONDER

G   C   G
When the trumpet of the Lord shall sound and time shall be no more,
                        D
And the morning breaks eternal, bright and fair;
      G   C   G
When the saved of earth shall gather over on the other shore,
               D   G
And the roll is called up yonder, I'll be there.

Refrain:

When the roll is called up yonder
      D
When the roll is called up yonder
      G   C
When the roll is called up yonder
      G   D   G
When the roll is called up yonder, I'll be there.

Verse:

On that bright and cloudless morning when the dead in Christ shall rise,
And the glory of His resurrection share;
When His chosen ones shall gather to their home beyond the skies,
And the roll is called up yonder, I'll be there.

Repeat Chorus

WHEN THE SAINTS

```
 A                 D                      A                E
I'm just a weary pilgrim, ploddin' thru this world of sin,
          A           D                      A            E     A
Gettin' ready for the Kingdom, when the saints go marching in!
```

Refrain:

```
   A                                                              E
O when the saints go marching in, when the saints go marchin' in
           A                   D                  A       E        A
O Lord I want to be in that number, when the saints go marching in!
```

Verses:

My pappy loved the Saviour, what a soldier he had been!
But his steps will be more steady, when the saints go marching in.

Up there I'll see the Saviour, who redeemed my soul from sin,
With extended arms He'll greet me, when the saints go marching in.

BIBLIOGRAPHY FOR VOCAL MUSIC

Boette, Marie (ed.), *Singa Hipsy Doodle* and Other Folk Songs of West Virginia. Parsons, W. Va.; McClain Printing Co., 1971.

Burton, Thomas G. and Manning, Ambrose N., *Collection of Folklore: Folksongs.* East Tennessee State University, Johnson City, Tennessee, 1967.

Campbell, O.D. and Sharp, Cecil, *English Folksongs from the Southern Appalachians.*

Child, Francis James, *English and Scottish Popular Ballads.* Boston: Houghton Mifflin, 1886.

Cox, John H., *Folk Songs Mainly From West Virginia.*

Cox, J. H., *Folk Songs of the South.* Harvard University Press, 1925.

Gainer, Patrick W., *W. Va. Centennial Book of 100 Songs.* Patrick W. Gainer, 1963.

Gainer, Patrick W., *Folk Songs from the West Virginia Hills,* Seneca Books, Grantsville, W. Va., 1975.

Leisy, James F., *Songs for Pickin' and Singin'.* Fawcett Publications, Inc., Greenwich, Conn., 1962.

Niles, John Jacob, *The Ballad Book of John Jacob Niles.* Bramhall House, New York, 1960.

Scott, John Anthony, *The Ballad of America: The History of the United States in Song and Story.* Grosset and Dunlap, N. Y., 1966.

Dances

Folk Dancing   Lois Hammer

THE DANCING BUTCHER FAMILY of Summersville has made a major contribution in preserving the dance heritage and renewing interest in folk and square dancing among young and old across the Mountain State.

Brookley R. (Rush) Butcher is a native of Braxton County, educated at Berea College and West Virginia University, where he received his Master's degree in Extension Education. His wife, Ruby Salyer Butcher, is a native of Kentucky, and a home economics graduate of Berea College.

Rush first became involved in folk and square dancing as a Braxton County 4-H'er in club and camp programs. At Berea College, he taught folk dancing as an assistant in the girls Physical Education Department. Here, he met Ruby and the dance team began. Rush and Ruby taught dancing at Eastern College and the University of Kentucky while instructing and participating in dance activities at Berea.

As a West Virginia University 4-H agent, dancing and instructing have been integral parts of the 4-H program for Rush (and Ruby) these past twenty-eight years. Both Judy and Keith from the very earliest, grew up in the family tradition assisting their parents in folk dancing. As time passed, they continued participation and teaching as 4-H club members, camp directors, and recreation instructors.

Judy, who graduated from Concord College in home economics, was employed as West Virginia University 4-H agent in Pleasants County, and has done graduate work at West Virginia University.

Keith, who holds a degree in music from Concord College and a Master's degree in education from West Virginia University, teaches in the Nicholas County school system.

The Butchers, out of their life-long experience, are ardent advocates of the values of folk dancing in personal development. They use folk dancing for: (1) Fun and fellowship, (2) Physical fitness, (3)

Music appreciation, (4) Social adjustment, and (5) Developing understanding of our cultural heritage and the characteristics of people from different cultural backgrounds. Dance, music, and laughter, are understood by everyone.

They teach dancing by demonstration and group involvement beginning with simple dances tailored to the experience of participants. Instruction is clear and simple. Great patience, along with enthusiasm and fun in a disciplined manner, is exercised in teaching. Out of practice, learners experience mastery and the satisfaction of individual and group achievement, all in an enjoyable social context.

Older 4-H club members are used for teaching and demonstrating—courteous, disciplined, dependable young people who love to dance and share with others. For them the satisfactions are doubled; not only from personal and group mastery, but even more from sharing with others and watching them grow, develop, and experience the pleasure and satisfaction of dancing.

Dance records with and without calls, are available from the three sources listed in the bibliography p. 344. Records should be ordered well in advance of need and filed for protection and ready use during dance sessions.

The fun, fellowship, joy, and enthusiasm for life shared by this Nicholas County family is surpassed (?) only by "Snoopy" in his suppertime dance.

FOLK AND SQUARE DANCING TERMS

Corner Lady - The lady on the gentleman's left side.

Swing - The dancers stand with right hips close together, both facing opposite directions. The man's right hand is around the lady's waist, the lady's left hand is on the man's right shoulder. The man's left hand and lady's right hand are joined. The right feet are kept together and the pivot point is between their feet.

Buzz step - Done in regular dance or swing position. Partners place outside of their right feet together, serving as a pivot. Weight is on ball of right foot. Left foot pushes right around.

Allemande Left - Corners facing each other, join left hands, walk all the way around each other and back to starting position. Simply: Gentleman turns lady of the left with the left hand.

Grand Right and Left - Partners facing, join right hands and walk past each other, passing right shoulders. Take the next person with the left hand and walk past each other, passing left shoulders. Alternate these actions until you return to your home position. Women move clockwise, and men move counterclockwise.

Weave the Ring - This movement is the same as the grand right and left, except that the dancers pass right and left shoulders alternately around the circle without touching hands with anyone, until they reach their home position.

Promenade - Two dancers stand together, side by side. Man's and lady's right hands are joined on top of the man's and lady's left hands. (Hands are crossed in front of the couple.) Promenade is done counter-clockwise around the circle.

Do-Si-Do - Two dancers walk forward, facing each other. They pass right shoulders, go one step past each other, take one step to the right, and walk backward to place.

See-saw - Just the opposite of the Do-si-do. Pass left shoulders, back to back, pass right shoulders.

Circle four, six, and eight - The active couple or couples join hands with the next couple and circle At the call the active man breaks hands and joins hands with the next couple.

Balance - Partners face. Each person steps on the right foot, and swings the left foot over the right. Then each steps on the left and swings the right foot over the left.

Two Ladies Chain - Two ladies meet and join right hands, walk past each other, passing right shoulders, and then join left hands with the gents. End with a courtesy turn.

Courtesy Turn - Gentleman holds left hand of lady with his left hand, puts right arm around girl's waist and gently turns her around. This is used as an ending for several movements: ladies chain and right and left through.

Four Ladies Chain - The four ladies make a right hand star and walk clockwise half way round, join left hands with opposite men and end with courtesy turn.

Sashay - Partners facing, with hands joined. A sliding step to the side, one foot leading, the other following: step, close; step, close; etc. Usually done to double-time.

Allemande Right - Gentleman turns his partner with right hand.

Right and Left Thru - Two active couples move toward each other. Each person joins right hands with the opposite person, and they pass right shoulders. Partners then join left hands and the man courtesy turns the lady. Repeat this movement, ending with couples in original positions.

Pass Thru - Two couples facing walk toward each other, passing the opposite person right to right shoulder and taking the opposite couple's position facing outward until the next call is given.

Cross Trail - Same as the pass thru except that after each person passes right shoulders with the one facing him, each man turns diagonally to the right and crosses behind his partner, who advances diagonally to the left. The movement ends with the couples facing away from the center, the lady on the left of her partner.

Right Hand Star - Usually performed by four people. All put their right hands to the center and join with the opposite person and circle.

Star Promenade - The men move to the center and make a left hand star and place their right arms around their partners waists. The ladies place their left hand on their partners waist or shoulder. (This star can be reversed so that the ladies make a right hand star and the men are on the outside.)

Two Hand Position - Partners face each other and join both hands.

Shoulder-hip Position - Partners face each other; women place hands on men's shoulders; men place hands slightly above women's hips.

Varsovienne or *Butterfly Position* - Partners stand side by side, facing counter-clockwise, lady on man's right. Man's right arm is behind lady; both right hands are joined above her right shoulder; his left hand holds her left hand in front of his left shoulder.

Wring the Dishrag - Two couples stand face to face and join hands in a circle of four. They hold hands throughout the figure. The leading couple walks forward and under the joined hands of the opposite couple, who have raised their joined hands in an arch. Leading couple immediately turn away from each other (man to the left, lady to the right), so that they are back to back. They then duck under their own joined hands which are raised as high as possible, continue turning (man to the left, lady to the right), and move back to their original positions by going around the other couple. At the same time they pull the other couple through the arch with their other hands (man's left, lady's right). The second couple, as they are pulled through, turn under their own joined hands, and all are back in a small circle of four again. REMEMBER: KEEP HANDS JOINED THROUGHOUT THE ENTIRE FIGURE!

ACE OF DIAMONDS
(Danish)

MUSIC: M102 4A

FORMATION: Double cirlce of partners, men with backs to center of the circle, facing their partners.

ACTION:

1. a. Partners clap own hands once, stamp right foot once, link elbows and swing with 6 skipping steps (8 counts).
   b. Partners clap own hands once, stamp left foot once, link left elbows, and swing with 6 skipping steps (8 counts).
2. Men fold arms on chest, ladies place hands on hips. Each hops into the air, extending right foot forward at the same time, left foot in place, pause; then on next hop, left foot is forward and right foot in place; pause. This hopping is continued. The rhythm for the hopping would be thus, from the beginning: ''And right (pause), and left (pause), and right and left and right and left and right (pause), and left (pause), and right and left and right.''
3. Partners join hands in skating position and do 8 polka steps (hop, step, step, step) counter-clockwise around the circle.

SUMMARY:

1. a. Clap, stamp, right-4-5-6-7-8;
   b. Clap, stamp, left-4-5-6-7-8.
2. Right-pause, left-pause, and right and left and right and left; Right-pause, left-pause, and right and left and right.
3. Polka.

VARIATION: The polka in Part 3 may be done in a waist-shoulder or closed-dance position.

1. a. Partners clap own hands and at same time extend right heel; then put hands on own hips and place right foot down beside left foot. Then *walk* with right elbows linked around 6 steps.
   b. Repeat with left heel and elbow.

Leader's Note: This is one of many versions of ''Ace of Diamonds.''

Record also available from: Folk Dance House, 108 West 16th Street, New York, N.Y.

ALL AMERICAN PROMENADE

MUSIC: Record - Winsor 7605

FORMATION: Double circle, boys on inside facing for promenade inside hands joined.

ACTION:
1. Walk forward 4 steps. (Start on outside foot both boys and girls.) Reverse direction by turning toward partner a half turn. Now move backward 4 steps. (This is the same direction as you started moving originally.)

2. Repeat No. 1. (This will put all back in original position.)

3. Face partner, join right hands, balance forward to each other two steps and back, partners exchange places as girls turn under the arch formed by the joined right hands.

4. Repeat No. 3 and move to a new partner on the right as you finish. (Both the boy and girl move right).

Repeat as many times as desired.

BINGO

This old Welsh-English ditty has become one of the best known and practiced song-dances of our Southern mountaineers. It is a favorite of all the huskins' and quiltin's and other play parties of the plain folk of the Southland. It is full of rollicking fun and should be danced with a chuckle.

WORDS:
A farmer's black dog sat on the back porch
And Bingo was his name.
A farmer's black dog sat on the back porch
And Bingo was his name.

SPOKEN: B, I, N, G, OH! (with a big hug)

SUNG: And Bingo, was his name.

MUSIC: RCA 45 6172

FORMATION: Couples in a double cirlce, facing counter-clockwise.

302

ACTION: Beginning on left foot, all couples march around the room with hands joined in skating position singing first four lines of song. On the chorus couples fall back into single circle, join hands, and continue sliding to the right.

On the spoken part, partners turn to face each other, taking right hands on "B" and continue with grand right and left in the direction they are facing to the next 4 people on each letter. Oh "Oh", they squeeze or swing their new partner with whom they begin the dance again.

This is a play-party game which is as much fun without recorded music as it is with recorded music.

BLACK HAWK WALTZ

MUSIC: MH 3002

FORMATION: Take partners in ballroom dancing positions. (Directions are given for boys; the girls will do the opposite.)

ACTION: 1. Balance forward, back and waltz once around.
            2. Balance forward, back and waltz once around.
            3. Balance forward, back and waltz once around.
            4. Balance forward, back and waltz once around.

            Partners face each other and join both hands.

            5. Swing right foot over left foot and shift weight.
               Swing left foot over right foot and shift weight.
               Swing right foot over left foot and step right,
               Step left, step right, and point with left.

            6. Swing left foot over right foot and shift weight.
               Swing right foot over left foot and shift weight.
               Swing left foot over right foot and step left,
               Step right, step left, and point with right.

            Repeat steps 5 and 6 and then go back and begin again with step 1.

BROWN EYED MARY

Record - MH 1106 or M 117 3A

> If per chance we should meet
> On this wild prairie,
> In my arms will I embrace
> My darling brown eyed Mary.

2. Turn your partner half way 'round.

3. Turn your opposite lady.

4. Turn your partner all way 'round.

5. And prom'nade right hand lady.

FORMATION: A circle of partners, faced for marching, man on the inside, girl on his right.

1. With hands crossed, partners promenade in a circle, with three or four feet between each two couples.

2. Partners join right hands, turn half around so that man is facing back, with right hand toward center, lady in opposite direction.

3. Each man joins left hands with the lady who was in the couple behind him, and turns her completely around.

4. Joining right hands with original partner, turn her entirely around.

5. Take lady behind in promenade position for a new partner and repeat from beginning.

This may also be sung (2 verses--words above) and danced as a play-party game.

CALICO POLKA

MUSIC: Record - MacGregor 756, or any good polka record.

POSITION: Side by side, arms around each other's waists.

START: All on left foot.

FIGURE: Weight on the right foot, place left heel to the side-front, lean
back. Place left foot beside right and put weight on it.

Place right toe back as you lean forward. Momentarily touch
right toe beside left foot. (This should be a brush). Weight still
on left foot, touch right heel forward - while leaning back
slightly then place right foot beside left and put weight on the
left foot.

Touch left heel to the side - touch left toe to the right of the
right foot (or just cross left over right in sweeping motion).

Starting on the left foot do four two-steps forward.

CIRCLE VIRGINIA REEL

FORMATION: Double circle of partners. Men on the inside, ladies on the
outside facing counter-clockwise to promenade.

MUSIC: Record - Blackberry Quadrille
RCA 456184 or M 103 6A
or any good fiddling tune.

ACTION: Promenade one and all

Face your partner and a right hand turn

A left hand turn

Two hands turn

Do-si-do right

Do-si-do left

Right elbow swing

Left elbow swing

Promenade the lady on your right (this is the girl behind
the boy as he promenaded the last time)

Repeat as many times as desired.

The caller might like to vary the above calls to suit his
group.

THE DASHING WHITE SERGEANT

FORMATION: This is a circle reel-time dance. Dancers stand in a circle round the room in 3's, a man between 2 ladies faces a lady between 2 men. The man between 2 ladies moves clockwise and the other 3 counter-clockwise.

ACTION: Bars 1-8: All six dancers make a circle and dance 8 slip steps round to left and 8 back again.

9-16: The Center dancer turns to right hand partner. They set to each other and turn with 2 hands, 4 pas-de-basque. Center dancer turns and does the same with left hand partner, and finishes facing right hand partner again.

17-24: They dance the reel of three, center dancer beginning the reel by giving left shoulder to right hand partner. 8 skip change of step. They finish facing their opposite 3.

25-32: All advance and retire, then pass on to meet the next three coming toward them, passing right shoulder with the person opposite to them.

The dance is repeated as many times as you will.

D'HAMMERSCHMIEDSGSELLN
(Dŭh-hahm'-mair-shmēēts-gŭh-zehln)
Th' Journeyman Blacksmith

(Bavarian dance for 2 couples or 4 men)

MUSIC: Record—Folkcraft 1485x45B and LP-5 (side B band 4).

FORMATION: Circle of four people: (a) two couples, women on partner's right, OR (b) four men (original form).

ACTION: Measure CHORUS—(Music A)

1-16 First opposites (men 1 and 3, OR the two women) do CLAP PATTERN* beginning on first count of measure 1, while the others (men 2 and 4, OR the two men) do CLAP PATTERN beginning on first count of measure 2.

FIGURE I—Circle (Music B)

17-24 Join hands and circle left with STEP-HOPS**.

25-32 Circle right in the same manner.

FIGURE II—Star

1-16 REPEAT CHORUS pattern above.

17-24 Right-hand star with STEP-HOPS.

24-32 Left-hand star in the same manner.

FIGURE III—Big Circle

1-16 REPEAT CHORUS pattern above.

17-24 Circles of four open out to form one large circle and circle left with STEP-HOPS.

25-32 Circle right in the same manner.

REPEAT ENTIRE SEQUENCE starting with new couple.

NOTE: *CLAP PATTERN: With both hands, slap own thighs (count 1), own chest (count 2), clap own hands together (count 3); opposites clap right hands (count 4), left hands (count 5), both hands (count 6).

**STEP-HOP: Step on one foot (count 1), pause (count 2), hop on same foot (count 3).

DOUDLEBSKA POLKA

MUSIC: Folk Dancer MH 3016

FORMATION: Either one big circle or several smaller circles scattered around the floor.

ACTION: I. Ballroom position. Couples do a regular polka around the circle, one couple following another. This should be a rather heavy two-step type of polka. Total of 16 polka steps. With beginners, a Varsovienne or Skater's position may be substituted for the ballroom position.

II. Men put their right arm around lady's waist as they stand side by side. Lady is to right of man. Lady puts her left hand on man's right shoulder of the man ahead of them. This closes up the

307

circle. Make sure that the men all move sidewards to the center to catch up with man ahead. Now in this position all march forward around the ring and sing loudly, la, la, la, etc. This takes 32 walking steps.

III. Men face center as ladies drop behind partners. Ladies face clockwise in an outer ring and with hands on own hips polka around the circle, AS AT THE SAME TIME, the men clap out a rhythm like this: Clap own hands twice.
Extend hands sidewards with elbows bent and strike palms with neighboring men once.
Repeat this pattern over and over again.

At the end of Part III, men turn around and take nearest lady for a new partner. It will turn out that someone may be without a partner, in which case such dancers should go into the center of the room to find the missing partner. Extra boys or girls can join the dance . . . the boys in Part II, the girls in Part III.

DOWN SOUTH MIXER

Record—Windsor 7122

MUSIC: "Down South"

FORMATION: Double Circle of partners, facing (girls facing center, men back to center).

ACTION: Step close, step close—slide, slide, slide. Both hands joined with partner. (Start boys left foot, girls right.)

Repeat in opposite direction.

Step point (4 times)—Boys step on left foot, point right toe back of left heel, swaying the body left, step on right foot, point left toe back of right heel, swaying the body right. Repeat left and right. (Girls do opposite.)

Do-si-do partners—End the do-si-do by facing new partner on right, both hands joined and ready to repeat entire dance.

GIE GORDONS

MUSIC: Methodist World of Fun Series.
Tune: White Cockade

FORMATION: Big circle of couples in a varsovienne position, facing counter-clockwise.

ACTION: I. Couples walk forward 4 steps in counter-clockwise direction (4 counts). With hands still joined, couples about face to the right (man now has left arm over the lady's shoulder), beginning turn on 4th count.
Couples walk backward 4 steps (still counter-clockwise). Do not turn. Stop. Walk forward 4 steps clockwise; then with hands still joined, about face to the left (man now has right arm over lady's shoulder) and walk backward 4 steps clockwise.

II. Drop left hands, hold right hands loosely for turning (lady holds man's index finger). Lady turns clockwise with 4 two-steps under joined hands, while man moves forward around the circle counter-clockwise with 4 two-steps (4 measures). In closed dance position, couple turns clockwise with 4 two-steps (moving counter-clockwise around the large circle) (4 measures).

Leader's Note: The movement is easier if each step of Part I is begun with the left foot for both man and lady. On last count of Part I, lady just touches right toe to floor. In Part II, man begins with left foot, lady with right foot. At the end of Part II, lady does a quick shift of weight so as to lead off with left foot.

A polka step can be used in action II.

HORA AND VARIATIONS (TRIPLE HORA)

(Jewish circle dance, no partners)

MUSIC: Record—Folkcraft 010x45A and LP-12 (side A band 1).

FORMATION: Single circle facing center, no partners.

Starting position: "T" position: arms extended sideward, hands on neighbors shoulders. Left foot free.

ACTION: Measure FIGURE I—Cherkessia (Music AA)

1-8 Three and 1/2 GRAPEVINE or CHERKESSIA STEPS* starting with left foot moving sideward right (counts 1-14), jump twice on both feet in place, keeping right foot free at the end (counts 15-16).

9-16 REPEAT pattern of measures 1-8 reversing direction and footwork.

FIGURE II—Double hora (Music BB)

17-18 Step sideward right on right foot (count 1), cross and step on left foot in back of right (count 2), step sideward right on right foot (count 3), hop on right foot swinging left foot across in front of right (count 4).

19-20 REPEAT pattern of measures 17-18 reversing direction and footwork.

21-32 REPEAT pattern of measures 17-20 three more times (4 times in all).

FIGURE III—Scissors (Music CC)

33 Leap onto right foot placing left heel forward (count 1), pause (count 2).

34 Leap onto left foot placing right heel forward (count 1), pause (count 2).

35-36 REPEAT pattern of measures 33-34 twice as fast (without the pauses) making four changes.

37-48 REPEAT pattern of measures 33-36 three more times (4 times in all).

NOTE: *GRAPEVINE or CHERKESSIA STEP (moving sideward Right): Cross and step on left foot in front of right (count 1), step sideward right on right foot (count 2), cross and step on left foot in back of right (count 3), step sideward right on right foot (count 4).

HOT TIME MIXER

MUSIC: "Hot Time in the Old Town Tonight"
                    Record—Folkcraft 1037

FORMATION: Partners in a single circle, all facing the center. Lady on the man's right.

ACTION: All join hands and circle left.
The other way back.
All in and out (four short steps in and four back to place).
Repeat in and out.
Ladies to the center and back.
Gentlemen to the center, turn left and swing the lady there.
Promenade this lady (she becomes the gentleman's new partner).

Repeat as many times as desired.

IRISH WASHERWOMAN MIXER

MUSIC: Record—RCA 45-6178

FORMATION: Partners in a single circle, all facing the center. Ladies on the gents right.

ACTION: 1. All join hands and into the middle.
2. And when you get there, keep time to the fiddle.
3. And when you get back, remember the call.
4. Swing on the corner and promenade all.
(Promenade 16 counts and begin again, repeating as many times as desired.)

DESCRIPTION:
1. All to the center and join hands.
2. Stamp foot 4 times in center.
3. All come back out.
4. Swing corner 3/4 round and promenade.

JIFFY MIXER

Round Dance—Mixer

MUSIC: Windsor Record 4684

FORMATION: Butterfly position, men's backs toward center of

hall. (Footwork for men and women is opposite throughout the dance; steps described are for men.)

ACTION: Introduction:
Wait; wait; balance apart, touch; balance together, touch.
Wait 2 measures; balance backward toward center of hall on left foot, touch right toe beside left foot; balance forward toward wall and partner on right foot, touch left toe beside right foot.

Dance:
Heel, Toe; Heel, Toe; Side, Close; Side, Touch. In Butterfly position, strike left heel to floor forward and toward left side, touch left toe beside right foot; repeat; step to left side with slide step; repeat.

Heel, Toe; Heel, Toe; Side, Close; Side, Touch. Repeat movement above, starting with right foot.

Chug, Clap; Chug, Clap; Chug, Clap; Chug, Clap. Releasing hands, partners do four "Chugs" away from each other with weight on both feet, men moving backward toward center of hall and women moving backward toward wall, clapping hands on the upbeat of the music following each chug.

Walk to the right-; two-; three-; four-(to butterfly). Start left foot and take four slow, swaggering steps forward diagonally to right, progressing to new partner, ending in Butterfly position, men's back toward center of hall, ready to repeat the dance.

Perform entire routine for a total of eight times ending with new partners bowing at the finish of the eighth sequence.

LILI MARLENE

MUSIC: "Lili Marlene"
MacGregor 301 or M113 1A

FORMATION: Partners standing side by side, holding inside hands. Lady on gent's right facing promenade direction.

ACTION: Walk forward four steps. (Both start on outside foot.)

Face partner, join both hands and slide to the gent's left four slide steps.

Repeat all of above in opposite direction.

Still facing partner both hands joined, balance in place. Step on left foot, swing right foot across it; then step with right foot and swing left across it; repeat this action.

Link right arm with partner and walk half way around each other, link left arms and return to place. Join inside hands as you face promenade direction.

Four two-steps forward—(boy start with left foot, girl right) this is a step, slide, step and a step, slide, step.

Now partners turn away from each other making a small circle. Girl turns right, boy left, with four two-steps boy coming back to girl behind as a new partner.

Repeat from beginning.

MARCHING TO PRETORIA

MUSIC: Record—Shaw No. 183/184

FORMATION: 2 concentric circles of couples (couple facing couple) lady on man's right. Square dancers are very comfortable with this formation.

ACTION: *Counts   Cues*

       8   TWO LADIES CHAIN
       8   CHAIN BACK
       8   RIGHT HAND STAR   Once around with the opposite couple.
       8   LEFT HAND STAR   Once around with the opposite couple; then, with the lady in the lead, single file, *WALK*. Note that at this point, the concentric circles are moving in opposite directions . . . (inside circle walks RLOD, outside circle walks LOD). *Get ready to start singing.*
       8   MARCH   in single file. (Sing through the

next 32 counts) "We are marching to Pretoria" . . . *reverse direction.*

8   MARCH THE OTHER WAY BACK   Back to the same couple with whom you started. "Pretoria, Pretoria."

8   RIGHT AND LEFT THROUGH WITH THE OPPOSITE COUPLE ". . . we are marching to Pretoria."

8   PASS THROUGH WITH THE OPPOSITE COUPLE "Pretoria, Hooray!" *and couples wheel to the left.*

NOTE: The "Pass Through and Wheel to the Left" is all accomplished in the last 8 counts, and a progression has taken place.

Start the dance over with a new opposite couple.

The "Marching to Pretoria" chorus takes 32 counts. You finish it as you wheel to face the new opposite couple.

The *chains* and *stars* also take 32 counts, which you dance without vocalizing.

MEITSCHI PUTZDI

MUSIC: Record—MH 1017

CHORUS: Couples face partner. Hold right hands high. Man takes one step to left, lady to right. And Bow or Curtsey. Repeat in opposite direction. Man stands still as lady turns under joined right hands to her own right (clockwise) with 4 step-hops.

Partners now hook right elbows, and place their left hands behind their own back where they will find their partner's right hand. Hold it. This is called a "back-grasp." In this position, both move forward, turning in place clockwise with 4 step-hops and finishing side by side, lady facing clockwise, man counter-clockwise.

Clap own hands on thighs; clap own hands. NOW turn to face partner and clap partner's hands 3 times quickly. This concludes the chorus.

314

FIGURE 1:	Partners hold each other by the upper part of the arm and do a schottische step sidewards to man's left, lady's right (step-together-step-hop). Then repeat another schottische step to man's right, lady's left. Then both turn with 4 lively step-hops, clockwise, but moving counter-clockwise around the circle. Repeat Part 1.
	THERE IS AN INTERLUDE OF MUSIC HERE during which you get into Chorus position and do the chorus.
FIGURE 2:	Partners join inside hands and starting on man's left, lady's right foot, move forward with a step-together-step-hop; step-together-step-hop (this means 2 schottische steps) and man now kneels as lady dances counterclockwise around man with 4 long step-hops. Do not drop hands during this part. Man rises and both dance forward with 2 more schottische steps. Man kneels again as lady dances around him with 4 step-hops.
	INTERLUDE OF MUSIC HERE to get you into Chorus position. Do chorus.
FIGURE 3:	Partners separate, man to left, lady to right, moving on a diagonal with one schottische step. Repeat to partner with another schottische step, moving diagonally forward toward each other. See diagram for this "diamond-shaped schottische." Now take partner in shoulder-waist position and turn with 4 step-hops. Repeat the separation schottische and return to partner again with 4 step-hops, at the end of which you toss the girl up in the air.
	Repeat dance from the beginning.
NOTE:	Free hands are held on hip in Swiss dances. Shout "yaho-hoo" on occasion. Swiss dances are very social and have delightful music and are therefore very popular with American folk dancers.

MEXICAN WALTZ

MUSIC: Record—Sonort M301

FORMATION: Couples facing each other around the circle with both hands joined.

ACTION: Swing in, swing out, swing in, clap, clap (own hands).

Swing out, swing in, swing out, clap, clap.

Move back together, and back, clap, clap.

Move together, back and together (putting arms around partner), clap, clap.

Waltz eight measures and repeat the dance.

NEBESCO KOLO

Dance from Balkan Countries.

MUSIC: Record—Balkan 513

FORMATION: Circle (no partners).

ACTION: Part I
Move 16 running steps to left
Move 16 running steps to right

Part II
Step in toward center of circle with right foot
Bring left foot in beside right foot
Step out of circle with right foot
Bring left foot out beside right foot

Part III
Cross right foot in front of left and balance, shifting weight from right foot to left foot to right and back to left—quickly
Cross left foot in front of right and balance, shifting weight from left foot to right foot to left and back to right—quickly
Repeat movement with right foot over left
Repeat movement with left foot over right
Stamp!

Repeat all three parts of dance until end of music.

OH, JOHNNY OH

MUSIC: Record—Folkcraft 1037 or may sing as a play-party game.

FORMATION: Big circle, partner on right side of gents.

ACTION: All join hands and circle left
Stop where you are, give your partner a swing (All swings should be two hand).
Then you swing that gal behind you
And swing your own before you get through.

Allemande left with that lady on the left.
Do-si-do your own
All promenade that cute corner girl
Singing Oh, Johnny Oh, Johnny Oh!

Repeat two verses as many times as desired.

OSLO WALTZ

MUSIC: Folk Dancer MH 3016

FORMATION: Couples in a circle, facing the center, lady to right of man. All hands joined.

ACTION: 1. All do one waltz-balance step forward. Man starts on left, lady on right. All take one waltz-balance step backwards. Man starts on right, lady on left. The men take 6 small steps in place as ALL the ladies move one place over to the right with 6 walking steps, making a solo turn to the right as ladies progress.
IMMEDIATELY all rejoin hands in a single circle. It helps if the man will take the lady at the end of his left hand and swing her over to the right during this part of the dance.
This balance forward and back, and lady progression to the right is done four times in all.

2. Face new partner (single circle formation). Lady to right of man is the new partner. Join both hands stretched out at shoulder level. Waltz balance to center of ring sidewards, then repeat away from center. Drop hands and turn solo toward

center of ring. Man to left, lady to right. Rejoin hands and waltz balance away from center, then toward center. Drop hands and turn solo away from center. Man to right, lady to left.

3. Resume two-hand hold and take two slow slides toward center and two slow step-slides toward the wall. Take ballroom position and do 4 waltz steps around the ring.

All face center in circle and repeat dance from beginning.

PATTY CAKE POLKA

MUSIC: "Little Brown Jug"
Record—Buffalo Gal, MH 1501 or M107 1B

FORMATION: Double circle, boys facing out, girls in, both hands joined.

ACTION: Heel, toe, heel, toe.
(Boy begins with left foot, girl right.)
Four fast slip steps counter-clockwise.
Heel, toe, heel, toe.
(Boy right, girl left.)

Four slip steps clockwise.
Boy holds hands up and girl claps three fast claps.
First right (clap, clap, clap), left (clap, clap, clap)
Both hands (clap, clap, clap), legs (clap, clap, clap)
(Both boy and girl clap own legs)
Right arm swing 1, 2, 3, and 4 count, and everyone move to the left as they finish the turn to a new partner.

Repeat as many times as desired.

POP GOES THE WEASEL

MUSIC: MH 1501 or M104 2A

FORMATION: Circle of partners, each boy has partner on right. Every other couple faces in opposite direction, making sets of four.

ACTION: Both couples join hands and walk to the left eight
steps;
Back to the right eight steps.
Stretch circle of two couples as large as possible,
then four steps to the center raising hands to apex,
Drop back into place.

Couples facing clockwise make arches,
Couples facing counter-clockwise go under arches.
Both couples move forward at the same time, Advancing to meet new couples.
Clap hands on "POP".

There are many versions of this game. When you want to use "Pop Goes the Weasel" as a play-party game (without music), these words may be sung:

1) A penny for a spool of thread
A penny for a needle,
That's the way my money goes,
Pop goes the weasel!

2) All around the vinegar jug,
The monkey chased the weasel
The monkey thought 'twas all in fun,
Pop goes the weasel!

3) Mary's got the whooping cough
Johnny's got the measles,
That's the way the money goes,
Pop goes the weasel!

4) You may buy the baby clothes,
I will buy the cradle,
That's the way the money goes,
Pop goes the weasel!

5) Round and round the market house
The monkey chased the weasel.
The preacher kissed the peddler's wife,
Pop goes the weasel!

6) Round and round the cobbler's bench
The monkey chased the weasel
The farmer kissed the cobbler's wife,
Pop goes the weasel!

FORMATION: Big circle of trios, facing counter-clockwise. The player in the middle takes a position slightly in front of his two partners, holding their two outside hands. These two partners join inside hands behind his back.

ACTION: 1, 2, 3—Skip in formation counter-clockwise 12 steps. 4. On "pop" they snap the center player under their raised arms to the players behind, who become his new partners.

ROAD TO THE ISLES

MUSIC: M110 3B

FORMATION: Double circle of partners in varsovienne position facing counter-clockwise (partners side by side, lady on man's right, their right hands joined above her right shoulder, left hands joined in front of his left shoulder).

ACTION: 1. a. Place left toe diagonally forward to the left (count 1,2), then step behind the right foot with the left foot (count 3), step to the right with the right foot (count 4), draw left foot to right (count 1,2), then place right toe diagonally forward to the right (count 3,4). Step behind the left foot with the right foot (count 1), step to the left with left (count 2), draw right foot to left foot (count 3,4).

b. Place left heel forward on the floor (count 1,2), place left toe backward on the floor (count 3,4).

2. a. Beginning with left foot, couple moves forward around circle with 2 schottische steps (step, close, step, hop). On the hop at the end of the 2nd schottische step, both do a hop-turn quickly to the right, by turning on the ball of the right foot and raising the left foot knee high. This brings the man's left arm across the lady's shoulder. Lift hands a little higher on the turn. Couple now faces clockwise in the circle.

b. Beginning on the left foot, couple takes 3 walking steps in clockwise direction and turns again (half turn quickly to the left), on ball of left foot, raising right foot knee high. Couple is now in original position.

c. Stamp three times in place; right, left, right.

SUMMARY: 1. a. Point left, back, side, together.
Point right back, side, together.
b. Heel forward, toe back.
2. a. Step, 2, 3, hop; step, 2, 3, turn;
b. Step, 2, 3, turn,
c. Stamp, stamp, stamp.

VARIATION: This is really a couple dance, and it is not necessarily done in a circle. A circle may be best while teaching the dance. To make progressive, use the circle formation and have man move forward on the 3 stamps while the lady stamps in place. Some leaders hold the "Road to the Isles" does not adapt well as a mixer.

In 2c., move forward 3 steps instead of stamping 3 times in place.

THE ROBERTS

MUSIC: M121 3-B or Folkcraft Record 1161 and Methodist World of Fun

FORMATION: Double circle of partners facing each other, man with his back to the center of the circle. May be done in free formation.

ACTION: 1. a. Join both hands, take 2 step-slides counter-clockwise around the circle, drop hands, each turns in place once around with 4 walking steps, man turning to the left and lady to the right.
b. Repeat A.
2. a. Couples face counter-clockwise. Starting with outside foot (man's left, lady's right) both do a heel and toe and a two-step (step, close, step) forward in a counter-clockwise direction.
b. Repeat with inside foot.
3. In closed dance position couples turn around the circle with 4 two-steps.

1. a. Step-slide, step-slide, turn 2, 3, 4,
   b. Step-slide, step-slide, turn 2, 3, 4.
2. a. Heel and toe and step, close, step,
   b. Heel and toe and step, close, step.
3. Turn with a step, Turn with a step
   Turn with a step, Turn with a step.

VARIATION: To make progressive: part 3 is done in the following manner:

a. Partners face, join both hands and take 2 step-slides counter-clockwise around the circle.

b. Man does 2 two-steps in place while lady turns under arch formed by her right arm and his left arm. Man's left hand and lady's right hand are loosely joined for turning.

Leader's Note: It will be easier for most groups to teach the variation of 3 first, then the closed turn.

SELJANCICA KOLO

MUSIC: Folk Dancer Record MH 1006

The word "kolo" means circle and is a dance form common to Yugoslavia, especially Serbia. This particular kolo was the first kolo to be introduced to American schools. The dance is somewhat simplified to enable even beginners to do it.

FORMATION: Circle, broken with a leader at one end, always a man, if possible. Joined hands are held straight down, and body is quite erect, tall, proud, almost arrogant in manner.

ACTION: Part I
Step to right on right foot.
Step on left behind right.
Step on right to right again.
Point left toe forward.
Step to left on left foot.
Step on right behind left.
Step to left on left foot.
Point right toe.

Repeat all of Part I again.

Part II

Step to right, then bring left foot up to it and step left, bring right foot up to it. Repeat this. During this figure, body should shake slightly up and down with each step like a tremble. It is fun also to sing as you go to the right the word "Desno" which means "right" and "Levo" which means "left."

Part III

Walk 8 steps to right and 8 steps to left, or else do a "lame-duck" step by hopping on left foot and almost simultaneously falling on right foot. Then step on left foot. Hop on left again, bringing right foot down quickly, and another step on left foot. Repeat for the whole phrase of music. Then reverse direction, but this time hop on right foot and come down on left foot, then step on right foot.

VARIATION: The authentic form of this dance is identical to these directions except for Part I, where the basic Kolo step is substituted. Those who are more advanced may want to try this:

Hop on left foot; drop on right foot in front of left. Step on left foot behind right foot; step on right foot in place.
Hop on right foot.
Hop on right foot again; drop onto left foot in front of right.
Step on right foot behind left foot. Step on left foot in place.
Hop on left foot.

NOTE: Steps should be close to the floor, tiny, with flexed knees. Movement is more up and down than side to side.

SICILIAN TARANTELLA

MUSIC: M118 6A

FORMATION: Sets of two couples in free formation, partners facing. Couples are numbered 1 and 2.

ACTION: 1. All step-hop on left foot and swing right foot across in front, clapping own hands on the step;

323

then step-hop on right foot and swing left foot across, clapping as before. (Cue: step-hop, swing, step-hop, swing; count: 1, 2, 3, 4.) Then do 4 tiny running steps in place (left-right-left-right; count 1, 2, 3, 4), snapping fingers with hands raised in the air. Repeat all of this action three more times, or four times total.

2. Bending low, partners walk toward each other 4 tiny steps, straighten up, and walk erect 4 steps backward to place, all the while snapping fingers. Move as close together as possible without touching (which is a foul!). Repeat three times, or four times total.

3. a. Man 1 and lady 2 meet in the center of the set and do a right elbow turn in 8 skipping steps. Then man 2 and lady 1 do the same.

   b. The same as 3. a., but turning with left elbows.

4. a. Man 1 and lady 2 do an Italian style right shoulder do-si-do, snapping fingers and slithering around each other, turning freely as desired. Other couple does the same.

   b. Repeat 4 a. but with left shoulders.

5. With hands on own hips all skip counter-clockwise around own set 8 steps, then 8 steps clockwise back to place.

6. Left-hand star, skipping counter-clockwise 8 steps, then right-hand star clockwise 8 steps back to place.

SUMMARY: 1. Step-swing, step-swing, run 2-3-4,
Step-swing, step-swing, run 2-3-4,
Step-swing, step-swing, run 2-3-4,
Step-swing, step-swing, run 2-3-4.

2. Down 2-3-4, up 2-3-4,
Down 2-3-4, up 2-3-4,
Down 2-3-4, up 2-3-4,
Down 2-3-4, up 2-3-4.

3. a. Right elbows, 2-3-4-5-6-7-8,
Right elbows, 2-3-4-5-6-7-8,
   b. Left elbows, 2-3-4-5-6-7-8,
Left elbows, 2-3-4-5-6-7-8.

4. a. Do-si-do right,
      Do-si-do right.
   b. Do-si-do left,
      Do-si-do left.

5. Hands on hips and circle counter-clockwise 5-6-7, reverse; Circle clockwise 2-3-4-5-6-7-8.

6. Left-hand star 2-3-4-5-6-7-8 reverse,
   Right-hand star 2-3-4-5-6-7-8.

SWEDISH MASQUERADE

MUSIC: MH 1055

FORMATION: Double circle. Couples, arm in arm.

ACTION: (:1-4:) Walking steps counter-clockwise; turn toward each other. Walking steps clockwise.

            (:5-12:) Tyrolean waltz.

            (:13-20:) Tyrolean hop-dance (like the chorus of Napoleon).

TEXAS SCHOTTISCHE

MUSIC: Record—MH 1055 or M102 4A (Swedish Schottische)

FORMATION: Double circle, facing counter-clockwise, partners side by side, inside hands joined (or skater's handclasp).

I. . . . . 4 measures
Moving forward in line of direction, begin on outside foot with

            Step-together-step (hold)
            Step-together-step (hold) . . . . 2 meas.

            Walk forward with 4 bouncy walking steps . . 2 meas.

II. . . . . 4 measures
Touch heel of left foot on floor, forward.
Touch toe of same foot back . . . . 1 meas.

Lady: 3 walking steps going around in front of partner
Man: 3 small steps in place . . . . 1 meas.

Both: Heel-toe, again (right foot) .... 1 meas.

Lady: 3 walking steps going back to the man of the couple back of her original partner. Give him R hand in his R hand; he takes L hand with his L hand as she swings into place beside him, ready to repeat dance.

Man: 3 small steps to meet lady from couple in front of him, who comes back as described above .... 1 meas.

Repeat all of I and II as many times as necessary to the end of the music, or until each lady has returned to her original partner.

THE MASON'S APRON

A charming progression mixer for two sets of trios
to the tune of "Star of Edinburgh."

MUSIC: Record—Folkcraft 1512

FORMATION: Circle of trios (one gent and two ladies), alternate groups facing.

ACTION: Music   Measures

A1   1-8   Circle left once around in circle of six.

A2   1-2   Gent balances (sets) right and left with his right hand partner.

3-4   Gent turns his right hand partner with a right elbow turn.

5-6   Gent balances right and left with his left hand partner.

7-8   Gent turns his left hand partner with a left elbow turn.

B1   1-4   Gent does a right hand star for three with his right hand partner and his opposite right hand lady.

5-8   Gents do a left hand star with left hand ladies (finishing in original lines of three).

B2   1-4   Lines of three go forward and back.

5-8   Lines of three go forward, pass

right shoulder with opposite, and progress to meet new group.

REPEAT DANCE WITH NEW GROUP.

VIRGINIA REEL

MUSIC: Record—MacGregor 735 or M103 6A

FORMATION: Longway for six couples, girls in one line, boys in other, facing partners.

ACTION:
1. Forward and bow: Hands joined in the lines, players advance three steps, bow to partner and back to place.

2. Repeat No. 1.

3. Right-hand swing: Partners advance, join right hands, and turn each other.

4. Left-hand swing: Partners join left hands and turn.

5. Both hands swing: Partners join both hands and turn.

6. Do-si-do right: Partners walk around each other, passing on the right and walking backward to place.

7. Do-si-do left: Partners walk around each other, passing on the left and walking backward to place.

8. Arm right: Partners hook right arms and swing around.

9. Arm left: Partners hook left arms and swing around.

10. Head couple join hands and do a side slip down center and return.

11. Reel: Head couple hook their right elbows and turn once and a half around. The lady will now hook left elbows with the first gent on the left and the gent will hook left elbows with the first lady in line. As they come around the partners will hook right elbows and swing and catch the

327

next lady and gent with left, etc., to foot of couple.

Continue until all couples have had their turn at the head.

WAVES OF TORY

MUSIC: M102 6A

FORMATION: Longways set of couples, men opposite partners, six feet apart. As couples face the head of the hall, ladies are at the right of men. Couples are paired into sets of two couples numbered 1-2, 1-2, all down the line.

ACTION:
1. The Waves: Men join hands in their line, ladies likewise; the two lines walk* toward each other 3 steps, pause, raising** joined hands high as they move forward; they walk backward to place with 4 steps, lowering joined hands. Repeat.

2. Whirlpools: Drop hands. The lines quickly come together again, and each man 1 gives right hand across to lady 2; each man 2 gives right hand to lady 1 to form a right-hand star. They walk around in star formation 8 steps back in a left hand star, ending in line in original place.

3. Repeat Waves as in 1.

4. Repeat Whirlpools, this time starting with a left-hand star and returning with a right-hand star to place.

5. Waves sweep out to sea: All face head of the set. Lady takes right arm of the man who is her partner, and the head couple turns sharply to the right, promenading down beside the ladies' line toward the foot of the set, all couples following. Head couple returns to original place, the others following, making a sharp right turn again before heading up the set.

6. Whitecaps: Couples do an under and over figure down and up the lines, returning to original positions. Couples go alternately under the arch formed by the oncoming couple, then over the

next couple with their own arch. All couples begin at same time: couples 1 moving down the set, couples 2 moving up the set; couple 1 begins going under the arch.

7. Waves of Tory: The head couple "casts off" (man turning to left and down the outside, lady to right), followed by the ladies' side and the men down the men's side. At the foot, the head couple makes a double arch by joining both hands and raising them high. All the other couples go through the arch and return to the place in the line. The second couple now becomes the head couple, and the original head couple remains at the foot of the set. Repeat as often as desired.

SUMMARY:
1. Forward-2-3-swish,
Back-2-3-4,
Forward-2-3-swish,
Back-2-3-4.

2. Right-2-3-4-5-6-7-8,
Left-2-3-4-5-6-7-8.

3. Forward-2-3-swish,
Back-2-3-4,
Forward-2-3-swish,
Back-2-3-4.

4. Left-2-3-4-5-6-7-8,
Right-2-3-4-5-6-7-8.

5. Couples cast off right and promenade the set.

6. Under and over.

7. Lines cast off; make an arch; return to place.

Leader's Note: While six or eight couples are usually used, Waves of Tory may be enjoyed where there are long lines of couples. Six seems best. Since the head couple stays at the foot, the right-handed and left-handed stars change because each couple has moved one position toward the head. If Waves of Tory is repeated, the group should check their stars to see who will be in each newly formed pair of couples.

*Sometimes a promenade step is used in Irish dancing: It is a two-step done with a leap on the first count (leap on left foot, step with right foot, step with left foot, leap on right foot, step with left foot, step with right foot, etc.).

**Authentic Irish tradition, by certain authorities, requires dancers to hold hands in line, shoulder height, elbows bent, preventing their being raised on the waves!

WEGGIS SONG

MUSIC: Record—MH 1046 or M101 7B

FORMATION: Couple dance in circle—woman on man's right—moving counter-clockwise.

WORDS: From Lucerne to Weggis on
                       Holdiridia, holdiria,
                       Shoes nor stockings need we don,
                       Holdiridia, holdia.

On the lake we all shall go,
                       Holdiridia, holdiria,
                       See the pretty fish below,
                       Holdiridia, holdia.

Weggis starts the highest hill,
                       Holdiridia, holdiria,
                       Boys and girls, cheer with a will,
                       Holdiridia, holdia.

ACTION:
  Form I.   Hands crossed, right over left.
      Measure I   -Partners separate—women to right—men to left—three running steps, on fourth count of measure lift (woman): left foot behind right and hold—(man): the opposite.
      Measure II   -Run back to partner.
      Measure III-IV-Man's hands on woman's waist—step, hop, turn clockwise.

REPEAT ALL CHORUS

  Form II. Woman facing man who is standing with his left to the center of circle—hands clasped together, arms stretched.
      Measure I   -Heel and toe toward center of circle; woman's

right and man's left—inside arms lowered—
outside arms lifted up.

Measure II   -Same—outside feet.

Measure III-IV-Repeat 1 and 2—then repeat all that

CHORUS—same as in Form I

Form III. Woman on man's right—hands crossed again.

Measure I   -Step to right on right—point left in front of right
to right.

Measure II   -Same to the left.

Measure III   -Polka step to the right—begin with hop on left.

Measure IV   -Polka step to the left. Repeat all 4 measures.

CHORUS—as in Form I

Form IV. Man with back to center—woman facing man—right
hands held—left on hip.

Measure I   -Step to right on right—point left across right.

Measure II   -Same to the left.

Measure III-IV-With two short polka steps change places with
partner—starting with right foot. Repeat all 4
measures.

CHORUS—as in Form I

Form V. Hold inside hands.

Measure I   -Description for man: woman does everything
with other foot. Give a swing with right hand to
partner's left and step forward on left foot, then
on right—at the same time turning with body
away from partner and pivoting on right foot.

Measure II   -Finishing the turn and stepping forward on left
again—facing partner and bowing deeply.

Measure III-IV-Same as measure 1 and 2 going back to starting
position.

CHORUS—as in Form I

VARIATION: This dance can be done so that after each Chorus the
man advances to the woman ahead and so changes
partners each time.

AMERICAN SQUARE DANCES

The square dance is everybody's dance. Square dancing is for fun—at least it ought to be! The square dance demands almost nothing of the individual dancer but a small sense of rhythm and the ability to follow instructions. Its basic steps and figures have come down to us virtually unchanged from colonial times when the square dance was the traditional celebration of work completed: a barn raised, a crop harvested, a flock sheared; when people, having worked hard and well together, found their joy and relaxation in dancing together, and anybody's kitchen was a dance hall as long as the fiddler was there. Square dancing was rest, relaxation, and social diversion all in its truest sense.

Square dances are a part of the true folk dance heritage of West Virginia. Particularly popular in the Appalachian Mountains have been the big circle dances and the "running set" squares. These running sets are a relatively pure form of the old circle dances of England.

In the section that follows, you will find a variety of the traditional calls and figures for both large and small (2 couples) circles. The large circle figures are used as the introduction, choruses, or breaks, and ending of the dance, and the small circle figures as the basic pattern or body of the dance. You will find these same figures as parts of square dance patterns in every section of the country.

GENERAL SUGGESTIONS FOR BETTER SQUARE DANCING

1. Square dancing is dancing, not wrestling. There is a difference between fast dancing and rough dancing. To get into advanced square dancing one must know the fundamentals, learn to dance smoothly and effortlessly and to follow the caller.

2. Listen to the caller. Yelling and clapping, contrary to many city people's idea about the square dance, is discouraged so that one can hear the music and the call. Do not anticipate the call.

3. Listen to the music. It has a beat and as in any other dance, steps are taken on the beat. The figure too is timed for a certain phrase in the music. Dancing to the music is half the thrill of square dancing.

4. If you get mixed up or make a mistake, don't worry about it. There's no time to make it up so square yourself away for the next figure and try it again.

5. Be graceful, be friendly and smile because you're dancing for fun and you're dancing with seven others who want to have fun too.

FIGURES FOR LARGE CIRCLES

CIRCLE AND PROMENADE

CALL: 1. All join hands and circle left,
2. Circle right,
3. Swing your partner,
4. Now promenade.

GRAND RIGHT AND LEFT

CALL: 1. Right hand to your partner,
And a right and left grand.
2. Right and left around that ring,
Meet your partner and give her a swing.
3. And promenade home.

SQUARE DANCE FIGURES FOR SMALL CIRCLES

The figures that follow are for small circles—that is, each figure is danced by two couples together. Most of the calls are self-explanatory. Where that is not true, the action is described. Any good fiddle tune will be appropriate.

BIRDIE IN THE CAGE

CALL: 1. Circle four in the middle of the floor,
2. Birdie in the cage,
And three hands around.
3. Birdie flies out and crow hops in,
Three hands around again.
4. Crow hops out and you make a ring.
5. Break that ring with a corner swing.
6. Now swing your own and move on.

ACTION: 1. Circle left.
2. Lady 1 steps into the center of the circle formed by the joined hands of the other three dancers. The three circle left around her.
3. Lady 1 steps back into the circle and man 1 goes into the center, while the three circle left around him.

4. Man 1 steps back into the circle and all four continue to move left.
5. Corner swing.
6. Partners swing and move on to next couple.

BUTTERFLY TWIRL

CALL:
1. Ladies twirl,
2. Gents twirl,
3. Everybody twirl a butterfly twirl,
4. And swing that corner girl.
5. Now swing your own and move to the next.

ACTION:
1. Ladies turn once around in place.
2. Men turn once around in place.
3. Everyone turns once around in place with arms raised above heads, hands waving.
4. Swing corners.
5. Swing partners and move on to next couple.

DIVE FOR THE OYSTER

CALL:
1. Circle four once more,
2. The other way back.
3. Dive for the oyster,
4. Dive for the clam,
5. Dive for the hole in the old tin can,
6. On to the next and circle four.

ACTION:
1. Two couples circle left,
2. Two couples circle right.
3. Couple 2 raise their joined hands and couple 1 walks forward four steps, ducks their heads under arch of couple 2, then moves back to place.
4. Couple 1 raises their joined hands and couple 2 ducks under, then moves back to place.
5. Couple 1 again moves forward and goes under the joined hands of couple 2, leading into a wring the dishrag figure.
6. When the two couples are back in place in the small circle again, they drop hands with the opposite couples and then move on to the next couple.

334

LADIES CHAIN

CALL:
1. Four hands up and away you go (circle left),
2. Head right back in the way you know (circle right),
3. Ladies chain across the set,
4. Chain right back, you ain't done yet.

RIGHT AND LEFT THROUGH
or
PASS RIGHT THROUGH

CALL:
1. A right and left through,
   And a right and left back.
2. Now circle left in a little ring.
3. Break that ring with a corner swing,
4. Swing your own and move on.

RIGHT HANDS ACROSS

CALL:
1. Right hands across (right hand star) and howdy-do,
2. Left hand back (left hand star), And how are you?
3. Corners swing.
4. Now swing your own.

TAKE A LITTLE PEEK

CALL:
1. Around that couple, take a little peek,
2. Back to the center and swing your sweet.
3. Around that couple, peek once more,
4. Back to the center and swing all four.
   or
   Back to the center and circle four.

ACTION:
1. Couple 1, hands joined, moves forward and peeks around behind couple 2.
2. Couple 1 returns to place and swings.
3. Couple 1 peeks around behind couple 2 again.
4. They return to place and both couples swing.
   or
   They return to place and join hands in a circle of four.

CLIMBING UP DEM GOLDEN STAIRS

MUSIC: Folk Dancer MH 1515 (with calls)
           Folk Dancer MH 1517 (instrumental)

FORMATION: Square dance formation; may be done with couples in a
            circle.

ACTION: Part I
           It's a left hand round your corner. Right elbow swing your part-
           ner (twice around) Sing: "Climbing up de Golden Stairs."
           Then left hand round your corner, two hand swing your partner
               (twice around) Sing: "Climbing up de Golden Stairs."
           And Do-si-do your corner, and Do-si-do your partner
               Sing: Climbing up de Golden Stairs."

           Part II
           Swing your corner lady, boys
           Then promenade your square   8 counts used for
           Let's sing that crazy song again,   each of these lines
           "Climbing up de Golden Stairs."
           Do parts I and II of this dance four times.

           Note that the call is phrased so that dancers are doing the figure
           while singing "Climbing up de Golden Stairs": each time
           with their partner.

DOWN TO THE CENTER AND DIVIDE THE RING

FORMATION: Four couples in an open square; number couples 1, 2, 3, 4
             counter-clockwise.

ACTION: A.   All join hands and circle to the left.
                  Circle back to the right to "home" (starting place).
                  Allemande left with your left hand grand.
                  Meet your partner and promenade home.

             B.   First couple out, down to the center and back.
                  Down to the center and divide the ring, the lady goes
                  right and gent to the left.
                  Meet your partner with a right hand around.
                  Meet your corner with the left hand around.
                  Do-si-do with the partner.
                  Do-si-do with the corner.
                  Swing your partner. Promenade the corner.

C. Same old gent with a new girl.
Repeat B.

D. Repeat A and continue B with second couple.

FIRST TWO LADIES CROSS OVER

FORMATION: Four couples in a square. Determine head couples and side couples in set.

DIRECTIONS: Two head ladies cross over, by the gentlemen stand.

Two side ladies cross over, all join hands.

Honor your corner lady,

Honor your partners all.

Swing the corner lady.

Promenade the hall. (Around the square and back to gentleman's home.)

Repeat above with 2 new head ladies beginning movement.

CHORUS

Do-si-do on the corner
Do-si-do with partner
Allemande left with corner
Grand right and left
When you meet your partner swing her
and promenade her home. (This will be your partner at
 beginning of chorus, not original.)

Repeat first verse with gentlemen crossing over.
Promenade back to girls home each time.

Chorus as before; except this time the boy will, when he meets his original partner in the grand right and left, swing her and promenade her home.

337

FORWARD UP SIX AND BACK

TUNE: "Camp Town Races"

FORMATION: Four couples in a square. Couples number to the right; head couples number one, next two, etc.

> First couple out to the right
> Circle four, circle four
> Leave that girl and go on alone
> There you circle three
> Take that girl alone with you
> Circle four, circle four
> Leave that girl and go alone
> Now you are at home.

> *CHORUS*
> Forward up six and back
> Gents go do-si-do
> Make that arch—and make it high.
> Let hand lady low. (Last time: Now you are at home.)

> (Each time chorus is repeated four times.)

> Repeat all for second, third and fourth couples.

GRAPEVINE TWIST

MUSIC: Any good fiddling tune.

FORMATION: Four couples in a hollow square.

INTRODUCTION:

> All eight balance and all eight swing
> Promenade the outside ring
> The right foot up and the left foot down
> Hurry up boys or you won't get around.

ACTION: Take your lady by the wrist, and around that lady with a grapevine twist (first couple moves out to couple on right)
Back to the center with a whoa, haw, gee,
And around that gent you didn't see.

> Circle up four . . . . .
> Take your lady by the hair and around

The lady over there
Back in the center on the same old track
Around the gent with the crooked back.

Circle up six . . . . .
Take your lady by the wrist and around
The lady with a grapevine twist
Don't forget your figure eight
Around that gent and don't be late.

Circle up eight till you come straight
Swing your honey like swinging on a gate,
And promenade her home.

CHORUS: Allemande left,
Grand right and left,
Meet your partner,
Promenade her home.

(Continue with 2, 3, and 4th couples)

HURRY, HURRY, HURRY

MUSIC: Windsor Record 4405 (with calls)
Windsor Record 4105 (instrumental)

FORMATION: Four couples in a square.

ACTION: Opener:
Everybody swing your corners, boys, swing 'em high and low
Swing the next girl down the line, don't let her go.
Now go back home and swing your own, swing-and-swing-and-swing,
Then promenade your pretty girl round the ring.

Figure:
First old couple lead to the right, circle four hands round
Leave her there, go on to the next, circle three hands round.
Take that couple on with you and circle five hands round.
Now leave those four and join the line of three.
(No. 1 couple goes to No. 2 circle four hands once around. No. 1 gent leaves his partner standing near her home position with No. 2 couple in a line of

339

three, then goes on to No. 3 couple to circle three hands once around, releasing his left hand from the circle and taking No. 3 couple with him to No. 4 couple where they circle five hands around just once. No. 1 gent then lets No. 3 and 4 couples make a line of four along No. 4 couple position and step across the square to his partner's side to make a line of four.)

The ladies chain across the hall, but don't return.
Now chain along that line, just watch 'em churn.
Now turn and chain across the hall, don't let 'em roam.
Now chain the line and swing your honey home.
(All ladies chain across the lines, chain down the lines, chain across the lines, then down the lines to partners and all swing to home position.

Break:
Allemande left with the old left hand, and around that ring you go.
It's a grand old right and left, boys, walk on the heel and toe.
And when you meet that gal of yours, just do-sa-do.
And then you promenade that pretty girl back home.

Repeat figure with second couple working.
Repeat break.
Repeat figure with third couple working.
Repeat break.
Repeat figure with fourth couple working.
Repeat break for closer.

HOT TIME IN THE OLD TOWN TONIGHT

MUSIC: Any good fiddling tune.

FORMATION: Hollow square. Four couples in a square facing the center.

ACTION: First couple out and circle four hands round
On to the next and circle six hands round
Take in two and circle eight hands round
There'll be a hot time in the old town tonight.

340

Allemande left the lady on the left (corner)
Allemande right the lady on the right (lady to right
of partner).
Allemande left the lady on the left.
And a grand right and left all around.

You meet your partner and do-si-do around.
Step right up and swing her round and round.
Promenade home, the sweetest gal in town,
There'll be a hot time in the old town tonight.

MY LITTLE GIRL

MUSIC: Any good fiddling tune.

FORMATION: Hollow square.

ACTION: First couple promenade the outside,
                    Around the outside of the ring,
                    Those ladies chain, right down the center,
                    And you chain them back again.
                    Those ladies chain, the right hand couples,
                    And you chain them back again.
                    Those ladies chain, left hand couples,
                    And you chain them back again.
                    All round, your corner lady,
                    See-saw, your pretty little Taw.
                    Allemande left your left hand lady,
                    And you grand right and left right along,
                    And when you meet, you do-si-do her,
                    And you swing her 'round and 'round,
                    Now promenade, just promenade her,
                    Promenade her 'round the town.

                    Repeat the action for second, third, and fourth cou-
                    ples.

NINE PIN

MUSIC: Any good square dance tune.

FORMATION: Four couples in a square with odd person in center
                    of square.

ACTION: One and three couples go forward and back

One and three couples circle around the 9 pin
Two and four couples go forward and back
Two and four couples circle around the 9 pin

9 pin swings No. 1 opposite (if 9 pin is lady, swings
No. 1 man; if 9 pin is man, swings No. 1 lady)
9 pin swings No. 2 opposite
9 pin swings No. 3 opposite
9 pin swings No. 4 opposite

AT THE SAME TIME 9 pin is swinging one person
in each couple, the person left in each couple goes
into center; a circle is formed in center of square of
those not being swung by 9 pin.
9 pin joins those 4 in center.

Music stops. Those in center grab a new partner.
The one left without a new partner becomes 9 pin.

Repeat with new 9 pin.

TEXAS STAR

MUSIC: Any square dance tune.

FORMATION: Four couple square.

STEPS: Square dance walk.

Introduction:
All join hands and circle left
The other way back
Swing your partner and promenade

Figure:
Ladies to the center and back to the bar
Men to the center and a right-hand star
Change to left hands and go the other way
Go by your partner and pick up the next
The ladies swing in, and the gents swing out
And form that Texas star again - - -
And swing the lady round and round
- - - - - and promenade - - - -

Repeat from beginning picking up a new partner
each time ("go by the last and pick up the next")
until original partners are reached.

Ending:
Allemande left
Grand right and left (all the way around)
Promenade your partner home.

NOTE: Men keep left hands joined in the center as they pick
up girls with their right arm. After circling around
they drop left hands and bring girls forward to the
center so that they can join right hands (still keeping
hold of the men).

RECORDS

SQUARE DANCE RECORDS WITH CALLS
    Climbing Up Dem Golden Stairs
    Forward Up Six and Back
    Grand Square
    Hurry, Hurry, Hurry
    Texas Star
    Trail of the Lonesome Pine

SQUARE DANCE RECORDS WITHOUT CALLS
    Boil Them Cabbage Down
    Golden Reel
    Orange Blossom Special
    Tennessee Wig Walk
    Up the Creek

BIBLIOGRAPHY

American Squares, 1159 Broad Street, Newark 5, New Jersey 07114
Michael Herman, Box 201, Flushing, Long Island, New York 11352
United Methodist Board of Education, P. O. Box 871, Nashville,
    Tennessee 37202